HOW TO BUILD
CHRYSLER, PLYMOUTH, DODGE
HOT RODS

By LeRoi Tex Smith/Rich Johnson

Printed And Bound In The United States of America

First published in 1990 by Motorbooks International Publishers & Wholesalers, PO Box 2, 729 Prospect Avenue, Osceola, WI 54020 USA

Motorbooks International books are also available at discounts in bulk quantity for industrial or sales-promotional use. For details write to Special Sales Manager at the Publisher's address.

Library of Congress Cataloging-in-Publication Data

Tex Smith / Rich Johnson
  How to build Chrysler, Dodge, Plymouth hot rods / Tex Smith / Rich Johnson
  p.   cm.
  ISBN 0-87938-459-X : $17.95
  1. Hot rods—Design and construction. 2. Chrysler automobile—Modification. 3. Dodge automobile—Modification. 4. Plymouth automobile—Modification. I. Title.
  TL236.3.C39 1990
  629.28'78—dc20   90-31173
                                                        CIP

Printed and bound in the United States of America

CONTENTS

TEX SMITH PUBLISHING

29 East Wallace, PO Box 726, Driggs, Idaho 83422

Publisher	LEROI TEX SMITH
Editor	RICHARD JOHNSON
Art Director	BOB REECE
Art Assitant	VICKY DAVIDSON
Copy Editor	BECKY JAYE
Circulation	JANET SMITH

Printed And Bound In the United States

Foreword

"Chrysler don't make no hot rods!" How many times I heard that phrase so many years ago, when I was getting into hot rodding. I worked around my father's body/fender shop, a place where race car builders and drivers tended to gather (usually because they were making their livings as mechanics in the same shop). There were some interesting people there, with names that would become legend in all forms of motor racing. Agabashian, Bettenhausen, Palamides... these were the people who knew everything about hot rodding. At least it seemed so to me. And none of them were very complimentary about anything that ever came out of the Chrysler camp.

Back then, hot rods were Ford, and Chevrolet, and GMC. Even the lowly Studebaker engine would creep in on occasion. Never a MoPar, the nickname given to all Chrysler products. (I always wondered why Ford/ Mercury/Lincoln wasn't collectively called FoMoCo!) But, while most of us were building our Fords and Chevys, there would inevitably be the nerd who came along wanting to build a 1934 Dodge coupe. "Hey, it's already chopped!" were the words we purists would hear. Yes, those cars did look chopped. But they also had semi-elliptic springs and when the fenders were removed, they looked super dorky. They hung up there in the air. Way up there. And that humongous grille shell! Jeeesh, what an ugly monster. True that we had to chop and channel a Model A or Deuce Ford body

to get it low, but at least we could get the chassis down to the ground. Real stud hot rodders built Fords. Weenies built Chevys. No one in his right mind built MoPars!

Then came the Detroit super-car cultural revolution. The 1955 Chevy OHV V8 engine changed our ways overnight. Suddenly the Weenies were in command. But Ford wasn't far behind, and the drag racing stock classes were crammed to overflowing with participants. And while no one was looking, something strange happened over at Chrysler Corporation. Someone over there made a car that could really haul.

Well, true there had been some rumblings along these lines as early as 1951. When Chrysler introduced the famous Hemi, race people knew there was tremendous potential in the engine. But Chrysler styling was still in the top-hat era. The cars were big, bulky, and they were affectionately labeled as "slugs". Although there were some very quick slugs at the fringes. Such as the really true first muscle car, the small Chrysler body with the biggest Hemi engine. This was in the very early Fifties. Although there were only a few of these cars on the road, they could blow the doors off Cad and Olds OHV V8s. Ford and Chevy didn't even apply for the contest.

But these boxes were not styling leaders (at least not at the time). And there was no attempt to get improved handling or braking. This car, the Saratoga series, only lasted a couple of years, but it was enough to get

Chrysler enthusiasts excited.

All of this does not mean that the older Chrysler product 6-and 8-cylinder cars were not good, because they were. And there were a few sporadic attempts to make them go very well. But, it remained for the new TorqueFlite automatic transmission of the late Fifties, and the new Wedge V8 of the Sixties to really ignite Chrysler.

So, while Chevy was boxing the ears off Ford, Chrysler quietly began an onslaught of the nation's drag strips that culminated in Chrysler products being crowned king of performance for the 1960s. Even so, when all of the nameplates from Chrysler could handily straight-jacket the best from the rest, there remained a huge legion of Chevy/Ford loyalists who simply would not throw in the towel. Which was good, for the Chrysler folks had to continue the performance march clear into the early Seventies.

Today, all of this high-performance interest from Chrysler's past, serves to keep the marque established as the car to beat. The car from "back then" to beat, because there has grown up around the 1960s an aura, a mystique that expands with age. New cars, modern cars may go fast. They may handle expertly. They may meet all government regulations. But they aren't exciting. Not in the way that muscles cars of the Sixties were. And no muscle cars were as exciting as the MoPars.

It's a nice place to be in, for a car that was once considered too dorky to be a real hot rod.

And another quiet revolution has been taking place. While every car enthusiast of the last 30 years will readily agree that Chrysler nameplates are the hottest of the hot for factory hot rodding, the earlier MoPars are rapidly gaining recognition in street rodding, in customizing, and in transition era cars (1949-1954). Much of this was spurred by the Resto-Rod craze in street rodding during the late 1970s.

As street rodding grew by great leaps during the Seventies, there was a change in attitude about how the early rods could/should look. Suddenly, it was very acceptable for a "real" hot rod to have full fenders. Instantly, this opened the door for those older Chrysler Products. Dodge coupes and sedans appeared overnight at rod runs everywhere, and people liked what they saw. True, most of those cars eliminated the early MoPar front suspension, which allowed a down-in-the-weeds appearance. But, builders discovered that here were cars slightly larger than traditional Fords, and the bodies were all-steel. The frames were bulletproof. Good stuff for big cross-country haulers.

Some of these early body styles, most notably the converts of 1933-34, were even turned into "highboy" roadster styles. Fenders were removed, the original MoPar front suspensions given the heave, and the cars were dynamite looking. Nothing dorky here. When these earlier chassis were combined with the late model

Wedge V8s, there was nothing dorky about performance, either. Chrysler Corporation retro-rodding was on a high. It is still on a high. At places such as the National Street Rodding Association Nationals, there is a special event called MoPar Country. This show within a show annually attracts hundreds of participants, with machinery that rivals the best ever in hot rodding.

Now, there is a craze on for "fat fender" cars. Essentially, these are the clamshell fendered cars produced from 1935 through 1948. Once again, the Chrysler styles are taking a back seat to Ford and Chevy, but things are moving along quietly in the Chrysler camp. Fat MoPars are not considered really styling leaders, at least not from 1935 through 1938. But the 1939-49 MoPar styles are catching on rapidly. There are a lot of these cars still out there, and a few enterprising builders have shown at major car events with chopped fourdoor 1947 Chrysler sedans and lowered business coupes (those strange huge-trunk models). These are instant favorites. Because they are different, and because as hot rods, they work.

But through all of this, the Chrysler product enthusiast has had precious little information in printed form. Car features here and there in the magazines have been spotty, at best. Trying to get information on building a Chrysler hot rod has been next to impossible. Yes, the factory has done wonders about getting great information on the streets about the muscle cars, those raging beasts of the Sixties. But practically nothing about earlier cars has been/is available. This book is designed to address that very problem.

No, this is not a complete, absolutely thorough compendium of information on MoPar hot rod building. We simply can't get all the information packed into the 200 or so pages allotted. But we can start, and that's why this is called Book 1. This is the beginning. In a couple of years, there will be Book 2, and perhaps Books 3 and 4. We'll do them until we feel we've covered the Chrysler products, end to end.

So, read How To Build CHRYSLER/DODGE/ PLYMOUTH Hot Rods. And read it again, and again. Because it is the beginning of another true revolution in hot rodding. A revolution of information. Information on a very favorite subject.

LeRoi Tex Smith
Publisher

Mopars Is

WHERE YOU FIND 'EM

Which is just about everywhere

by LeRoi Tex Smith

At the time, I was driving a 1948 Chrysler 7-passenger sedan, newly built and beautiful with wide whitewall tires and a custom maroon paint job. I was enroute to the Street Rod Nationals in St. Paul, the year of 1974.

I had built this particular car more out of frustration with the pre-1949 street rod rule that was then-fresh, than for any purely aesthetic reason. The rule said (says) that a true street rod had to be a car of 1948 or earlier manufacture or appearance. So I went to the extreme. On a vacant lot in a small Montana cowtown, I spied the big car, later nicknamed Walter P. Chrysler. It was pre-1949, it had a flathead engine, and it had wide whitewall tires. Could anything be more traditional hot rod? Well, yes, but out of spite, I bought the car for $200 and did a thorough rebuild. Not a restoration, but something between renovation and hot rod updating.

Mopars of that era are especially bulletproof machines. Slugs in performance, marginal in handling, but strong. Very, very strong. Especially suited to hot rodding.

At the time, I had a southern California colleague who had an identical Chrysler, into which he had stuffed a B-block Wedge 383 V8 and automatic transmission. Nothing else was changed on the car, which meant there was interference between the left side exhaust manifold and the steering gearbox/shaft. In this case, the engine was simply moved 3 inches to the right. This was a perfectly parallel move, meaning the line drawn through the crankshaft/transmission output shaft was moved an equal 3 inches. Instant clearance, and the power made the car truly exciting. But, as with all the older Chrysler Corporation vehicles, the brakes were terrible. Worse than terrible.

In my case, I elected to stay with the original Flathead 6-engine. During those years, there was an 8-cylinder inline engine as well, but years before, while working in a Chrysler agency, I had been around a number of engine swaps. Virtually new 8-cylinder Chryslers regularly got 6-cylinder implants, because the owners wanted better fuel economy. Those 8-cylinder cars were longer, about 9 inches in wheelbase as I recall. Besides, during the late 1940s and early 1950s we routinely used this particular 6-banger as a hop-up base. The smaller Plymouth 6 wasn't (still isn't) good for performance increase, because it had a soft crank, the bigger Chrysler 6 was (is) the engine to use.

While at a swap meet, I stumbled over a pair of Edmunds finned aluminum heads for this particular engine; I bought one. To the transmission I added an overdrive from a mid-50's Plymouth. This particular car had been used as a VIP tourer by the Yellowstone Park Company. In the steep Rocky Mountains, it needed a 4.30:1 rear end gear, and a standard clutch had replaced the old fluid-drive. So, it had too much low-end gearing, but with the overdrive of 28 percent, the rearend ratio was in the modest 3's. Perfect for low engine RPM highway cruising. The fresh engine rebuild, with its new 8.5:1 compression ratio, an engine oil cooler, and the OD trans combined to give a big and heavy car that would cruise all day at 85 mph. And cruise it did, everywhere in the U.S. and Canada, until it finally moved over to the garage of Skip Readio, a MoPar enthusiast in Massachusetts.

Did that car need a later OHV V8 engine? Yes, it could have been a more pleasant car with more power, an automatic trans, air conditioning power steering, power disc brakes, etc. But it was the very epitome of "period" driving as it was. A bit of hopping up, and it was totally compatible with modern driving. Too, it got 21 mpg! For those rod runs, this car hauled my family of between 5 and 7 people perfectly. The right car for the right time.

Now, down to just two people, we are looking at a 1948 Plymouth coupe. Of course, in the meantime a 1960 Chrysler New Yorker has come to live in my garage. It has a zillion miles on the odometer, but the faithful old 413 engine just takes another gulp of oil and climbs the mountain passes. Even tired, this engine will still haul the car over 100 mph. With a new hopped-up 440, a fresh automatic, a later model 8 3/4 rearend, and a later model MoPar disc brake swap up front, this is going to be one fearsome ride. Pure hot rod. Fins and all. But, there is also a 1972 Imperial in the garage. It gets a bit of rebuilding, some zoomie exhaust, and later perhaps a bit of engine work. Great ride, marginal

mileage. Yet, when the numbers on cost per mile are run, this is still far less expensive than going with a new car.

Anyway, back to the time I was driving the '48. I had just finished the rebuild, putting a whopping 2 miles on the car (down to the gas station to fill up, lube, etc.) before leaving southern California for Minnesota, (via the more interesting northern route through Montana). We had stopped in Big Timber for fuel. While checking everything out, the young station attendant commented "Gee, I wish I could find an old car like this to fix up." So, I told him to follow me. We walked about 30 feet, to the back of the station, where in a vacant lot there sat an exact replica of my car. It had been there for at least 15 years that I remembered. "Gosh", he said, "I never realized that it could be fixed up as nice as yours!"

And, there, is the crux of the matter of finding old MoPars to fix up as hot rods. All too many would-be car enthusiasts can't see beyond the ravages of time. They can't see shiny paint where there is dirt and rust. They

don't understand that any kind of engine can be shoehorned into any kind of space. They haven't spent time doing homework to realize what hot rodding is really all about. The result is a continent bulging with great, superb hot rod building material. Chrysler/Dodge/Plymouth/DeSoto hot rod building material.

But, all this won't be forever. Currently, there is an awakening of the masses in the value and beauty of Chrysler products. This is being fueled largely by the burgeoning muscle car awareness, since MoPar has been such a major factor in factory car performance in the past. Perhaps even more important to this new interest is the world-wide passion for fin cars. American fin cars of the late Fifties/early Sixties. No cars represent this era better than Chrysler. Because of this interest, it is now common to see radical MoPar products going oversees for prices in the Six Figure area. All of which means that if you're into Chrysler products, now is the time to find/get/stash your favorites. While they are plentiful, while the prices are reasonable.

In the traditional street rodding circles, Chrysler products of the early 1930s are much more popular than those of 1935-1939. These "early" MoPars have a great deal going for them, as basis for street rods. During the 1920s, Chrysler products - especially Dodges - were very popular in the western states. Particularly mining areas, where the stronger Dodge chassis/body/engine combinations were well suited to the rough terrain. For this reason, you can expect to find a lot of Dodge touring cars of the Twenties throughout the Rocky Mountain states. Roadsters of the era are less common, while the closed bodies for Dodges from about 1928-1931 are in good supply. But, these are big cars, so if you're planning a rod then you need to keep this in mind.

The open cars, tourings and roadsters, produced during the Twenties are wider than the Model T Fords, and slightly deeper from floor to door top. For this reason, the cars make a nicer envelope than the T's if the builder is large. The roadsters have the turtle deck area molded to the body, as well. It is in the fender area where these cars tend to lose favor with rodders. The Dodge fenders are bulky. However, if 1928-29 Ford fenders are used with the Dodge roadster/touring bodies, the effect can be stunning.

Dodge open bodies of the early Twenties have a "necked-down" cowl, much like Model T and other cars of the same era. Anyone building a track roadster might want to use such a narrow cowl body. Later in the Twenties, the cowl became larger (where the hood fits), again more in line with what other builders were doing.

While these open cars from Dodge are excellent rod material, the Chrysler products have been pretty well devoured by the restoration enthusiasts. Even Plymouths have become very popular in restored trim.

Starting in 1933, Chrysler designers changed the cars significantly. They had been leaning toward the new design from about 1931 (with DeSoto) so that with the '33 Dodge sedans and coupes, some really nice and solid cars were available. These cars feature the "suicide" style doors that today's hot rodders consider so neat. That is, the doors hinge at the rear, open at the front (as with 1932 Ford 3-window coupes and 1933-34 bodies of all types). Unlike Chevy, which was filled with wood, and Ford which still used some wood, the Chrysler Products were very strong, reinforced metal throughout. The bodies are larger than Ford, and the 1931-34 designs have tops that look chopped. The lower glass area has always been intriguing to hot rod builders, but the semi-elliptic front suspension system and bulk below the grille was earlier on considered ugly. Today, however, with fenders being considered "in", and front suspension swaps common, these cars are very much in vogue. Even when run fenderless, with some minor metal work around the grille lower surround, the cars are considered very handsome. Most all of this is due to the building techniques that lower the chassis/body in relation to the wheels.

The Chrysler products through 1934 can still be considered a part of the Square styling era. Things changed in 1935, across the car building industry, as cars began to take on the rounded turret-top styling. Interestingly, Chrysler products from 1935 through 1939 have very low appeal with hot rodders and customizers. The exceptions would be convertibles and Airflow series cars. This is holding true, even with the recent interest in "fat fender" hot rodding. However, the 1940 through 1948 Chrysler products are gaining favor by leaps and bounds, while the 1957 through 1961 fin cars are hurtling past Ford and gaining on Chevrolet. The muscle era cars of 1962 through the early Seventies are reasserting themselves as champions of the American performance car era. Very exciting indeed.

The "box" styling that started in 1940 and carried

through undisguised until 1948, and then in "sort-of" fashion through 1956, has taken off in popularity in recent years. Much of this is due to the continued use of the "suicide" front opening rear doors. But the fact that these cars have excellent independent front suspensions is being recognized as a major plus factor. Although the Chrysler Corporation brakes are notorious for poor performance, it is possible to swap later model MoPar and aftermarket disc brakes to the earlier chassis. The result is good stopping, good riding, and good handling. The torsion bar suspension used from the later Fifties, when combined with late model disc brakes, proves a superior hot rod platform.

Interestingly, very few of the always-scarce Chrysler product 2-door sedans remain. Coupes are relatively rare, and convertibles are really scarce. These shortages ease somewhat after the mid-Fifties.

There are sections of the U.S. and Canada where the term MoPar Country really applies. While the Pacific states and portions of the Midwest can be identified as Ford areas (when talking about Fords through the early Fifties), and much of the South (as far west as Texas) can be considered Chevrolet territory, the Rocky Mountain states and some of the northern South is definitely in the Chrysler camp. It is in these areas where so much of the usable early Chrysler products are coming from. Of course, MoPars from the performance Fifties and Sixties can be found almost everywhere, but the problems of rust in the midwest and eastern states means that even these cars will be coming from the West or South.

We don't talk a great deal about DeSoto as a particular brand name, simply because it is rarely seen, even in Chrysler product events. The Plymouth is a lot rarer than one might think, since the car was the low-price leader for Chrysler Corporation through the years. It may be this no-value perception that has caused too many Plymouths to disappear through the years. Whatever, among the earlier MoPars the most common are Dodge and Chrysler, with the very early Chrysler nameplates so popular with restorers, that very few are available for rodding.

Plymouth and Dodge pickups of the Thirties are not uncommon, but they are rare enough so that a builder of such a vehicle will find parts hard to locate.

The bottom line is that MoPar building material is actually easier to find, and often far less expensive, than Ford or Chevrolet. Which means that the currently emerging interest in Chrysler products as great hot rods is going to gain momentum in the early 1990s. Get on the bandwagon now!

Note: Just to prove our point about the great amount of MoPar tin hiding out in western hills, we took an hour from work one day and drove around our eastern Idaho mountain valley. The photos that accompany this section are typical of Chrysler products to be found throughout the entire Rocky Mountain area, including those reaches far into Canada.

Mopar
BONEYARD

Where used and abused Chrysler products go to await resurrection.

If you were an old Chrysler product trying desperately to avoid the crusher, chances are very good you would want to find a way to Freeman's Auto Parts, 138 Kountz Rd., Whitehall, Montana 59759, telephone (406) 287-5436.

Because if there is a spirit world for faithful old MoPar vintage tin, this is the place. Neal Freeman is the guardian angel to over 1000 pieces of Chrysler/Plymouth/Dodge/DeSoto relics, pieces rescued from scrap heaps and backyards across much of western America. If you browse the pages of Hemming's Motor News, you've come across Neal's ads for spare parts, ads that have been appearing for years. Yes, there are similar specialty junkyards scattered across the nation, but perhaps none with such a collection of excellent condition sheetmetal (rust is not a major problem in the intermountain west), nor with such variety.

Interestingly, it is the sheetmetal and small parts that make these old cars so valuable to the growing legion of Chrysler product builders/restorers. The heavier mechanical parts such as rearends, transmissions, and engines are readily available just about everywhere. Even so, when the occasional good early Hemi 392 engine comes along, Neal has a ready list of customers waiting including drag racing legend Don Garlits.

Because of the growing interest in specialty cars of the Fifties and Sixties, Freeman keeps a crew of mechanics busy assembling rare machinery, particularly Chrysler 300's. Convertibles, hardtops, uncommon body styles; every possible Chrysler form passes through the yard at one time or another. Although there are also high-demand Buick and Cadillac hulks lurking in the underbrush, it is the MoPar product that gets most of Freeman's attention.

Browse through the accompanying photographs to see exactly what a visitor to Neal Freeman's emporium is likely to find. Always interesting, sometimes amusing, surely captivating for anyone who is in desperate need of a very specific part.

LATE MOPAR REAR-WHEEL-DRIVE TERMINOLOGY

by Ron Ceridono

If you have been wondering about the proper designations of late-model rear-wheel-drive MoPar equipment, here is a guide to help you figure out which combination of letters and numbers refers to the various body types, engine types and transmission types.

BODY TYPE

A Body 1964 - 1976 Valiant, 1964 - 1969 Barracuda, 1964 - 1976 Dart, all Duster/Demon/Sport/Scamp/Swinger

B Body Coronet, Satellite, Road Runner, R/T, GTX, Charger, Belevedere, Super Bee, Cordoba (before 1980), 1976 - 1978 Fury, 1977 - 1978 Monaco, 1978 - 1979 Magnum

E Body 1970 - 1974 Barracuda, all Challenger

F Body 1976 - 1980 Volare and Aspen, Road Runner and R/T

J Body 1980 - 1983 Mirada and Cordoba

M Body 1977 - 1986 Diplomat and LeBarron

R Body 1979 - 1981 New Yorker and St. Regis

Mopar
IDENTIFICATION GUIDE

1929 Chrysler Series 65 Business Coupe

So there you are, standing in the junkyard staring at a bunch of stuff that the guy at the front desk said is supposed to be his MoPar pile. But how do you know if those headlights are '33 or '34, and what about the bumper, hood, fenders, etc.? Maybe it doesn't matter, but then again, maybe it does. It all depends upon what you have in mind for your particular project.

To help out with identification of MoPar pieces, John Lee has gathered this collection of photographs of MoPar vehicles — Chryslers, Dodges, Plymouths and DeSotos — ranging from fairly early to fairly late models. Although we don't show every model for all makes, or even every year, these photos should be somewhat helpful for identifying quite a variety of MoPar vehicles.

Among MoPars the Chrysler and DeSoto were the "big" cars, while the Dodge and Plymouth were the "small" cars. There is frequently a broad range of parts interchangeability among the different makes. Just because your car is a DeSoto, doesn't mean that you necessarily have to shop for DeSoto parts and overlook Chrysler pieces. Likewise with the Dodge/Plymouth stuff.

photos by John Lee

CHRYSLER

1933 Chrysler Imperial CQ Convertible Sedan

1954 Chrysler New Yorker Club Sedan

1947 Chrysler Windsor Convertible

1955 Chrysler 300

1947 Chrysler Royal 6-passenger 2-door Brougham

1961 Chrysler 300-G Hardtop

1950 Chrysler Windsor Club Coupe

1955 Chrysler New Yorker Deluxe 2-door Hardtop

1961 Chrysler 300-G 413 Cross-Ram

1965 Chrysler 300 2-door Hardtop

1961 Chrysler 300-G Swivel Seats

1968 Chrysler Newport Convertible

DODGE

1928 Dodge Victory Six Coupe-Brougham

1932 Dodge Convertible

1949 Dodge Wayfarer Roadster

1937 Dodge Coupe

1946 Dodge Station Wagon

1949 Dodge Wayfarer Business Coupe

1948 Dodge Business Coupe

1949 Dodge Coronet 4-door Sedan

1950 Dodge Coronet 4-door Sedan

1955 Dodge Coronet Club Sedan

1952 Dodge Coronet Club Coupe

1956 Dodge Custom Royal Lancer 2-door Hardtop

1959 Dodge Royal Lancer 2-door Hardtop

1953 Dodge Coronet Club Sedan

1959 Dodge Coronet Club Sedan

1960 Dodge Dart Phoenix 2-door Hardtop

1961 Dodge Polara 2-door Hardtop

1962 Dodge Custom 880 4-door Hardtop Station Wagon

1963 Dodge Custom 880 2-door Hardtop

1964 Dodge Custom 880 2-door Hardtop (with non-stock grille)

1965 Dodge Coronet 500 2-door Hardtop

1965 Dodge Polara 2-door Hardtop

21

1965 Dodge Custom 880 Convertible

1969 Dodge Charger

1966 Dodge Monaco 500 2-door Hardtop

1971 Dodge Challenger R/T Hemi

1967 Dodge Coronet 440 2-door Hardtop

1971 Dodge Charger R/T

1969 Dodge Coronet 440 Coupe

1971 Dodge Polara 2-door Hardtop

PLYMOUTH

1933 Plymouth PD Coupe

1934 Plymouth PF Coupe

1936 Plymouth DeLuxe Convertible Coupe ('37 DeSoto bumpers, '50 Plymouth wheel covers)

1936 Plymouth DeLuxe 4-door Touring Sedan

1939 Plymouth DeLuxe Touring Sedan

1941 Plymouth Special DeLuxe Convertible

1942 Plymouth Special DeLuxe Town Sedan

1949 Plymouth DeLuxe Business Coupe

1949 Plymouth Special DeLuxe Club Coupe

1949 Plymouth Special DeLuxe Convertible

1950 Plymouth Special Deluxe Station Wagon

1951 Plymouth Concord Business Coupe

BEST EVER!

HOT RODDERS THE WORLD OVER SAY HRMx IS THE BEST EVER.
We think they're right!
And there's only one way to get us.

We don't try to be sophisticated. We're not brilliant. We certainly are not empty glitz. We're just plain old hardcore, basic, useful, practical. Which is right on target, because over 95% of street driven hot rods have between 5000 and 10,000 actual dollars invested...and a zillion hours of labor. HRMx is about that.

HRMx is the How-To Magazine.

Lots of other super magazines give you great photos of cars. Good stuff, and the hobby needs them. But, we think the hobby needs us even more! We show how these cars are built, how they are put together. Hot rodding hasn't become a kind of mystical black art, it is still something that happens one bolt at a time.

HRMx is written by the legends of hot rodding. By the pro's. And by the hundreds of thousands of back-yarders who know what it is to save, and scrounge, and invent, and create. HRMx is about everything in hot rodding, just as long as it is fun.

We don't try to dazzle you with dollar signs, and big names. We're for the average rod builder. We cost a bit more, but we're worth it.

YOU GET US ONE WAY ONLY- BY SUBSCRIPTION.

1952 Plymouth Belvedere 2-door Hardtop

1953 Plymouth Belvedere 2-door Hardtop

1954 Plymouth Belvedere Suburban

1955 Plymouth Belvedere 2-door Hardtop

1956 Plymouth Belvedere 2-door Hardtop

1957 Plymouth Belvedere Convertible

1957 Plymouth Savoy 2-door Hardtop

1958 Plymouth Belvedere Convertible

1959 Plymouth Belvedere Convertible

1961 Plymouth Valiant V-200 4-door Sedan

1961 Plymouth Fury Convertible

1961 Plymouth DeLuxe 2-door Suburban

1962 Plymouth Valiant V-200 2-door Sedan

1962 Plymouth Sport Fury 2-door Hardtop

1965 Plymouth Satellite Convertible

1967 Plymouth Belvedere II Hardtop

1968 Plymouth Sport Satellite Convertible

1968 Plymouth Barracuda Fastback

1969 Plymouth Road Runner Coupe

1970 Plymouth Road Runner Superbird

1971 Plymouth Barracuda

1972 Plymouth GTX Hemi

1975 Plymouth Duster Coupe

DESOTO

1936 DeSoto Airflow

1948 DeSoto Custom 4-door Sedan

1955 DeSoto Firedome 2-door Hardtop

1953 DeSoto Firedome Club Sedan

1956 DeSoto Firedome Convertible

1954 DeSoto Firedome Convertible

1959 DeSoto Firesweep Convertible

A Tour of
MOPAR COUNTRY

Grille of the '32 DeSoto was as good looking as any of the '30s. Art Mason, Dryden, Ontario, had to rebuild his with 3/8" stainless steel tubing forming the bars. Original 3/8" rolled steel bars were too far gone to rechrome.

by John Lee

A person can literally walk for days looking at cars at the NSRA Street Rod Nationals and still not see them all. The problem is compounded if your main interest is "minority" makes like MoPars. You have to wade through tons of Fords, Chevys and other types to find them.

To promote the use of its products as street rodding material, and to give its fans an opportunity to concentrate attention on MoPar iron, Chrysler Corporation sponsors MoPar County at the Nationals every year.

In St. Paul during the 1989 gathering, MoPar County was designated at a particular site on the fairgrounds on Saturday morning. A record number of 308 Chrysler Corporation bodied and/or powered vehicles gathered for judging, from which five "MoPar Picks" were selected and drawings were held for a Chrysler engine and transmission assembly and other merchandise prizes.

But for most, the important thing was being able to closely scrutinize other pentastar machinery and talk things like slant sixes, Torqueflites and torsion bars with rodders of like mind.

We spent most of Saturday morning in MoPar Country in order to bring you some of the scenes.

We'll just have to say, they may not be the biggest in numbers, but many of the Chrysler-based street rods can rival the best being assembled from other makes. And with some of Chrysler's unusual models, like the neat mid-'30s pickups and 3-window business coupes of the '40s, there's certainly great opportunity to build a different kind of rod.

Those appear to be '40 Chevy headlights tucked into the fender valleys of Jack Giachino's '35 Plymouth sedan from Green Bay, Wisconsin.

Bright red '33 Plymouth coupe is powered by a 360-inch small-block.

Restored on the outside, rodded on the inside is Al Schonert's beige and blue '34 Plymouth convertible. Creve Coeur, Illinois rod runs a slant six and features dual side mounts and a rumble seat.

A top chop and opened up wheel wells set off John Zechbauer's black '47 Plymouth business coupe from Roseville, Minnesota.

A big 392 cu. in. early Chrysler hemi overflows the engine compartment of Bill Miller's Kokomo, Indiana '27 Model T sedan!

Dodge humpback deliveries like Kent Schnell's '34 from Des Moines are hard to find, but make roomy, unusual rods. Kent's is small block MoPar powered.

Dallas Triebenbach, Osakis, Minnesota has his '47 Plymouth coupe well underway with Volare front suspension and a 360 small block under the hood.

Grille, bumpers and all trim are painted black on David Rice's LaPorte, Indiana '48 DeSoto club coupe. Interior is red velour.

Brian Dreger of Lane, Saskatchewan powers his '28 Dodge coupe with a slant six boasting headers, an Offy manifold with a Holley 4-barrel and torsion bar suspension.

This is the Canadian version of the '41 Dodge business coupe as customized by Barrie, B.C. resident Keith Pearsall with wheel flares, a mesh grille and Cibie headlights.

Six-pack 340 is wrapped in a louvered stainless steel engine shroud in James Schultz's candy red '33 Dodge two-door from Wilber, Nebraska.

Harry Ruthrauff of Coldwater, Michigan was out to prove a 354 Chrysler hemi with four carbs would, indeed, fit under the hood of a '36 Ford.

A 440 big block powers George Fabry's metallic bronze '32 Dodge panel delivery out of Arvada, Colorado.

Above left- How do you like your '34 Dodge many door, chopped or stock? Black resto-rod is Al Johnson's from Milwaukee, Wisconsin. Light copper low-lid belongs to Rich Thacker, Kokomo, Indiana.

Above- Tony Schimka, Des Plaines, Illinois gave his '41 Plymouth business coupe the pro-street treatment with widened rear fenders and repro '37 DeSoto bumpers by Briz. Power is from a small block MoPar with dual quads on an Edelbrock tunnel ram.

Left- Maroon and burgundy '33 Chrysler sedan is Bill Fodrie's handiwork from New Bern, N.C. Behind the hood doors is a 340 six-pack.

35

Mopar
CUSTOM IDEAS

1938 Plymouth sedan with a top chop, tunneled headlights and nerf bars looks ready for action. Check out the chromed hand crank!

by John Lee

Consider this: If you combined all of the most popular custom components derived from Chrysler-built cars into one car, you should have a fantastic custom. It would have a toothy '54 DeSoto grille, '57 Chrysler quad headlights, '49 Plymouth ripple bumpers, '55 DeSoto side trim and '56 Chrysler taillights, and it would be powered by a 392 Chrysler hemi.

Come to think of it, maybe it's a good thing no one has tried it.

But the fact remains, the principal styling components of many a fine custom have come from Chrysler products, yet cars with the pentastar that have been customized are few and far between.

One reason is that Plymouths, Dodges, DeSotos and Chryslers were a bit stodgy during the decade following WWII, when street customs and rods were in their heyday. There wasn't much you could do to make a flathead six run with a Ford flathead.

Too, MoPar products were more family oriented.

There were more four-door sedans than anything, and few hardtops and coupes, which make the neatest rods and customs.

Still, there's a lot of hot rodding that can be done to these cars, especially given the resources and knowledge available today that make it easier to update the running gear of any make.

Except for some lapses in quality control from 1957 to 1960, and styling from 1961 to 1964, these cars were solidly built, which means there are still quite a number of them around. The rarest and most muscular models are out of sight on the price scale, but the rest are much more reasonably priced than comparable models from Ford, Chevrolet, Pontiac and others.

Even though there isn't an abundance of examples to choose from, here are some of the MoPar restyling ideas we've run across at various shows in recent years. Maybe they'll get you started thinking about how to customize your own MoPar.

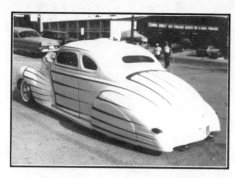

Guy Root chopped and subframed this bulky '39 Dodge coupe and covered it with a wild scallop pattern. See how skirts have speed lines like those stamped into the fender.

Dechroming this '47 DeSoto sedan extended to painting the front bumper and removing the rear.

One of the slickest jobs done on a postwar MoPar in recent years is this Dodge sedan with a '57 Buick grille set into a molded shell. Top is chopped just enough.

Bob Vaira has had his period-restyled '47 Plymouth business coupe at most of the KKOA Leadsled Spectaculars. Burgundy coupe has '50 Plymouth bumpers with a '49 Chevy license guard in back and early accessory Imperial-style taillights set on the gravel pan.

The hood is shaved, windshield V-butted and headlights tunneled on Frank Vaira's '47 Plymouth.

This '46-'48 Plymouth club coupe has the benefit of a top chop, stylish wheels and modern V8 under the hood. .

Lots of people leave the Plymouth grille alone because it's hard to change. This owner built a neat one out of small-diameter tubing.

The '49-'52 Dodge Wayfarer was a "compact" (shorter wheelbase), economy model. This one's been treated to a top chop, tunneled taillights, dechroming and custom-built skirts.

This '49 Dodge Wayfarer has the stock bumper tucked in close to the body and molded in. Triple-lens taillights are set into tunneled openings. License housing is stock but with chrome trim and handle removed.

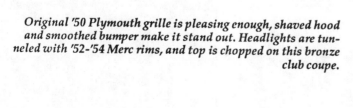

Original '50 Plymouth grille is pleasing enough, shaved hood and smoothed bumper make it stand out. Headlights are tunneled with '52-'54 Merc rims, and top is chopped on this bronze club coupe.

There were only 322 '32 Chrysler 2-door convertible sedans built. Ken Mutch of Grundy Center, Iowa powers his with a late MoPar small block.

From Canal Fulton, Ohio, Tom Burger won't see another like this '33 Plymouth coupe with its wild graphics and 330-inch '56 DeSoto hemi with dual quads and pushbutton Torqueflite.

Above- Power comes from a 340 and a Torqueflite with B&M shifter to propel Wayne Edwards' brandywine '33 Plymouth coupe from Lees Summit, Missouri.

Right- Grille insert in Art Heffernan's '33 Plymouth from St. Paul, Minnisota is stainless steel. Are these available somewhere as repros?

Leo Whitman, Brainerd, Minnesota restored his '41 Plymouth business coupe with period accessories — skirts, whitewalls, flipper caps and sun visor.

Chrysler, DeSoto and Dodge all offered this 3-window business coupe body style during the 1940s. This is the '41 Chrysler version.

Henry Bargenquast, Oshkosh, Wisconsin owns the red '35 Dodge pickup in the background, while the yellow '34 is David Hinck's handiwork from Red Wing, Minnesota.

Cream yellow '32 Plymouth coupe of Jerry Delzer, Bismarck, N.D., is chopped and powered by a 340 six-pack.

Rick Smith from Camby, Indiana installed four bucket seats in his russet and black '37 Dodge coupe.

Town sedan, with rearward-opening doors, was a new Dodge body style in 1941 and had a run of only 16,000 vs. about 120,000 regular 4-doors. Mildly rodded version is Jeff Korol's from Harwood, N.D.

A late MoPar small block powers Charmie Steine's neat beige '37 Dodge convertible from Loveland, Colorado.

1933 Dodge pickup like this restored version is excellent rodding material.

Chopped top and filled quarter windows change the character of this '41 Plymouth business coupe.

Here's how a fat-fendered '47 Plymouth looks with stock grille and rectangular quad headlights. Dallas Triebenbach of Osakis, Minnesota also built directional lights and license housing into the '49 Plymouth bumper.

Above right- Wild graphics in dark and light blue and black break up the bulkiness of Pat Newell's light gray '40 Plymouth sedan.

Right- Norm Kyhn, Longmont, Colo., makes a fashion statement with his '47 Plymouth's two-tone pink paint scheme with graphics. Flathead six has dual carbs, high-comp head.

39

Already on a 131-1/2 inch wheelbase, the '52 Chrysler New Yorker hardtop looks even longer with a mild top chop. A bunch of chrome has also been ditched from hood, grille area, doors and rear fenders.

Ernie Barrett saw the custom possibilities of the '51 Plymouth Suburban two-door wagon. Fender flares from a '56 F-100 pickup have been grafted on, framing Enkei wheels.

1955 DeSoto bar floats in Ernie Barrett's '51 Plymouth, surrounded by the stock top grille bar frenched in. Note the '49 Plymouth bumpers and reverse hood scoops.

Custom grille bar in Leon Mills' 1952 Dodge club coupe appears to be derived from a Chevy bumper guard. Cordoba parking lights are frenched like headlights.

The '52 DeSoto multi-tooth grille works as well in its natural habitat as it does in some other make. Scallops on this dechromed four-door are dark green over light green.

1955 Plymouth Plaza club coupe had no side chrome to begin with, which means fewer holes to fill; '54 Dodge of '55 DeSoto trim could be applied if desired. Stock grille needs no modification.

A continental spare installation with extended fenders also works well on the '55 Plymouth. Bubble skirts are recessed into the body.

This is Doug Shoemaker's cleaned-up '55 Dodge with filled bumper, '55 Olds headlight doors, hood scoop filled, and corners rounded.

Neat lines of the '56 Chrysler New Yorker hardtop don't need changing. This one benefits from shaved hood and doors, skirts and lowering.

Built a number of years ago, this '58 Plymouth station wagon takes on a strictly business look with cut-out rear wheel openings and filled top quarters with opera windows.

When her KKOA duties allow, DeVona Titus likes to cruise in her red '58 Chrysler Windsor hardtop. Dechroming and painting the bottom sections of the bumpers body color make it look less heavy.

Ron Meyers made his '60 Plymouth hardtop even more radical looking than it was originally by painting it white with candy blue scallops.

How about a dechromed and lowered '68 Chrysler Newport hardtop for a slinky cruiser? Note how skirts are filled to the lower body line.

Yours truly applied this treatment to a '69 Coronet. Grille bar from a '66 Galaxie separates rectangular sealed beams.

CHASSIS/BODY

This is the traditional hot rod front end — a Ford beam axle with transverse leaf spring. In this case, where a "suicide" front spring perch allows the axle to be level with the frame, tie rod clearance is achieved by reversing the pre-1949 Ford spindles side for side. Problem with this is that the Ackerman steering principle is tossed out the window.

FRONT SUSPENSION

by Tex Smith

Chrysler products have long utilized excellent front suspension components, whether semi-elliptic springs with drum brakes that reach back to the Thirties beginnings, or torsion bars with discs that are used on contemporary models. Much of this is the result of engineering emphasis, which has always been a strong suit at Chrysler. Those early cars, even the so-called lightweights of the Twenties, have very strong frames for their time. This, coupled with elliptic springs, produced a solid ride and good handling. Later, into the '30s when the independent front suspension came on board, the same battleship frame approach was used. The result of all this is that you don't have to do a lot of front suspension swapping with MoPars to get excellent results. The major Chrysler weak point, brakes, can be cured with a brake swap.

On the earlier Chrysler products with semi-elliptics, the major drawback is the same as with any similarly sprung car — it rides too high. GM vehicles have been plagued by the same problem. The I-beam axles are very strong, but they already have a significant factory

designed drop. When these axles are dropped even more, the result is a "leverage arm" that can adversely affect handling. More simply, the distance in horizontal measurement from the axle mounting point (at the spring) to the spindle centerpoint on a dropped axle becomes so long, that braking and road condition actions cause this section of the axle to distort (try to twist). This problem of distortion is controlled if a special tubing dropped axle is used, but the forces are still there. Also, when an aftermarket dropped axle is used on these cars, steering tie rod clearances become a major problem.

Dropped springs should not be ruled out on the leaf spring MoPars, but they will create some additional frame/suspension problems to solve. One of these problems will be axle/frame clearance. It is possible to relocate the leaf spring rear shackle mount higher on the frame. This effectively drops the front end without an aftermarket dropped axle. But, when this is done, the axle is moved closer to the frame rail bottom lip, a distance that is already minimal (usually between 3 - 5 inches). To gain more axle working room (vertical), it is possible to make a "C" section in the frame, above the axle. Because the Chrysler product frames are strong to begin with, this modification reduces overall frame strength only slightly.

If the dropped axle is used (and the traditional Ford axle aftermarket builders can definitely modify one of their axles to fit semi-elliptic springs), there will usually be no need to alter the original spring attachment points at the frame.

Neophyte rod builders sometimes make the mistake of mounting the factory or dropped axle above the elliptic springs. This seems like a quick and logical way to get an additional 2-inch drop. The problem is that the already minimal axle/frame clearance is nearly eliminated with this axle placement. It doesn't even work well with the frame C'd for clearance, and since the axle must have pads welded to the bottom end, this entire scenario is a wash.

The earlier MoPar frames, into the early Thirties, are of the traditional industry "flat" style. That is, the ladder frame style has flat side rails, when viewed from the side. Early in the '30s, however, the frame started to take on a decided swayback appearance. Engineers found this a good way to lower the vehicle body and center of gravity (for better ride and handling). Race car builders of the period took this practice farther by dropping the frame center area even more, by cutting V-shape notches in the frame just ahead of the body firewall and just ahead of the rear spring kick-up. While this is not a common practice in building early model MoPar hot rods, it could be considered. This would require some reshaping of the body flooring at the rear kick-up, and in the transmission tunnel area.

The Chrysler products used three-quarter elliptic springs at the rear during the early '20s, then changed to the industry standard semi-elliptic rears. This spring style has been carried through (on rear drive cars) to the present time, but the springs have not remained the same. Early springs will be narrower, and the distance from axle centerline to front/rear attachment of the spring (at the frame/shackle) is often the same. If the distance from the axle forward to the front pivot point is shorter than the rear section of spring, resistance to axle wind-up under acceleration/braking can be good, while the longer (thus softer) rear portion of spring helps ride comfort. When building a rod and there is some concern about rear spring swapping, keep this in mind.

The independent front suspension system used in Chrysler products from the 1930s into the 1950s was/is a good basic design. The upper A-arms are shorter than the lower arms, and camber adjustment is built into the lower arms at the steering knuckle attachment point. The MoPar steering boxes are good, although the steering ratio is almost always too slow for most performance-minded builders. The solution is to make up a longer pitman arm for the gearbox, or find a longer arm to use as a swap. Keep in mind that any time this ratio is changed, the idler arm ratio should also be changed.

Because the Chrysler products all used inline 6 and

During the late 1930s, MoPars came with their own versions of the tubing axle (Ford had tubes on some cars/trucks in 1939-'40). These axles have long been known to traditional hot rodders who have used them under a variety of cars. Shown are two Fords with the axles in place. The giveaway to the MoPar tube axle is the extra bend at the center area.

8 cylinder engines until the 1950s, the earlier cars tend to have a narrow frame configuration around the engine compartment. For this reason, when a late model V8 engine is used, most builders decided to change the Chrysler original steering gearbox and go for the steering box out of a later MoPar. Often, the steering gearbox can be mounted outboard an inch or two, but the easiest way to get steering gearbox/steering column shaft clearance is to offset the engine 2 - 3 inches to the right. Most builders of Chrysler product rods in the "fat" category also decide to go with the later model MoPar power steering gearbox.

As mentioned, the big drawback to using the Chrysler type independent front suspension is poor brakes. Disc brake conversions are possible, and some hot rod aftermarket suppliers are now beginning to create special disc brake kits. See the section on brakes for more information.

It is possible to cut the front off a MoPar frame and replace it with a "frame clip" from another, later-model MoPar or other make of car. This is a lot of work, however, for a minimal gain, since the problem is brakes, not the independent suspension system. To keep the car all MoPar, this kind of front clip swap also requires some extra work at the torsion bar rear mounting points (assuming the front clip will be post-1956 MoPar). However, we have seen a very interesting swap where a 1960s era mid-sized MoPar front clip was welded to a '40 Dodge frame. The late MoPar unit was an abbreviated frame section, of course, since these are unit-construction cars. But the interesting thing was that, in this case at least, the front body mount bolt hole in the late frame clip was identical in placement to the earlier Dodge! Some planning with a measuring tape just might prove very beneficial to anyone going the frame clip swap route.

When a frame clip is being made, the donor clip is cut off at a convenient point, usually right at the donor car firewall. If the frame is a perimeter type (bulges outward at the firewall) or a wasp type (necks in at the firewall), the idea is to cut the donor frame at a point where it is flat and going under the body flooring, and where it is almost the same width as the recipient car.

The exact wheelbase of the original car must be used as the guidepoint for this swap, and the donor front clip is positioned to get this wheelbase before the two frames are welded together.

All of this is assuming use of a non-MoPar front clip. If the MoPar torsion bar front suspension is used, you get the added feature of having a large amount of front end height adjustment, something that non-MoPar front ends don't have. On older Chrysler products that have fat fenders, but do not have IFS, the Gibbon Products MoPar torsion bar front end kit would be a good possibility. While this kit has been designed for fat fender Fords through 1948, it would take only a small amount of modification to get the unit under something such as a 1935 Plymouth. Gibbon can be

When the Mustang/Pinto independent front suspension is being put under a non-Ford frame, specially built crossmember usually fits flush against lower lip of frame rails. Mounts for upper A-arms come in kits, or must be fabricated by builder.

The popular Jaguar independent front suspension kits can be adapted to all early MoPar frames. Kit crossmember can be moved to give different heights to the finished product. But, since these kits are made mostly for Ford products, the builder has to do some engineering.

STEERING GEAR

Chrysler Corporation has had a good reputation with steering systems since the very beginning. However, since the 1950s, when power steering became universally available, the common complaint against MoPar power steering has been that it is not sensitive enough to road feel. This is usually a complaint of Ford and GM product owners who are more used to a factory built-in front end feedback that is heavy to the driver's feel.

Because the Chrysler products have tended to be heavier than Ford or Chevrolet, the steering gearboxes have tended to be of a slower gear ratio. The bigger the MoPar, the slower the ratio. Much of this was compounded during the 1940-'54 era, when the big Chryslers and Dodges and DeSotos were wearing the largest tires on the road. Coupled with huge steering wheels, the MoPar boxes could be trusted to park the car. But they also tended to give a kind of vague feel to the steering at speed.

Since the MoPar steering gearboxes are strong, the quick fix for steering ratio is to lengthen the pitman arm slightly, and reduce the steering wheel size. Pitman arms of various lengths were produced through the years, so it is possible to find longer arms in the junk yards (we're talking cross-steering here). Smaller diameter aftermarket steering wheels are about the only thing available at specialty parts stores now, so steering wheel size is automatically reduced. Just keep in mind that the easy steering of a stock MoPar box will go away when the longer pitman arm and smaller steering wheel are installed.

Not so well known is the fact that the Dodge van drag link (side) steering gearboxes work very well when a drag link steering is used. This type of gearbox goes through the frame (or over/under it) just ahead of the firewall, and connects to the left front spindle via a drag link. The Dodge van box has been used by non-MoPar rod builders for years, but it is nowhere near as well known as the Mustang or Vega gearboxes. As good as this box is, this type of steering has almost disappeared from modern rod building practices.

A note: Some of the Chrysler vehicles imported from Japan have great cross-steering gearboxes. Smaller in overall size than the American MoPar units, these boxes compare favorably with the popular Vega box in size. They are smoother, and are even available as very compact power units.

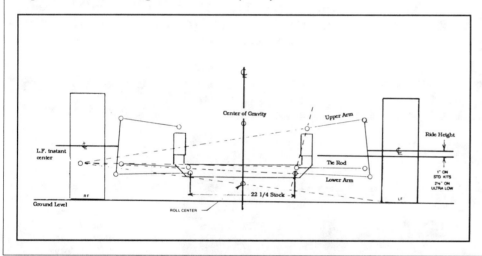

There are a great number of different factors involved in front end geometry, and a change in one usually results in a change in the others. Factory engineers have figured out solutions to most of the problems. Hot rodders can make good things bad.

contacted at PO Box 490, Gibbon, NE 68840. This particular kit has been developed using the fore/aft torsion bar system common to the mid/large size MoPar vehicles built since 1957.

While the Mustang/Pinto independent front suspension has found great favor among Ford and Chevy enthusiasts during the past several years, the Volare cross-chassis torsion bar front end has been making great inroads with pickup owners. Pickups of all makes. No wonder, since the Volare front suspension is an all-inclusive design worked up around a stamped sheetmetal K-member, that is held to the frame by just 4 bolts.

Since all independent front suspension MoPar vehicles have a good front end to begin with, only the cars of the early 1930s with Chrysler Corporation trademarks get much in the way of Mustang IFS swaps. The Mustang front suspension can be cut from a donor car and the entire sheetmetal crossmember unit adapted to the MoPar frame. Better yet is to make up a new crossmember, or buy one of the special kits made for Ford and Chevy cars. These kits can be adapted to the Chrysler/Dodge/Plymouth/DeSoto frames very easily, simply by cutting away the stock MoPar front crossmember. When installing these kits, be sure to set the angle of the top A-arm inner mount at the stock Mustang factory setting. As a rule, the crossmember will fit flush against the bottom edge of each frame side rail, but it can be tilted slightly. When setting up a bare frame, set the frame at a slightly downhill angle, rear to front. The front of a rod that has the "just right rake" will usually have the frame front end about 2 inches lower than the rear end (from level). When the Mustang A-arms are set at the correct angle (about 6 degrees from level, front end high), the front end will then have built-in anti-dive characteristics common to new cars.

Weld the Mustang front crossmember in place, and gusset it well. Strength should take precedence over pretty!

Part of the desirability of the Mustang IFS is the rack and pinion steering. The R&P can be positioned properly, and still eliminate much of the engine clearance problems common to the more traditional steering gearbox.

This clearance is generally not a problem with the Volare front end, since the gearbox nestles nicely down inside the K-member, usually well out of the way of exhaust headers and accessories. Although there are not currently any aftermarket kits that adapt the Volare front suspension to cars or trucks, it is only a matter of time before they are available.

The drawback of the Volare front suspension as a swap is the width of the transverse (cross-chassis) torsion bars. Whereas the traditional MoPar torsion bar has been front-to-back, when the entire unit is made as a single component, the transverse bar works better. But, when the Volare suspension is used in cars and trucks of older years, the wheels/tires tend to be right at the edge of the fender opening (as viewed from front or back). This extra wide stance can be reduced by cutting a section from the K-member, but the torsion bars must also be shortened, a problem for most

builders. When someone builds a good K-member replacement, along with shortened (and diameter reduced) bars, this will become one of the most popular front ends for hot rods ever. Partly because with such a front suspension, it is possible to adjust the vehicle front end height through a full range of 7 inches! This adjustment simply is not available with any other type of independent front suspension.

We haven't seen the Volare front end used under MoPar products, even though it is a natural. The Volare front suspension K-member can be bolted below ladder frames with the factory insulator rubber biscuits, or it can be welded directly to the frame rails. Very popular among Chevy pickup owners of the 1955-'62 variety is the use of a Volare K-member set into the lower frame rails 2 inches, then welded. This allows the pickup front end to be lowered so that the bumper practically drags the pavement, but with torsion bar adjustment the front end is brought up to a more practical street-use height.

Obviously, after the torsion bar appeared on Chrysler products in the 1950s, most of the engineering went into product refinement. Rodders and customizers building post-1956 MoPars do little more to the front end than add disc brakes, and perhaps an aftermarket large-diameter anti-sway bar.

4-BAR & CROSS-LEAF SPRINGS

Left- Perhaps the most popular of the early MoPars in hot rodding would be the 1932-'34 body styles. These cars have semi-elliptic front suspension, and with the larger fenders most any kind of late model independent front suspension can be installed. However, should the builder want to go with something like a 4-bar Ford type cross spring beam/ tube axle front end, it is possible. This car has such a unit.

Right- In this case, a SuperBell 3-1/2" dropped tube axle replaced the stock MoPar beam axle/semi-elliptic spring setup.

Left- One of the great features of early Chrysler products is the beefy frame. Note how bulky the front crossmember is. If an independent suspension, such as from a Jaguar or Mustang were to be used, the side rails would need to be straightened the same as in this Ford swap, and the large front crossmember replaced.

Below- Here the frame rails have been cut off just behind the stock front crossmember. Extensions of 3x4-inch rectangular tubing have been added. These extensions run well ahead of the Ford front crossmember to give mounting points for front of fenders and front bumper. This 4-bar radius rod kit is from a 1932 Ford design.

The Ford front crossmember should be tacked in place until new spring is in place, since this spring sets at a slight angle (about 5 degrees, front high). Weld and gusset the crossmember where it meets the side rails.

MoPar drag link steering is as close as any Dodge van. The gearbox can mount through the frame, as shown, or above the frame. Mustang gearboxes can also be used, laid on their side.

With the fenders and radiator back in place, all you see of the Ford type front suspension is this.

FAT MOPAR SHOCK KIT

New from Mr. Street Rod, 17459 Kranenburg Ave., Bakersfield, CA 93312 is a shock absorber kit to replace the aging units found in all MoPars since the Thirties. One of the neat things about Chrysler products has been the inclusion of tube shocks long before other car makers. The stock shocks usually are dead, and need replacing.

Right- The Mr. Street Rod kit includes new shocks, lower attachment brackets, and new frame upper brackets.

Left- The lower and upper stock shock absorber studs must be cut from the A-arms and the stubs ground smooth.

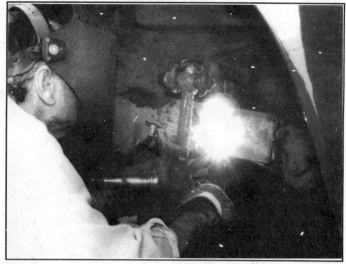

Upper Left- Area on the frame where the new upper shock brackets will be welded in place must be ground clean.

Above- While the upper mounts could be bolted to the frame, it is much easier to weld them in place.

Left- The lower bracket is attached to the lower A-arm, to the inboard side of caster adjustment zerk fitting.

Below- This new shock mounting gets better utilization of the shock than did original Chrysler type mounts.

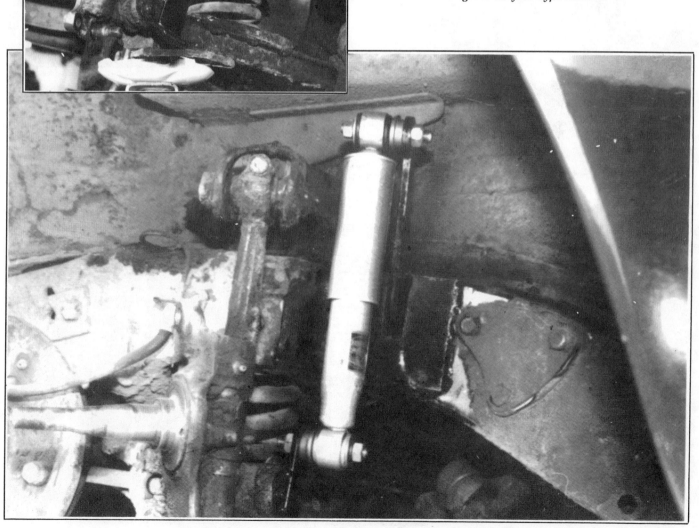

49

VOLARE SWAPS

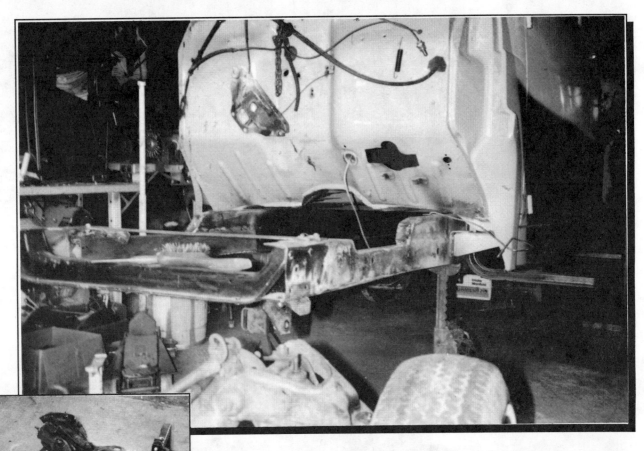

Above- The Volare front suspension is held to the vehicle with just 4 bolts. When it is removed as a unit, everything comes out attached to the K-member. Steering is tucked tight against left side A-arm tower. Torsion bars are across chassis ahead of the K-member.

Left- Any frame can be straightened with channel or tubing extensions. Here an early pickup straight frame has original crossmembers removed and top part of frame notched for working clearance of Volare upper A-arms. If the unit were to be positioned lower, that is the entire car would be lower to the ground, the notch could be on the bottom. Some frames are narrow enough, others must be modified to accept the Volare K-member.

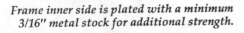

Frame inner side is plated with a minimum 3/16" metal stock for additional strength.

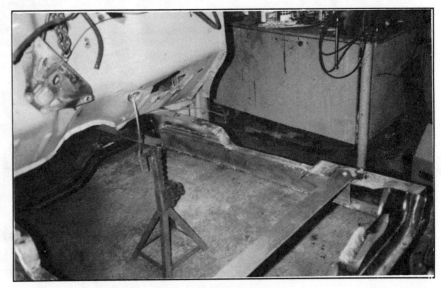

Above- This photo shows why the frame rails were notched. Volare A-arm towers are wider than A-arm pivot point, which is the problem.

Above- Note how the K-member nestles up against flat bottom of the frame. The K-member can be welded to the frame. Most builders prefer to build brackets off frame and bolt K-member in place at original points.

Left- The steering is tucked out of the way. Here an extra rod was welded across the notch in the frame rails for additional strength.

Below- In this installation, the K-member has been fit up into the frame notch on the lower edge of the frame, then everything welded in place.

INSTALLING A MUSTANG
IFS IN A '37 PLYMOUTH

Doc cut the '74 Mustang II front suspension from the donor car, then split the front crossmember so it would slip over the front of the Plymouth frame. The crossmember was welded back together at its original width, which is about 2-1/2 inches less than the Plymouth's original 60 inches. This allows room for 6-1/2-inch-wide rims (original Plymouth rims were 4 inches wide).

by Geoff Carter

If there's one thing an older MoPar can use to advantage, it's an updated front end that gives it disc brakes, advanced independent front suspension, and a late-model steering system.

Here's an example of a '37 Plymouth that is getting the upgrade just mentioned. This car belongs to Jim Goddard of Los Angeles, and it is having a '74 Mustang II front end swapped in. The work is being performed by Doc MacDougall at Doc's Hot Rod Welding in Long Beach, California. Here's a run-down on what is being done in these photos.

The engine is an '86 Camaro 305 V8 with all factory accessories. It rests on mounts made by Doc with Datsun 510 control arm bushings.

Doc made new lower strut mounts from 1/2" steel, boxing them with 3/16" plate for additional strength. The rest of the suspension — including the power rack and pinion steering — is stock salvage yard Mustang II. All that's needed to combine Chevy pump and Mustang steering is a set of custom hoses.

A '78 Granada 8-inch rearend at stock width is slightly narrower than the '37 Plymouth. Swap required merely cutting off spring pads, then re-welding them to align with the original springs. Doc made his own lowering block style pads of 2x3-inch rectangular tubing and de-arched the springs 1-1/2 inches to make the main leaf straight and keep the car from riding too high. Then he hung everything with new stock shackles and U-bolts in their original positions.

The Mustang's 9-inch brake rotors gave way to '78 Granada 11-inch discs. Then Doc modified a commercial mounting kit and adapted '83 Camaro/Chevelle calipers.

With '78 Granada brakes on all four corners, matching the rest of the components with a '78 Granada "combination valve" is simple. A '78 Fairmont master cylinder with 7/8" piston makes booster unnecessary.

Left- The '87 Cadillac Cimmaron steering wheel slips onto the '78 Chevy van tilting column. Doc added the Plymouth medallion. An additional 2-1/2 inches of sheetmetal on the bottom of the dash gives room for switches and air conditioner outlets.

A new firewall was built 4-1/2 inches back to go with the new passenger compartment floor. The interior will be finished with Cimmaron front seats and original rear seats covered with matching material.

SPRINGS

Suspending a vehicle axle from the frame is done by employing some form of spring system, which may be a leaf type, coil type, torsion bar, hydraulic, or air. In hot rodding, the first three are the most common, but air and hydraulic will certainly become predominant in rodding as factory units finally make it to the boneyard.

The leaf spring is most common, and modifications/repairs are the same for both semi-elliptic and transverse types. An old spring will need to be rebuilt before being pressed into service, but the rebuild process is fairly simple. Place the spring in a vise and squeeze it adjacent to the centerbolt. Remove the centerbolt and open the vise. To soften the spring rate, one rule of thumb is to remove every other leaf, counting the main leaf as number one. However, this is only a starting point and it will be necessary to experiment with altering the spring rate after the springs are installed on the car. If a heavy engine (such as a Hemi) is in the car, most of the original leaves will need to be used.

Wirebrush and grind each spring leaf until it has all rust removed. The end of each leaf, where it contacts the leaf below, should be rounded so the leaves don't dig into the each other. Place strips of something like Teflon between each leaf and bolt the spring pack back together, with the aid of the vise. Alignment clamps toward the end of the spring will help keep the leaves running true.

The vehicle can get a kind of free lowering job of about an inch, if the main leaf has the eyes reversed. The best advice here is to have a spring shop re-arch the main leaf so that the eyes are on top, or make up a new main leaf. There are other ways to do this at home, all difficult and not nearly worth the small amount of cost the spring shop will charge.

Semi-elliptic springs usually don't need more than a couple of the shorter leaves removed, and sometimes not even that. But they do need to be cleaned and have the leaf ends tapered. Use Teflon on these springs as

The torsion bar and the coil spring are the same type of spring but in different configurations. Coil springs of many varieties are used on rods. Local suspension shops can wind springs with different rates for special applications.

Torsion bars are the most simple of springs and they can be adapted to rods very easily. The most common types run parallel to each frame rail and connect to the axle by a lever arm. The arm must have shackles for free movement. The rear end of the bar can be made adjustable to control frame height.

well. The main leaf may also have the eyes reversed, but keep axle/frame clearance firmly in mind before doing this.

Semi-elliptic springs, as used at the rear of a rod, can pose some real problems. For the most part, trying to find something to use yields springs that are far too long for the early car chassis. If the car is a non-Ford, the stock springs can almost always be used. These springs will be narrower and shorter than modern semi-elliptic, thus they will be stiffer. You want to make them as soft as possible and still hold the frame high enough.

The semi-elliptic spring for rearends will normally have a short front section and a long rear portion. The short (stiffer) front piece helps control torque wrap-up of the rear axle, while the long section provides a soft ride.

Coil springs work exactly the same way as a leaf, it's just a different shape. While coil springs can be made to work on a solid front axle, appearance never seems

quite right. The exception is the coil/shock design where the spring wraps around the shock absorber. Coil spring rate is dictated by coil wire diameter, total coil diameter, wire cross-section, and coils per inch. Through trial and error, coil-over manufacturers have come up with coil rates for the most common types of hot rods. If you're working with something uncommon, you'll have to go through the same trial and error.

Weight of the car determines the appropriate spring rate. A roadster, minus fenders, and running a small-block V8, may have a total weight of about 2200 pounds. A coupe with fenders will come in a couple hundred pounds heavier. Most early rods will weigh between 2500 - 3000 pounds. Cars of the '50s and later will be right around 3200 pounds. The weight of early cars will be distributed almost equally, 50% front and 50% rear. Cars produced after 1937 will have a weight distribution closer to 60% front and 40% rear. This weight distribution has a bearing on the spring rates as well as

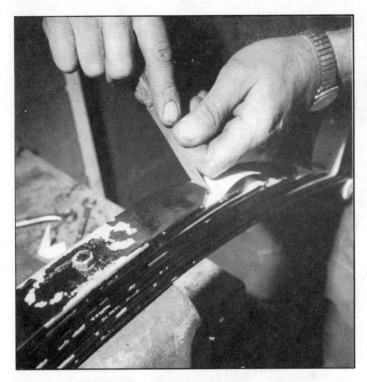

Teflon sheet stock has been placed between the spring leaves and is being trimmed. This reduces friction between spring leaves and makes a dramatic improvement in ride, making the leaf spring almost as good as the coil or torsion bar.

Quarter-elliptic springs are used on either the front or rear of the car. An upper locater bar must be used to control axle wind-up. This is a good system where space is at a premium but the springs must be strong. The spring acts as one of the suspension locating members.

on braking.

The torsion bar is a kind of straight coil spring, or a leaf spring that twists. In fact, some of the earlier Volkswagen torsion bars were simply stacks of flat spring stock that twisted in use. Torsion bar length and diameter, as well as actuating arm, determines rate.

A common problem in rodding is trying to match an existing coil spring to an older car. Find a car with a very similar corner weight requirement, and the coil spring wire diameter will be close. The length will probably be way off.

Rod builders make the common mistake of cutting coil springs to fit a particular application without regard to spring rate. Usually, the cut-down coil is too strong.

If a junkyard spring cannot be found, spring shops can wind a coil spring to fit. Unfortunately, they will also be working mostly on a trial and error basis, so you may have to go through a couple of springs to get exactly what you need.

Torsion bars can be modified by changing the actuating bar length, bar length or bar diameter. If the bar diameter must be reduced, have a machine shop do it in small increments until you get what you need. Again, the best advice when selecting a torsion bar is to find one on a vehicle with similar weight characteristics to the car being built. Suggestion: look hard at the torsion bars under some Japanese import pickups. They bolt to the back of the lower A-arm, and it takes very little imagination to see how they could be made to work with either independent or solid front ends (or rear ends). The entire IFS from these trucks could very

well be adapted to earlier cars.

There is one kind of elliptic spring that sometimes is used in rodding, usually as a space consideration. It is most normally found at the rear, but it can be used at the front. The quarter-elliptic is simply a single semi-elliptic spring cut in half just behind the centerbolt. The big end of the spring is bolted to the frame rails (parallel) and the small end is bolted to the axle. A common mistake is to make this spring too short, resulting in a very firm ride. Early in American car production, the quarter-elliptic was used at the front.

There is a growing tendency among more sophisticated rod builders to try to hide as much suspension componentry as possible, starting with the springs. This has lead to the use of cantilever A-arm designs, with the coil/springs mounted inside the frame rails (usually hidden by a grille shell or race car nose piece). This is not a new or unique idea, since it has been used by road racing cars for many years. Here, the inside of the A-arm extends beyond the mounting point at the frame and connects to the spring/shock. It can be a very effective system, but it does take a lot of planning.

One interesting offshoot of such a system is that either hydraulic or air suspension can also be used. Since the hydraulic designs are still rather uncommon, the air units offer the most promise to the exotic rod builder. These can be found on some of the older import cars and some massive units are used on trucks. You would probably have to work with a manufacturer to create a homebuilt air suspension system, but it does work, and quite well.

With any kind of spring, the idea is to connect the spring as close to the axle end as feasible. This way the slightest movement at the wheel immediately interacts with the spring. You want the spring action to be smooth and to become increasingly stiff as the wheel

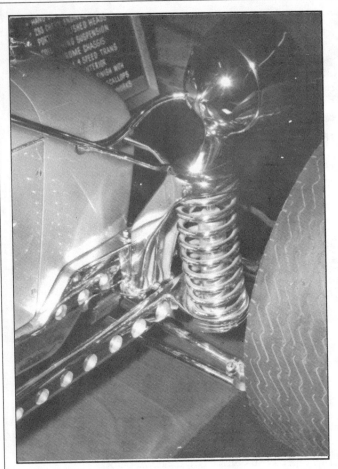

We show a variety of coil spring types here to give ideas of how coil springs and coil-over shocks can be used. These are popular on rods because of their compact size and smooth ride quality.

The closer the springs are to the ends of the axle, the better the ride control. This was not a bad approach on a show car several years ago.

The coil-over shock and spring combination surfaced during the '60s on race cars. These on a Jaguar rearend are now seen on just about every type of car, from race to street. Springs can be "stacked" by adjustments on shock bodies, and all kinds of different spring rates are available. The big advantage is in space and weight savings.

Seldom seen in rodding is a fenderless rod with semi-elliptic front springs, but it was common practice with old-time race cars.

This is how a single-leaf semi-elliptic spring can be used. Locater bars will be advised with sing leaf spring.

moves upward from its static position.

The new generation of leaf springs (and probably coil and torsion springs as well) will be made of some kind of non-metal, like the "plastic" spring in the Corvette. It would seem entirely feasible with current technology to make a multi-leaf plastic spring that would work very well in the older rods. The Corvette single leaf spring might even be adapted to the semi-elliptic design.

THE ACKERMAN PRINCIPLE

Consider the car as it turns in a constant circle. The inside front wheel is turning a smaller-radius circle than the outside front wheel. Something must be done in the front steering mechanism to allow this to happen. This something is called the Ackerman principle, and if you look at a set of spindles you see that the steering arms on the spindles have the tie rod end holes closer to the center of the car than the kingpin holes.

If you draw a line from the center of the kingpin to the center of the rear axle, the line should pass directly through the steering arm rod end holes. If not, the car does not have perfect Ackerman effect. Current mass production technology is beginning to ignore this principle somewhat. Some new cars with rack and pinion steering ahead of the front axle centerline actually have the outer tire turning tighter than the inner wheel. Tire technology is offsetting some of this problem and so is wheel offset, but for our purposes, stick with making a pure Ackerman effect on your rod.

If it is necessary to bend a spindle steering arm for any reason, be sure and set it so that the Ackerman check line described is obtained. Sometimes, when a crossleaf spring is used on a frame with a suicide spring perch, the tie rod runs into frame interference. Rodders have cured the problem by reversing the spindles side-for-side. This puts the tie rod in front of the axle. And the Ackerman goes out the window, resulting in very poor turning control at higher speeds. If there were enough room, the spindles could be heated and bent outward so that the tie rod holes would again line up for the Ackerman check. Not really conceivable, so better to find another way and keep the tie rod behind the axle.

One method is to mount a rack and pinion steering gear directly to the solid axle. This is usually a simple matter of two sturdy brackets between the rack and pinion unit and the axle. This creates a problem with the steering shaft, however. As the axle travels up and down, the effective length of the steering shaft changes. Some new cars use spline sections in the steering shaft, and rodders cure the variable-length problem this way.

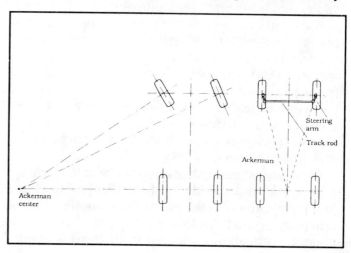

SCRUB LINE

One of the more important checks in any vehicle safety test would be that of the scrub line. That is, any part of the chassis/body that hangs below the wheel's diameter. Unfortunately, a large percentage of hot rod builders violate this basic safety tenet, with both early and late model vehicles.

The reason for not wanting to have anything hanging lower than the bottom wheel lip is obvious. Given a flat tire, the offending part(s) can cause serious problems. One example would be a steering pitman arm that is too low. It digs into the pavement and the car can go out of control instantly. A bracket or such grinding against the pavement sends up sparks and a fire can result.

While it is true that a flat tire seldom lets the wheel rest on the road surface, good building sense says never take chances. To check for scrub line violations, have a buddy hold the end of a long string while you hold the other end. Start by running the string between the bottom edges of the two front wheel. Then move the string diagonally from one front wheel to the opposite rear wheel. If there seems to be something hanging too low, it is worth a further check, and repair if necessary.

ALIGNMENT

Once you have the suspension system installed, all would seem well and good. It is ... almost! Now, you must make the wheels roll true, and do what they should do in a turn.

Leave the final wheel alignment to the professional shop. However, there is a lot of alignment that you can do at home to get things at least in the ballpark. Since most projects are a long time from first movement to final drive-away, this initial alignment will help things considerably.

A note here: If you have an independent rear suspension, it is vital that this unit be aligned by the professional. Such systems have a lot to do with how the vehicle will handle, and they are not simply set with the wheels parallel to the chassis and vertical to the ground.

Rearend alignment is supposed to be right on the money if you have measured carefully when attaching all the mounting brackets. Quite often it is. But to find out, measure diagonally from the leading edge of the rearend housing at the outer brake backing plate flange, to some known point on the opposite frame rail, well forward. Do this on each side to the opposite rail. If the frame has measured square, this will give exact true to the rearend. Measure across the chassis from the rearend housing flange to make absolutely sure the rearend is centered under the frame. If the rearend must be moved, now is the time to do it.

Front end alignment is similar. The axle at the spindle should measure identical on a diagonal to a frame point. Adjustment at the radius rod mount(s) or the A-arm mounts will bring this into "square". Now, lay the kingpin inclination backward until there is about 5 degrees of caster in the spindle. The wishbone or 4-bar set-up can be adjusted, and shims are available to be placed between A-arm mounts and the A-arm itself. Since there are a number of different adjustments in the A-arm system, ask the front end professional for adjustment points with your particular system.

Wheel camber, or the amount the wheel leans in at the bottom versus the top, is not important at this time, although a sighting down the wheel line from in front should show the bottom tilted in slightly from the top.

If you have decent caster, and the camber is usable, then the only other factor is toe-in/toe-out. Measure across the wheels from one side to the other, using a tire sidewall or tread mid-point as reference. Generally speaking, at this early stage, something like 3/8" toe-in will work. That is, the measurement across the front of the tires will be closer together by 3/8" than measuring the same place at the rear of the tires. If you do not have a toe-in or toe-out factor in the front end, you'll feel a lot of shimmy in the steering.

Trying to measure the rear of the tires can be a problem (as in the front, if there is sheetmetal in the way). A quick solution is to tape plumb bob weights to the center of the tire, front and rear, then measure from these (near the floor).

Sometimes, no amount of toe-in work seems to remove shimmy from a front end, especially one using a solid front axle. Try as much as 1/2" toe-out. This often cures the problem. Of course, shimmy can also be caused by excessive play in the kingpin bushings, or excess play in the tie rod ends. Also check the steering gearbox for wear. *Diagrams on next page*

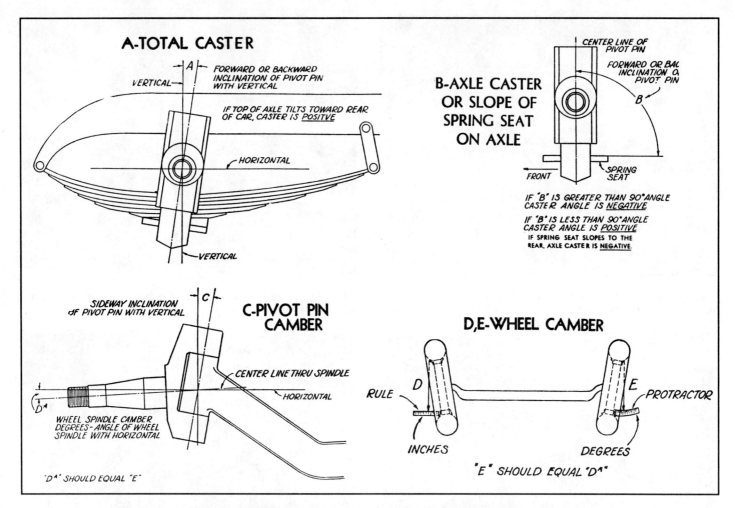

A-TOTAL CASTER

VERTICAL
A
FORWARD OR BACKWARD
INCLINATION OF PIVOT PIN
WITH VERTICAL
IF TOP OF AXLE TILTS TOWARD REAR
OF CAR, CASTER IS POSITVE
HORIZONTAL
VERTICAL

B-AXLE CASTER
OR SLOPE OF
SPRING SEAT
ON AXLE

CENTER LINE OF
PIVOT PIN
FORWARD OR BAC
INCLINATION O
PIVOT PIN
B
FRONT
SPRING
SEAT

IF "B" IS GREATER THAN 90°ANGLE
CASTER ANGLE IS NEGATIVE
IF "B" IS LESS THAN 90°ANGLE
CASTER ANGLE IS POSITIVE
IF SPRING SEAT SLOPES TO THE
REAR, AXLE CASTER IS NEGATIVE.

SIDEWAY INCLINATION
OF PIVOT PIN WITH VERTICAL
C
C-PIVOT PIN
CAMBER
CENTER LINE THRU SPINDLE
HORIZONTAL
D
WHEEL SPINDLE CAMBER
DEGREES-ANGLE OF WHEEL
SPINDLE WITH HORIZONTAL
"D" SHOULD EQUAL "E"

D,E-WHEEL CAMBER

D
RULE
INCHES
E
PROTRACTOR
DEGREES
"E" SHOULD EQUAL "D"

A MIRADA SUBFRAME
INTO A '53 DODGE TRUCK

photos by Gerry Charvat

Here's a great approach to building an early '50s MoPar pickup into a neat piece. This example involves a 1953 Dodge pickup that gets the full front end makeover, leaving it with a more powerful engine, smooth-riding independent front suspension and a lot of other late-model equipment.

The donor car, whence came most of the neat new stuff, was a 1980 Mirada. Parts scavenged from the Mirada include the engine, wiring harness, pedal assembly, parking brake, K member, rear springs and even some of the nuts and bolts. The rear axle came from a big Chrysler, because the Mirada was too narrow. In the capable hands of the guys at The Hot Rod Shop (5706 Industrial Rd., Fort Wayne, Indiana 46825; (219) 482-7473), this old truck was given a chance to live again.

The total project took 123.5 hours for a turn-key truck that is safe to drive home. And what a driver it turned out to be! Smooth, soft and comfortable. Not at all like the original '53 pickup — which was all truck, through and through. Of course, the trick cosmetics are due to come later.

Under all that glamorous sheetmetal, this is what a '53 Dodge truck looks like. Pretty straightforward truck stuff, guaranteed to shake your spine loose.

Stage one of this project is to remove the front suspension pieces, including the crossmember.

With the front of the truck supported on jackstands, the stock frame rails are ready to be cut off.

Measure forward eleven inches from the front body mount, and make a vertical cut through each frame rail at that point.

A trial fit of the K member from the 1980 Mirada looks good. This swap is going to give the old truck upgraded suspension, steering and brakes.

In order to mate the old Dodge frame with the new Mirada front end, 2" x 4" rectangular steel tubing is used to join the two.

Overall length of the tubing is 26 inches. Measuring forward, 7 inches of the rear portion of the tube is welded to the top of the frame rail. Coming forward another 6.5 inches, we find the centerline for a 2-inch-diameter hole that must be cut through the inner side of the frame extension to permit access to a mounting bolt.

NEW! NEW! NEW!

SPECIALTY BOOKS FROM TEX SMITH

FROM THE PRO'S WHO KNOW ALL ABOUT BACKYARD BUILDING. MEGA PAGES, HEAVILY ILLUSTRATED, PLASTICIZED ENAMEL COVERS, CRAMMED AND JAMMED WITH USEABLE INFORMATION ABOUT BUILDING HOT RODS AND CUSTOMS.

Warning! These are not golly-gee-whiz books, these are hard core building manuals for people who need to know how to make cars and trucks. You don't skim through these babies in 30 minutes and toss them. You keep them. You refer to them time and time again.

SPECIAL PRE-PUBLICATION PRICES ON SOME TITLES, GOOD UNTIL THE BOOK IS IN PRINT.
(PRINT DATES ALL IN 1990)

HOW TO BUILD REAL HOT RODS, *Tex Smith*	$15
HOW TO BUILD CUSTOM CARS, *Tex Smith/Rich Johnson*	$17.95
HOT ROD/CUSTOM/KIT CAR ELECTRIC SYSTEMS, *Skip Readio*	$13
HOW TO DRAW CARS, *Denny Krist*	$17.95
HOW TO CHOP TOPS, *Tex Smith*	$17.95
HOW TO BUILD CHRYSLER/PLYMOUTH/DODGE HOT RODS, *Tex Smith/Rich Johnson*	$17.95
HOW TO BUILD CHEVY HOT RODS, *Tex Smith/Rich Johnson,*	$17.95
HOT ROD HISTORY, PART ONE, *Tom Medley, (Pre-Publication)*	$12.95

(On all orders, add $2 postage for each book)
Payment for book orders by check/MO or credit card only.
Please send me the books checked, I enclose a check/money order, or use my Mastercard/Visa

\# _____ Exp. _____

Signed _____

Name _____ Ph. _____

Street _____

City _____ State _____ Zip _____

CREDIT CARD ORDERS BY TELEPHONE 1-800-782-0539 during normal working hours.

Tex Smith Publishing, PO Box 726 Driggs ID. 83422

ZOWIE!

Send a SASE for information about the terrific new line of Tex Smith CAR CLOTHES. Bomber jackets, roadsters, authentic signature stroker caps, scarves...all the zoomie stuff you need for real hot rodding!

63

On the bottom side of the tubing, a 5/8-inch hole is drilled at the centerline of the previously-mentioned 2-inch hole. This 5/8-inch hole is for the mounting bolt to the K member. Note the marked area of the tubing to be removed for a clearance notch.

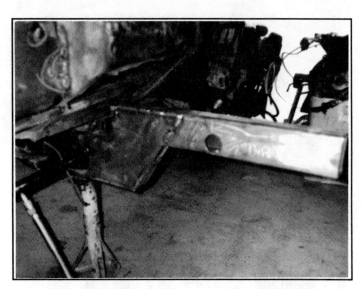

After welding the frame extension in place, reinforce it with steel plate welded to each side. Box across the end of the frame and the gusset plates for additional strength.

The first section of the frame extension has been completed, and the truck is ready to receive the Mirada front end for a trial fit.

Use the original mounting bolts and the rubber mounting pads when fitting up the K member to the new frame extensions.

The second section of frame extension is made of 2" x 4" rectangular steel tubing, with clearance notch and holes drilled for access to mounting bolts. (See accompanying sketches for exact dimensions).

The new extensions are installed with a 2-inch off-set to the outside. The K member now bolts to the frame extension just as if Dodge designed it that way. Neat!

Note the K member mounting bolts inside the access holes in the frame extensions. Note also how the clearance notch in the forward extension section fits over the mounting pad.

The firewall is now cut to allow clearance for the 318 V8 engine from the '80 Mirada.

Left- After surgery to the firewall, the big engine fits with all the stock equipment still attached.

Below- With the front sheetmetal installed, the K member torsion bars were adjusted down so the truck would sit about 2 inches above the floor. That's not practical for driving, but it demonstrates the range of suspension adjustment available with the Mirada front end.

Mirada radiator, wiring, power brake unit and everything fit like it belonged in this engine compartment.

The rear end came from a big Chrysler because the Mirada was too narrow. However, the '80 Mirada leaf springs were installed, along with Monroe air shocks. Note the steel tube cross member installed for upper shock mounts. Angle iron spring mounts made this an easy bolt-on.

Above- The Mirada leather bucket seats fit perfectly in the truck's cab, and the driver now has the advantage of a tilt steering column and a comfortable wheel.

Above- The steering column and pedal assembly from the 1980 Mirada fit easily into the '53 Dodge truck.

Left- Except for the cosmetics, the truck is now ready to roll. Total shop time was 123.5 hours for a turn-key job. Ride and handling were phenomenal, and it was amazing how easily everything fit together.

DISC BRAKES

Early Chrysler products suffer from very poor original drum brakes. Trying to adapt disc brakes has been a major problem until this solution came along. On MoPar products of the '50s and later, it is possible to swap spindles from newer MoPars that have discs.

by Ed Gross

When I was putting my 440-powered '48 Plymouth sedan together, I recognized that the front brakes, which needed to be rebuilt, would be inadequate. When looking at the available kits for this model, you better have deep pockets because the only kit I found was $650 plus. So, the only other answer was to be creative (also known as cheap). When my brother-in-law offered to give me the backing plates, rotors and calipers from his early '70s Blazer, I couldn't pass them up. But these units, originally from a 4-wheel drive 16-1/2"-wheeled Blazer, proved to be too massive to fit inside of 15" wheels. So, it was back to the drawing board.

By looking around an auto recycling center (junkyard), I found that the '79-'85 Oldsmobile Toronado used a front rotor that does not have a hub attached. I believe the same rotor is used on the front of Eldorados and front and rear of Rivieras.

Originally, I planned to have the '48 Plymouth hub machined to fit inside of the rotor, but it fit without any machining. To attach the rotor to the hub, I first removed the brake drum from the hub and used it as a drilling template for the 29/64" holes in the rotor. Note: there's enough material for at least two attempts to get it right. Next, the rotor was tapped for the 1/2" clearance holes to allow the studs to pass through and attach to the rotor. I assembled the hubs and rotors and then had the rotors turned. It may be necessary to disassemble the hubs and rotors and shim them to make up for any imperfections.

The backing plates I used came from the early Blazer 4-wheel drive. They're made of formed 1/4" plate and could adapt to other applications. It was easy to fit them to the three mounting bosses on the spindle. Alignment was made on the center, and three 9/16" holes were drilled in the backing plates. I then attached the calipers (with new brake pads) and slid them over the rotors. After straightening and trimming the mounting ears, I tack welded them in position. They were removed and finish welded on the bench.

Final assembly was made with new wheel bearings, oil seals and hoses. You can have hoses custom made, or look through the cross reference books for a car using the same caliper for a hose that is less bulky than the Blazer's. You will only be able to use 15" wheels intended for use on disc brake cars.

Any questions, contact Ed Gross, Down 'n Dirty Rod Shop, 221 N. Elias St., Wales, Wisconsin 53183.

The '48 Plymouth spindle is very similar to a full range of Chrysler products from 1940 on.

There is enough area in the Toronado hub to allow making two sets of wheel bolt holes, in case of mistake.

The Plymouth drum with hub removed is shown alongside the Toronado rotor. The hub fits inside the Toronado rotor without any machine work. Rotor must be drilled to hub bolt pattern.

The Toronado rotor is drilled and tapped 1/2"-20 for wheel studs.

Above Left- Blazer backing plate was drilled to mount to Plymouth spindle (arrows, three holes), and the caliper ears were cut and repositioned.

Above- Dotted lines show where caliper mounting ears were cut and rewelded.

Left- Installed, the discs clear 15" passenger car wheels that were designed for disc brakes.

LATE MOPAR
DISC BRAKE CONVERSION
by Ron Ceridono

Chrysler has given us some amazing cars over the years. The big wedge engines and, of course, the legendary hemi would give you a ride not soon forgotten. But sometimes trying to stop, left a lasting impression too. It was possible, for example, to order an E body ('70 to '74 Barracuda and Challenger) with a 440 engine and drum brakes — lots of go , not enough whoa. Chrysler did not require "packaged options" such as disc brakes to be an integral part of some performance engine options. Many examples survive today with high-performance engines and low-performance brakes.

Installing factory disc brakes on the front of your MoPar is not a simple matter of trash-canning the drums and bolting on discs. The spindles are different and must be changed as well.

Enter Duane Frederickson and his company, California Suspensions (936 Detroit Ave., Suite C, Concord, California 95418; (415) 685-7487). Duane, along with JFZ, has developed a disc brake conversion that is a bolt-on for '67 to '72 B and '70 to '74 E body drum brake spindles. The kit consists of 12-inch vented rotors that fit the stock hubs, 4-piston calipers, caliper brackets that bolt to the drum brake spindles, and necessary hardware. Everything you need to get the whoa more equal with the go. And if you're in search of the ultimate in braking ability, a rear disc conversion is under development and will be available soon.

In addition to brake kits, California Suspensions offers front and rear suspension parts, urethane bushings, sway bars, steering components, and custom torsion bars.

71

MASTER CYLINDER

The master cylinder you use is critical to how well the system will work. If you have a late-model car, you will use the master cylinder common to that car, unless you add disc front brakes. In that case, you can use a master cylinder from the same make car, but from a later year when discs were introduced. If you must install a different master cylinder, the best thing to do is select one of the dual master cylinders, the kind that have separate brake lines for front and rear.

It is in the older rods where some confusion exists over the master cylinder. As a rule, the master cylinders common to the older cars will not work well with the more modern brakes. Mostly, it will be a matter of both capacity and pressure. For the typical modern brake system, the master cylinder bore should be 1-1/8". Lightweight cars with small calipers can get by with the 1-inch master cylinder bore.

With the proper pedal ratio and master cylinder bore, 90% of all cars will have excellent line pressure, therefore a power assist unit may not be needed. The pedal ratio will be somewhere between 6:1 and 6.5:1. It is vital to carefully select and install the brake components on the heavier car, and this is especially true of the master cylinder.

The key is the volume of the fluid moved at a certain pressure. The pressure will be determined by the master cylinder bore multiplied by the stroke. If you put discs on the front, find what the car's original master cylinder bore was (for the front brakes). Meaning the car from which the disc brakes were taken. This will tell you roughly the size of master cylinder you need.

The master cylinder selected for drum brakes all around should be as near what the brakes originally required as possible. This holds true with a power brake unit as well. With a true power brake, as opposed to a power assist, engine vacuum reduces the amount of brake pedal pressure needed to operate the master cylinder. This is a direct action on the pedal/master cylinder, rather than indirect, since the power brake fits between the pedal and the master cylinder and the brakes. However, and this is important, if you have a maximum performance car, you may not want to include a power system of either type, since this will be utilizing engine vacuum, one of the major principles of engine performance.

For rod building, the size of the power brake chamber in diameter is a determining factor. Most of the power brakes have a very large diameter, too big for the older engine compartments. Some of the mid/small size cars have longer, smaller diameter chamber housings (such as Dodge). Many experts feel that these power brake systems from the factory are much better than aftermarket boosters. If the master cylinder is mounted beneath the floorboards, there is the problem of fluid feedback on the lines, especially if the cylinder is below the height of the brakes. A master cylinder used with drum brakes must have 10 psi residual pressure in the lines at all times. A residual pressure valve is normally built into the drum brake master cylinder. Some disc systems keep about 2 psi in the line to reduce pedal slack and give a kind of "instant on" feel to the brakes.

Rod builders remove the residual valve in the master cylinder when a combination of drum and disc brakes is used. If this residual valve is not removed, it will cause the disc pads to drag severely. When residual pressure is required, it is achieved through valves placed in the line between master cylinder and drum brakes. For instance, with a drum/disc combination, the master cylinder might have a residual valve with 2 psi built in, then a secondary valve would be placed in

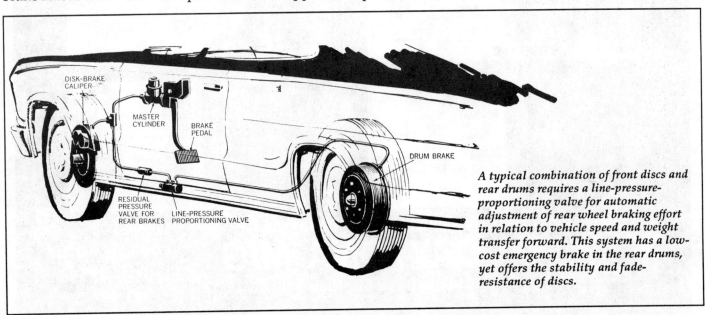

A typical combination of front discs and rear drums requires a line-pressure-proportioning valve for automatic adjustment of rear wheel braking effort in relation to vehicle speed and weight transfer forward. This system has a low-cost emergency brake in the rear drums, yet offers the stability and fade-resistance of discs.

the line to the drums giving 10 psi. Or two valves would be used, 2 psi to the discs and 10 psi to the drums. In addition to the residual valve, a drum/disc combination would also include a proportioning valve between the master cylinder and the drums.

Starting in the early '70s, most American production cars have a block somewhere near the master cylinder (on the firewall or frame rail) that receives the brake lines from the master cylinder, then sends the lines to the brakes. This block will be involved when drum/ disc brakes are used, and it will usually incorporate a metering valve, proportioning valve, and residual valve (there is no proportioning valve when 4-wheel disc brakes are involved). This unit can be used on rods of all years.

Incidentally, if the discs seem to drag and you are wondering if it is a matter of too much residual pressure, just open the bleed screw. Too much pressure is immediately apparent.

REAR AXLES

Boneyards are full of old MoPar rear axles that can be had for a fair price. Often, you have to remove the axle from the car, but sometimes you can find them just lying loose like this. Take careful measurements when searching for an axle to fit under your rod.

When building a rod, you can choose from five different MoPar axles. They are designated by referring to the ring gear diameter (in inches) as 7-1/4, 8-1/4, 8-3/4, 9-1/4, and 9-3/4. These axles fall into two distinct groups — banjo axles and carrier tube axles, and they are easily distinguished from each other. All of the MoPar axles with the exception of the 8-3/4 are carrier tube axles. Only the 8-3/4 is a banjo type.

Looking at the axles from the rear, the banjo type has a single-piece housing, and there are no bolts or cover plate to the rear of the center section. For service or replacement, the third member is removed from the front side of the housing.

On the other hand, the carrier tube type axle consists of separate housing tubes that are pressed into the center section. The third member is removed from the rear of the housing, after removal of the cover plate. Identification of the ring gear diameter of the carrier tube axles can be accomplished by simply counting the bolts in the cover plate. The 7-1/4 has a 9-bolt cover, the 8-1/4 has a 10-bolt cover, the 9-1/4 has a 12-bolt cover. The 9-3/4 Dana 60 axle has a 10-bolt cover, but is easily distinguished from the 8-1/4 by size of the overall unit. Additionally, the 8-1/4 is distinguished from the 9-3/4 by the arrangement of the cover bolts. The smaller axle has the bolts in a perfect circle, while the larger axle has the bolts in somewhat of a hexagon pattern.

The first carrier tube axle used in Chrysler production vehicles was the 7-1/4. Introduced in 1960, it was used in lightweight cars with small V8 and 6-

73

After disassembly, the housing should be thoroughly cleaned with solvent to remove any sediment inside. Check for metal shavings when draining the oil, which is evidence of wear or damage to internal components. New seals must be installed in the ends of the housing tubes.

Factory ring gears have the gear ratio stamped on the edge. An alternate method of determining the ratio (in the event the ratio is not stamped on the edge of an aftermarket ring gear) is to count the teeth on the pinion, count the teeth on the ring gear, and divide.

cylinder engines. Standard production ratios range from an economical 2.76:1 to a performance-oriented 3.91:1, but there are half a dozen additional performance ratios available through the Direct Connection program including, 4.10, 4.30, 4.50, 4.80, 5.10, and 5.30:1.

The 8-1/4 axle came along in 1969 and was generally overlooked by Chrysler performance enthusiasts until about 1973 when it was included as standard equipment in the 340 Duster and Dart. Since then, it has also seen duty on the 318/340/360 Road Runners and Chargers. As far as a production unit is concerned, the best performance ratio available is 3.91:1 and the best economy ratio is 2.71:1. There is a 2.45:1 ratio available, but it requires a special differential case for installation.

Using a dial indicator, check the backlash of the ring/pinion set. While holding the pinion immovable, try to turn the ring gear. Watch the dial indicator to see how much backlash registers. Too much movement indicates gear or bearing wear, or poor initial set-up of the differential. If backlash is only a few thousandths in excess of factory specs, it may be corrected by tightening the spanner nuts on each side of the carrier. More than a few thousandths over, and you have to replace parts.

There is a bearing on the pinion shaft below the yoke and seal. After removing the yoke nut, yoke and seal, check this bearing for any visible indication of wear or damage.

A new seal must be installed over the pinion shaft. The neck of the yoke protrudes through this seal, so care must be taken when reinstalling the yoke to prevent damage to the seal.

If the car originally had the 2.45:1 ratio, and the owner desires to install a higher numerical ratio, the case has to be changed to the standard unit. High-performance ratios available through the Direct Connection program will fit the standard cars, however it is necessary to use a notched cross-shaft for axle assembly. The cross-shafts are included with the special-order 4.10:1 to 5.30:1 ratios. Note: the 4.5" bolt circle for A-body cars came along in 1973 for disc brake models with 8-1/4" axles only and will not fit the 8-3/4 units.

In 1973, the 9-1/4 axles were introduced with standard production ratios ranging from 2.71:1 for economy to 3.5:1 for performance. The same higher numerical ratios are available from Direct Connection for the 9-1/4 axle as were previously mentioned for the smaller units.

The 8-3/4 banjo style axle (last produced for A-body cars in 1972, and for E-body cars in the 1974 Barracuda and Challenger) feature three different types of ring and pinion sets. One has a small stem (1-38" diameter shaft), another has a large stem (1-3/4" diameter shaft), and the third has a tapered pinion (1-7/8" diameter shaft). Identification numbers for the ring and pinion sets can be found cast into the driver's side of the case. Two numbers identify the small stem — 1820657 (up to '64) and 2070741 (later). 2070742 identifies the large stem unit. Then in '69 the tapered pinion replaced the large stem unit with 2881489. Two different axle shaft assemblies also exist, and the three ring and pinion styles are interchangeable when used with these two different shaft assemblies. (However, pinions, bearings and cases are not interchangeable between the three different units. Be very sure of the parts interchangeability before swapping a new gear set into the old case). The earlier assembly (in use up to '64) has tapered axle shafts and the brake assembly is attached to the shaft with a keyway and a large nut. (Note: when disassembling these axles, it is almost impossible to remove the shaft. One way to release the shaft is to loosen the nut a couple of threads, then drive the car a few blocks, turning corners often. This seems to successfully release the tapered shaft and allow easier disassembly). From 1965 on, the axle has flanged shafts which are easier to work on. A wide range of special high-performance ratios are available for the 8-3/4 axle. Following are the ratios and the axles they will fit:

1957 - 1968 vehicles with case #2070742 (1-3/4" shaft) 3.91, 4.10, 4.30, 4.57, 4.86, 5.12, 5.33, 5.50:1

1969 - 1971 vehicles with case #2881489 (1-7/8" tapered) 3.91, 4.30, 4.57, 4.86, 5.12:1

Check the neck of the pinion yoke for indication of wear around the seal area. There may be a dark ring around the neck that is not necessarily wear. Feel with a finger to make sure. If minor wear is detected, it may be possible to clean it up with emery cloth.

1957 - 1968 Chrysler standard series 8-3/4 axle
4.10, 4.30, 4.56, 4.89, 5.13, 5.38, 5.57:1

1969 - 1973 Chrysler standard series 8-3/4 axle
3.91, 4.10, 4.30, 4.57, 4.86, 5.13, 5.38:1

Chrysler 8-3/4 axle (with 1-3/8" small shaft)
3.91, 4.10, 4.56, 4.89:1

Since 1966, Chrysler Corporation has used the 9-3/4 Dana 60 axle for heavy duty and high-performance applications. Ratios for this axle range from 3.54:1 to 6.50:1, but for ratios above 4.56:1, a different case is required. The standard series of ratios for the 9-3/4 axle are 4.10, 4.56, 4.88, 5.13, 5.38, and 5.57:1. Beyond that, there is the Pro Series (made of high-strength material) with ratios of 4.10, 5.86, 6.17, and 6.50:1 which

AXLE DIMENSIONS

Stock Axle & Body	Std. Track	Housing Flange-to-Flange	Spring Seats Center-to Center
7-1/4 A-body	55.56	53.2	43.02
7-1/4 A-body	55.56	51.4	43.02 w/10x2.5 brakes
8-1/4 A-body	55.56	51.4	43.02
8-1/4 B-body	62.00	57.8	47.30
8-1/4 B & C body	63.40	59.2	47.30
8-1/4 F-body	58.50	54.34	44.46
8-3/4 A-body	55.60	——	43.00
8-3/4 B-body	59.20	——	44.00 '62-'70
8-3/4 E-body	60.70	——	46.00
8-3/4 B-body	62.00	——	47.30 '71-'74
8-3/4 body S.W.	63.40	——	47.30
9-1/4 B-body	62.00	57.8	47.30
9-1/4 B & C body	63.40	59.2	47.30
9-3/4 E-body	——	56.5	46.00
9-3/4 B-body	——	54.936	44.00
9-3/4 Race Only	——	52.5	loose
9-3/4 Race Only	——	44.0	loose

CENTERLINE OF AXLE SHAFT TO CENTER OF REAR U-JOINT OR YOKE

7-1/4	10.09"
8-1/4	11.69"
8-3/4	12.35"
9-1/4	11.69"
9-3/4	13.47"

Torque the pinion nut to factory specs. Depending upon the rear end you're working on, instruction for this torque procedure may vary. Here, Wayne Atkinson holds the pinion yoke with a large wrench while torquing the nut.

Reassemble the axle shaft with the threaded bearing preload adjuster assembly going on first, followed by a seal (actually, the seal fits into the adjuster retaining ring), then the bearing race and bearing cone, and finally the retainer ring.

can be purchased from Direct Connection. Early axles ('69 and older) had a 23-tooth spline, while the later units (after '70) have a 35-tooth spline. An interesting note is that the 35-tooth shafts can use the axle bearings and seals out of a 8-3/4 axle. Part numbers for the earlier shafts are 2881010 (right shaft), 2881011 (left shaft) and 2852514 (side gears). For the later shafts the numbers are 3507160 (right shaft), 3507161 (left shaft) and 2944837 (side gears). A special high-strength ring and pinion set is available for heavy-duty applications, and the part number is P3690226.

SURE GRIP UNITS

For maximum traction, there have been three different limited slip differentials used the the MoPar axles over the years. They are the Trac Lok, the Power Lok, and the Borg-Warner Spin Resistant. The Power Lok and the Borg-Warner units were used in the 8-3/4 axles, with the Power Lok in use from '62 to '69 and the Borg-Warner unit entering the scene in '69 and continuing thereafter. The part number for the Power Lok is 2881487, and the part number for the Borg-Warner unit is 2881343.

In the 7-1/4 axle from 1964 to '66, a unit that was similar to the Power Lok was used (part number not available). The 8-1/4 sure-grip has a part number of 3432598, and the part number for the 9-1/4 axle is 3723014. For the 9-3/4 axle, from '66 to '69 the Power Lok was in use, then in '70 and '71 the Trac Lok was employed. The 9-3/4 axle sure grip part number is P3571027 which comes with the special offset case for the ratios above 4.56:1.

A completed axle assembly looks like this. Only the right side shaft has the adjustable bearing preload mechanism. The left side simply has a retainer that gets bolted to the housing flange.

PREPPING A REAR AXLE FOR THE STREET

To photograph the kind of typical work that needs to be done to a stock MoPar rear axle in preparation for running on the street, we visited Wayne Atkinson, noted axle guru who preps rearends for everything from street rods to Bonneville racers. For our photo session, we used a MoPar 8-3/4 banjo type axle.

In the disassembly phase, it is important to look closely at the oil for evidence of metallic particles that indicate wear or damage to some of the internal components. After the axle is disassembled, clean up all the parts with solvent and inspect for signs of wear or damage. Then, it is time to replace any worn or damaged parts and reassemble everything. So, let's start with pieces scattered all over the garage floor and work through the assembly process one item at a time.

Basically, all Wayne does to the housing is to clean it thoroughly with solvent to get rid of any sediment, and inspect for damage. Of course, if a customer wants a narrowed rearend, that work is done, but here we're working with a stock-width housing. If there is no damage to any part of the housing, Wayne installs new seals and it is ready to receive the third member.

The third member is checked for bearing wear, ring/pinion wear, and proper initial adjustment. A dial indicator is used to make these checks. With the third member securely bolted to a workstand, place the dial indicator against one tooth of the ring gear. Then, while holding the pinion so it can't move at all (critical), try to turn the ring gear back and forth while watching the dial indicator. There should be no more than about .008" movement shown on the indicator. If the backlash is within tolerance, and there are no signs of metal shavings in the oil, it isn't necessary to tear down the third member any farther. Just install a new pinion seal and reassemble in the housing. If the backlash is excessive, but just a few thousandths over, it is possible to correct this situation and bring the unit within tolerance by tightening the spanner nuts on each side of the carrier. However, if the excess backlash is more than a few thousandths over, this indicates wear to the gears and/or bearings and it is time to think in terms of replacement.

By the way, as long as you have the ring and pinion staring you in the face, you can double check the ratio (if you are in any doubt). If the ring gear is a factory unit, the ratio will be stamped on the edge of the gear. If it is an aftermarket ring gear, it may not be stamped with the ratio, so you will have to count the teeth on the ring gear and count the teeth on the pinion — then divide the lower number into the higher one. Example: 17 teeth on the pinion, 47 teeth on the ring gear. The actual ratio is 2.76:1.

Any time the ring and pinion are disassembled, reassembly may result in a change in relationship between the pinion teeth and the ring teeth. This causes a new wear pattern to begin and can result in a noisy third member. Adjustments of the ring/pinion are made in two ways. The pinion depth is altered by using shims, and the backlash is altered by adjusting the spanner nuts at each side of the carrier. When setting up a third member properly, these two adjustments are manipulated over and over again, constantly checking the way the ring and pinion teeth interface, until a perfect wear pattern is achieved.

When inspecting the pinion, you want to take a close look at the pinion bearing. To do this, remove the nut that holds the yoke in place, remove the yoke, remove the seal, and look at the bearing. At this time, inspect the neck of the yoke where it passes through the seal. What you are looking for (and feeling for) is any indication of wear around the neck. You will likely see a dark-colored ring where the seal fits around the neck, but this is not necessarily wear. Feel the neck to detect any actual wear. You may clean up the neck with a light application of emery cloth prior to reinstallation. Of course, a fresh seal should be installed at this time. The last item is to torque the pinion nut to 210 ft. lbs. Use a new pinion nut, because the old one is likely to pull threads. Check the pinion drag torque to see how close it is to the stock specs. Then, if necessary, increase the torque on the pinion nut until the pinion drag torque is within plus/minus 5 in. lbs. of spec.

Assuming that everything is now correct with the third member, it can be reinstalled in the axle housing. That leaves us with the axle shaft assemblies to install. First, install new seals in the housing tubes. The 8-3/4 axles have adjustable end-play systems built into the right-hand shaft, utilizing the wheel bearing preload adjusters. If the shaft assembly has been completely taken apart for replacement of the bearings and general clean-up, the first thing back on the shaft is the threaded adjuster and retainer (right-hand shaft only — the left-hand shaft gets a retainer only). A seal is installed in the retainer (lips up). Next the bearing cup goes on the shaft, followed by the bearing cone. Right after the bearing cone is a bearing retainer ring, and that finishes up the assembly.

A metal gasket goes on the axle housing flange, and then the shaft is inserted into the housing (taking care when passing through the seal) and is bolted in place at the flange. As the splined end of the shaft enters the third member, it may be necessary to turn the shaft until the splines mesh and the shaft can be slipped all the way in.

Now it's time to make the end-play adjustment to the right-hand shaft. First, install the left-hand (non-adjustable) shaft and bolt it in place at the flange. Then install the right-hand shaft and make the adjustment. Begin by threading the adjuster ring all the way into the retainer ring until the face of each is flush with each other. Now bolt the axle into place. Tighten the adjuster until there is zero end-play, then back the adjuster off approximately 4 notches or until there is .013" to .023" of end-play. Use a dial indicator to verify the correct end-play. The two shafts are butting up against a thrust spacer in the center of the third member, and this adjustment is making the tolerance between the shafts and this spacer correct.

That's all there is to it. Fill the housing with oil, and the MoPar 8-3/4 rear axle is set up for most street applications.

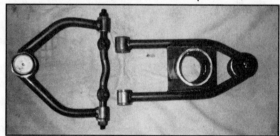

79

BOLT PATTERNS

Axle flanges can be drilled for different wheel bolt pattern, providing there is enough diameter.

One thing about wheels is that they either fit or they don't. There is interchangeability in wheels, but remember that while the bolt pattern may be the same, the lug nut taper may differ. It is a small thing, but you should be aware of this fact. Which is why the lug nuts may keep working loose on your trick set of steel wheels.

To measure the bolt pattern, measure from one stud across the wheel to the farthest-away opposite stud. Normally, the distance will be anywhere from 4 to 5 inches. You may be able to find a wheel interchange chart somewhere, but since these go out of date with the introduction of each new year's cars, get practice at measuring wheels. One outstanding tool for measuring

bolt patterns is the Ident-A-Wheel measuring caliper (5290 S. Helena Hwy., Napa, California 94558 for information). This tool has two tapered locaters on a sliding scale, and when the locaters are registered in the wheel holes, you simply read the scale to find what cars have similar wheel bolt patterns.

Even though the bolt patterns may be the same, the center register hole may be smaller, or larger. This is important because this register hole fits snugly over an axle flange on some cars. Also, some axle flanges will have a pin locater that sticks through a register hole in the wheel. The solution is to drill a hole in the wheel to match.

Stock drum will have a basic bolt pattern and can easily be drilled with a new pattern.

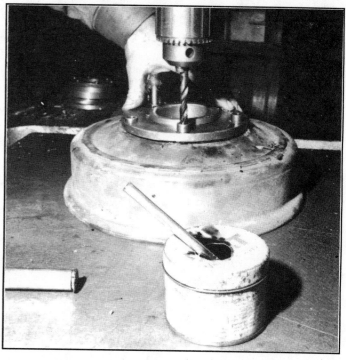

Use a special jig or axle flange as a drilling guide on the drum. Center hole is alignment guide.

Here is the drum with old and new bolt patterns. This can be done at home on a drill press.

Now the redrilled axle flange and the newly drilled hubs can be mated with different wheels.

Use top-grade bolts or lug bolts for the axle flange. Make sure the wheel fits the drum flush.

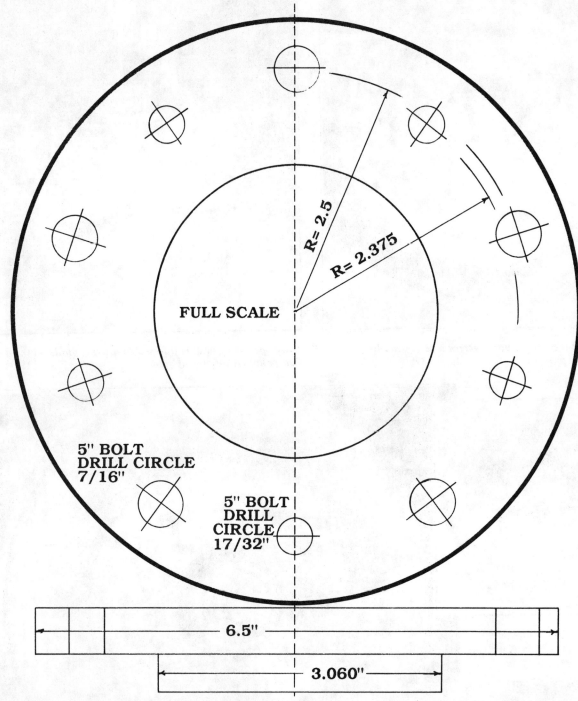

FULL SCALE

R= 2.5

R= 2.375

5" BOLT
DRILL CIRCLE
7/16"

5" BOLT
DRILL
CIRCLE
17/32"

6.5"

3.060"

Special thanks to Laurie Teichrow and the Canadian Street Rod Association for information about redrilling axles/hubs. Start by finding the center of the hub. Cardboard works fine for a template. From this center, make a circle the diameter you want. Now get the straight line distance between the center of any two holes. To find the straight line distance, multiply the circle diameter by the number that follows:

4 holes — 0.707107
5 holes — 0.587785
6 holes — 0.500000
7 holes — 0.382683

Suppose this wheel has a 5-bolt pattern with a 4.75-inch bolt circle diameter. Multiply the bolt circle 4.75 x 0.587785 and you get 2.793, rounded to 2.8. Start at any point on your cardboard template and mark off a distance of 2.80 inches. Then from this point repeat the 2.80 measurement and you should end up smack dab back at the starting point, with centerpoints for the 5 new bolt holes.

BORGESON UNIVERSAL COMPANY INC.

Borgeson offers a variety of universal joints, splined intermediate shafting, and couplers which fit almost every Mopar application. The joints can be furnished with both ends unsplined for welding and are also spot drilled for pinning, with one end splined and one end plain, or with both ends splined in any of the available sizes we offer.

We also offer "Double D" configuration (a round shaft with two parallel flats) in both the 3/4" and 1" sizes (this will fit the collapsible Chevy system).

For the serious street rodder who wants to have a "driver" as opposed to having the car trailered, we recommend the needle bearing style joint. Our joints use the same bearings as those used by General Motors.

Our splined shafting is stocked in 2" increments up to 36" in length and is very easy to measure, easy to install, safe, and removable if necessary. This allows your steering to be a bolt-together system. Our shafting is 3/4" OD which is stronger than the 5/8" OD shafting.

Borgeson universal joints have less than 1/1000" of backlash, are made exclusively for steering in high performance vehicles, and are the strongest for their size.

Borgeson offers a smaller (1-1/4" OD) non-needle bearing style joint for those who do not intend to drive their cars much or where size is restricted.

For Chrysler products, we do have six different splines as well as the 3/4" "Double D" configuration. Those who work with Mopar parts usually find little rhyme or reason to how things are done there. Therefore, we do request that you measure the OD of the shaft across the teeth of the column, box or rack and pinion. We would also need a count of the number of teeth for the application. If any teeth are missing we would need a count of half way around where there are teeth in that full semi-circle. This will enable us to accurately determine the proper spline needed.

Borgeson offers a double universal joint in either style for those who have up to 60° of mis-alignment.

Please call Borgeson Universal Company, Inc. at (203) 482-8283 and our competent sales staff will be happy to assist you with any technical questions.

BORGESON UNIVERSAL COMPANY INC.
1050 South Main Street
Torrington, CT 06790
(203) 482-8283

PRO-STREET PLYMOUTH

Although this particular Pro-Fat frame is for an early Plymouth, the basic building theme works for all older cars having full frames. Note that the frame now has a new tubing X-member with an oval mid-point which doubles as a driveshaft safety yoke. The transmission mount is square tubing between the frame.

If you're ever in the mood to build a pro street '49 Plymouth, here's how it's done. "Squeak" Bell of the Kiwi Konnection at 1331 Flower Street in Bakersfield, California 93305 took us through the steps of frame preparation to squeeze a set of 15x12.5 fats under the fenders.

In order for the wheels to fit under the '49 Plymouth, total width of the rear axle, with the wheels mounted, has to be 57 inches. For this project, a Ford 9-inch rearend was borrowed from a '64 Galaxie. Squeak recommends '66 and earlier axle housings because they have oil filler plugs. From '67 on, the plug is in the third member. When you use a '66 third member and a '67 housing, there are no filler plugs. You are able to fill the housing through an open axle end, but he doesn't recommend this.

The Ford rearend was narrowed 17 inches to get the 57-inch total width with the fat tires and wheels installed. Of course, you'll need to measure your own vehicle to find out exactly what the total width will be. Then add the mounted tires to your total width and measure from the mounting flange of one rim to the other. This is your axle flange-to-flange width. It is wise to leave a couple of inches between the tires and body to allow for body sway and/or using larger tires or offset rims. You may someday want to go bigger than what you started with. Double check and remeasure everything.

The Ford third member is offset to one side about 2-1/2 inches, so the pinion will align with the transmission. When Squeak narrowed the housing, he shifted the third member to the center. Even though the driveline no longer runs down the centerline, that line and the line that the crankshaft rotates on are parallel to each other (though they are not in alignment). You can offset a single driveline in any direction.

Next, the body was modified with large fender wells (though this could be done after narrowing). Again, Squeak allowed at least 2 inches to the inside for body sway and wheel swap. Add at least 2 inches from the tire tread, fore and aft, in the new well for racing tire growth and wheel diameter change. The fore and aft measurement is sometimes a compromise because of body mounts, as in this case. There was just enough room, barely, without removing the mount. Now measure the new bodywell distance to figure out how far to move your rails in. Measure again to be sure.

First, Squeak measures the frame for square. This is habit with any frame he works on for any reason. In this case, it has to be square so that the cut will be square to the frame, when measured on the frame. To measure, it is easiest to pick a body mount hole or fender mount hole at the front that has a matching hole in the opposite side. Using the same reference holes, measure diagonally across. Measure with the utmost accuracy and always use the same reference points. If the two measurements are the same, the frame is square. (Editor's Note: Many older frames were produced to a tolerance of plus or minus 1/8". Measure your frame at several diagonal points to get an idea of what the tolerance might have been). If not, it has to be straightened. This could be a real chore, but it must be done. Double check your measurements.

It is not uncommon for stress to build up in the frame from daily driving. This condition is compounded if the car was in an accident and the frame restraightened. To keep the frame from twisting hopelessly out of shape when the rails are cut, tack weld angle iron, channel, or tubing from rail to rail. A bulletproof method to secure the rails in their same relationship before cutting is to crossbrace the rails. When tack welding the braces in, be sure they touch where they cross each other because this point is welded. Weld braces on the rear section also.

Because his concrete floor is relatively level, Squeak places the frame on the floor. You may place your frame at any level, but it must be secured so it can't move or shift. It is critical that it does not move from the time you start measuring until you start welding. If you can leave it secure until after you weld, it is easier to remeasure when finished. Squeak prefers a plumb bob to lay out and recheck the frame cuts, but a combination square with an integral level will also work. To double check a line measured with a level, use a plumb bob.

The angle at which you cut the frame is not important. That the angle is identical on both rails is the secret. All you want to do is move the rear rails in but at the same angle for each side, so the frame rail as a whole has not changed its shape when looking at it from the side. Also, measure the exact height of the rear frame horns to the floor. They will be rewelded at this height.

After scribing the lines on the rails where they are to be cut, scribe a second set 3/16" apart. There will be a 3/16" steel plate added here and we don't want to change the length of the frame. About every half-inch, centerpunch your scribed lines. This is so you don't lose your line when torching off the rear section. The rails could also be sawed or cut with an abrasive cut-off

The Critical measurements are determined by tire width and clearance between outside edge of tire and fender opening. Once this has been determined, the rearend flange-to-flange measurement gives amount rearend housing must be measured. Note here that there is enough clearance between inside edge of tire and relocated frame to allow for some wheel/tire size changes to be made for racing.

After following the procedures outlined in text for cutting and relocating rear portion of frame, note new square tubing crossmember and frame horn crossmember are in place. Here a Ford rearend was chosen.

The type of rear springing used is a personal preference, this owner wanted coil/shocks. Pay attention to how beefy the lower shock is, and that it also serves as mount for lower locator bar.

Upper shock/spring mount has additional mounting holes drilled so the spring angle can be changed. Note that frame has been cut just behind body mounting pads.

Right- The key to narrowing a frame is making the new attachment points very strong, that's the reason for the large triangle shaped gusset plates. Here the plate angle has been designed to correspond to angle of upper radius rod.

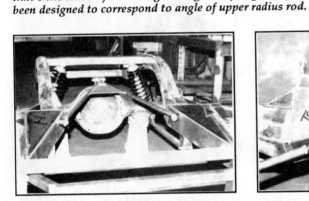

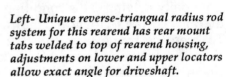

Far Left- Check the text for information on blind nut mounting for rod ends, necessary since the new boxing area is complete on bottom.

Left- Unique reverse-triangual radius rod system for this rearend has rear mount tabs welded to top of rearend housing, adjustments on lower and upper locators allow exact angle for driveshaft.

saw as long as you stay dead on line.

If you need to, especially after using a cutting torch, grind the main rail ends with a disc grinder. Check with a level or plumb bob to be sure they are square to gravity. The rear rails are just ground with care to the centerpunch line. A straightedge, whether a steel rule or a virgin section of healthy angle iron that is wider than your frame, is placed on both front and rear rail ends to check for high spots and to be sure the two rail face ends are on the same plane (parallel to each other). Now, cross-measure from the outside corner of the new end to a reference point at the front of the frame. These measurements should be the same.

Measure the total width of the frame and height of the rail at the cut. You will need a flat piece of 3/16" plate with these dimensions, with at least one long edge being straight. This edge is important, as it will run from the horizontal rail surface (or body side) on each side. With the rear rail ends being the same height as the plate, they can only fit one way; square to the plate.

Tack weld the plate so the long edge is flush with both rail surfaces. Now you can see the plate is on a perfect geometric plane through the frame. No matter how far you move the rail ends in, they will butt up against the plate at the same angle as when they were attached to the rails.

If your frame has a rear crossmember (most do), remove it either by unbolting or grinding off the rivet heads (or using a cutting torch) and driving out the rivet shank with a drift punch. If the crossmember was riveted, it is better to weld it back in. If it was bolted in, rebolt it or weld it if it's permanent. Put the crossmember in position before you tack weld as it helps locate the new distance between the rails. Whatever way you narrow or make a new crossmember is up to you, but it has to be exact.

You can now mount the body on the frame and use the body to align the rear rails like a welding jig. The other way is to measure in how far the rails are to be set and scribe the lines on the plate with a square. After tack welding or bolting the rear crossmember in the rails, check for square. Next, pull the rear section against the plate. Use a furniture bar clamp, a strap clamp or any way you can to get the new section to pull up flat against the plate. It's got to be snug. Now place each rear rail on the scribed lines on the plates and made sure the rails are squared to the top edge. Cross-measure and tack weld. Remeasure, and if it's off square, square it up by moving the new section sideways at the very rear tip. Measure from the floor to the rail ends and match your previous measurement. If it isn't right, work with it until it is, but it should be real close to start with. When you have the right height and it is square, remeasure and recheck the rail sides to be 90 degrees from the top edge of the plate. When it checks out, tack weld it all, top, bottom and sides and then remeasure. It's gotta be right.

Next, Squeak gussets the 90-degree angle by moving the rails, plus he boxes the gussets. The gusset on the fenderwell joint was an arbitrary size, but the inner gussets were planned. As you see in the photos, the upper radius rods run parallel to the gusset. Squeak drew an imaginary line from the outside of the rearend upper radius rod bracket to the inside edge of the narrowed rails to the frame. Cardboard patterns work well in helping shape the gussets from 3/16" plate. The large gussets also make good pads for roll bars (on top) and radius rod brackets (underneath). Cut the plate out between the narrowed rails before tack welding the gussets flush with the rail surface. Recheck your angle.

The particular advantage to this radius rod system is that besides having similar geometry to a four-bar, the upper bar also acts as a rearend locater. Squeak chose a 25-inch radius rod end center-to-center. The upper and lower rearend bracket centers are on the same vertical plane as are the forward bracket centers. The radius rods are .356" wall seamless mild tubing. The tubing ends are drilled and tapped for 5/8" National Fine rod ends from Pete and Jakes. The top radius rod gusset is 3/16" plate. All the rod end brackets are also made from 3/16" steel.

Measure and cut the inner gusset box from 3/16" steel plate. With the radius rod centers you chose, mark it on the box plate on the gusset. The rod centers must be far enough from the edge to allow a nut to be welded to the inside. The center is the same on both plates, but the nuts must be welded on opposite sides.

Squeak first welds a 5/8" National Fine coupling nut to the plate, then tap drills through the nut. Then a tap is run through the nut first, screw in the bolt and run the nut over it, then tighten. When the nut is welded to the plate, you have the same result as our first method. Now tack weld the plate into place with the nuts inside the boxed gussets. Squeak uses 5/8" National Fine grade-8 bolts except for the 3/4" on the rearend top radius rod bracket. A coupling nut is about twice as long as a standard nut and has much less chance of the bolt rocking in the nut under load.

Squeak uses 5/8" National Fine grade-8 bolts with an unthreaded shank the length of the rod end bushing. This is so the threads will jam tight in the plate, yet allow the rod end to work. A loose bolt will snap at the point where the threads start. Drill a hole in the bolt head for a safety wire or fabricate a lock washer. Cut a piece of sheetmetal about 5" x 1" long and put a 5/8" hole in it about 5/8" from one end. Place the bolt into the washer and tighten the bolt into the threads. Be sure the washer is in such a position that the long leg is anchored to something stationary like the frame. The other ear is folded against one of the bolt head flats.

Left- Pete & Jake's rod ends, normally destined for traditional street rod front ends, work very well for the late model as well.

Big mistake that many amateur builders make on frames is using brackets from too-thin plate. If in doubt, go bigger! Rearend locators mount to brackets welded to lower gusset plate.

To weld the frame, Squeak uses a MIG (wire welder) with A.W.S. Spec. E70S-6 .035" wire. The wire has been triple deoxidized and thin copper-coated to first clean the wire and then seal it to keep moisture out. The gas shield around the arc keeps moisture out and allows a porosity-free weld. It will give you a 70,000-pound tensile-strength weld, the same as 7018 Low Hydrogen arc rod. Uncoated wire will oxidize and hold moisture and leave a porous weld. Basically, if the wire is copper-coated, that is what you want.

Not everybody has a MIG welder, but an arc will work just as well except the weld is hotter. 6011 and 6013 have the same steel core as Low Hydrogen 7018 except the flux is different on Low Hydrogen. Low Hydrogen flux creates its own gas shield to produce a porosity-free weld. The fumes are toxic, so weld in a ventilated area. Low Hydrogen rod comes in sealed containers with a moisture content of no more than .01%. If you leave your Low Hydrogen rod exposed to the air, it will absorb moisture and you won't get a good weld. The ideal machine is an AC/DC with reversible polarity. Welding DC reverse is best but what most guys have is an AC buzz-box. If your buzz-box does not have an open circuit voltage of 73 volts minimum, you don't have enough power to run AC 7018, which is designed for these low-power machines.

Before welding, double-check and remeasure everything. It is wise to weld an inch or two at a time on any one seam, then go to the other side and weld the same amount. Go back to the first rail and pick a seam that is cool. This method is time consuming, but the heat generated by the weld must be kept very low to prevent distortion. Not so hot you can't lay your hand on it after it cools for a minute or so.

Remember when you were learning to arc a bead on an innocent steel plate? After you burned a pound of rod on the hapless victim, the only amazing thing that happened was the unbelievable degree of heat warpage and distortion. The same can happen to your frame by running a long bead. After it is cold, remeasure for fun because if it isn't right, it won't be fun.

NOTE: *When adding large rear tires to a car, you are disturbing the original design for handling as well as braking. The large rear tires may adversely affect the way the vehicle corners and rides.*

Right- This particular frame modification was done on the shop floor, proving that while huge and expensive frame jigs are nice, they are not mandatory.

Try to allow enough fore-aft distance at front of frame modification so that larger diameter tires can be used at a later date. Here the determining factor was a body mount pad.

The new triangular gusset boxed frame area may look massive, but it is not heavy, and the extra strength it gives is vital.

This is a highly modified Corvette frame, set up with the narrow rear frame section by Gene Reese in Dallas. Note how the area where the narrow frame extension attaches to the original frame has been beefed up considerably, which is especially important on an open car where no added structural strength is derived from the body. Keep in mind that all work on the frame must have a constant check/cross-check to make sure that the frame is square and not twisted.

INSTALLING A MODERN
GASOLINE FILLER DOOR

by Geoff Carter

Sometimes the simple things are easiest to overlook. Here's a simple technique for installing a modern gas filler door, and you can use the following procedure when installing those recessed door handles and other neat stuff you find in salvage yards these days.

Start by deciding where you want your new gas filler to go. Is the surface flat or curved? Will a round or square door look best there? You can do most of your research on the street, then call around and ask if any of the local yards have a car with the filler door you're looking for.

When you find it, cut it out with a hacksaw or snips. Be sure to get everything all together, not just the door, and leave plenty of metal around it.

When you get home, trim the piece, lay it out on your car, then hammer-weld it in, and you're done.

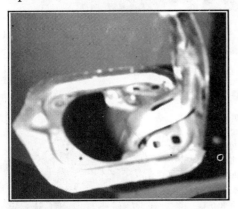 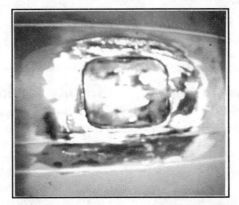 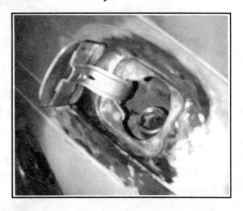

This complete unit is from a '72 Ford Galaxie, complete with spring, finger slot and everything.

Hammer-weld in place as a unit. Note that the relationship to the original hole requires only minor re-routing of the tank filler neck.

And there you have the whole thing — one complete working unit, no extra design or fabrication required.

HANGING
SHEETMETAL IN JIG TIME

by Geoff Carter

The big trend in the past few years has been subframe swapping. Several stories have already been published about how to cut them off and weld them on. Of course, then you have figure out how to hang your old sheetmetal on that foreign stub. What usually happens when the sheetmetal is ready to go back on is guesswork. You jack it up and shim it to try to get all the body contours squared and lined up.

Orv Elgie of Norwalk, California has come up with a solution to this problem. When he decided to adapt a Corvette front suspension cradle to his '40 Plymouth, he foresaw this problem and decide to solve it before starting to work on the swap. What he came up with will work for any subframe swap, so if that's what you're planning to do, follow along. It's easy to accomplish and you can use all scrap materials. Orv used 3/8" steel straps, but most anything will do.

The secret is in knowing that the point where the radiator sits centers all your front sheetmetal. So before you cut your frame off, build a jig that locates your radiator mount. With the jig to locate it, that point is never going to change.

Before cutting anything off your frame (after is shown here), remove the front sheetmetal and radiator, and bolt a piece of flat metal to the radiator mount. Next, run several strips of strap metal from various locations on the firewall and weld to the radiator-locating pad. Then unbolt the jig and set it aside.

First, bolt a plate to the radiator mount. Then select four to six locations around the firewall (existing holes, or you can drill some holes to be filled later). Then start running the metal straps. Bolt one end to the firewall and weld the other end to the pad you bolted to the radiator mount. This becomes your jig.

Now, unbolt all these pieces from the firewall, and from the radiator mount, and set it aside. Then cut the front end off.

After you've finished grafting the new subframe onto the existing frame, reinstall the jig, being sure to bolt each end to the original holes. You'll probably have to build a crossmember to meet the radiator pad on your jig. Copy the mounting adjustment slots exactly. Now you know exactly where the radiator has to go. Then when you set your front end sheetmetal back on, it'll fit precisely in the original position.

After grafting on your subframe, reattach the jig to the firewall. The radiator locater will probably hang out in space in front of the chassis.

Construct a radiator-supporting crossmember from box tubing or flat stock. Note slots cut to match original crossmember.

After attaching the new crossmember to the chassis in the position dictated by your jig, you can install the radiator, followed by the rest of the doghouse, all in its exact original location.

INTERIOR - INSULATION
FOR QUIET & COOL

Far Left- Before starting to tar, cut padding to exact shapes required, then set aside. Holes in the floor should be patched, and your carpet layer will thank you if all depressions are filled (unless you've already built a new flat and smooth floor).

Left- Here's the master home-builder himself. Wear old clothes because this gets very messy, but you'll be glad you did it ... guaranteed.

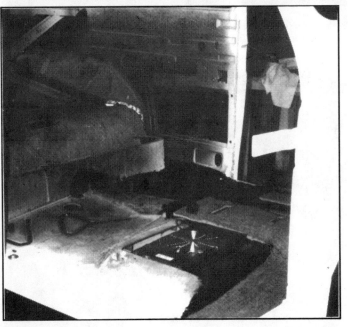

Directly to the rear of the Big Al's under-seat heater we can see several original floor depressions filled and smoothed with plastic body filler. This little trick makes a much more satisfactory carpet job (and upholsterer's bill).

Don't forget the trunk. Any heat or noise inside the body is too much.

by Geoff Carter

Although Orv Elgie's cars look as smooth and shiny as any you'll ever see, there's some decidedly unglamorous stuff below the surface. You see, Orv drives his cars, and he knows that crossing the desert with heat and road noise droning around the inside of his sedan is not the kind of fun street rodding is supposed to be. So, he liberally tars the underside of his car bodies, then tars and pads the floor before final assembly.

He recommends Henry's roofing tar because it's cheap and it dries quickly. It should be available just about anywhere hardware or home improvement supplies are sold. He gets the carpet padding at upholstery stores; remnants or medium-sized scraps will do. Nobody but you and your trimmer will ever see them again. Just remember to cut them all to fit before you start spreading that sticky tar.

If you skip this step, or start wiring or any of those other fun jobs first, you'll probably regret it. It's the most important step to hot rodding happiness.

Another important thing to remember is to wear clothes you never want to wear again. And follow the instructions on the container.

Your air conditioner will actually keep you cool, and you can hear your music at something lower than pre-detonation volume level.

BEST EVER!

HOT RODDERS THE WORLD OVER SAY HRMx IS THE BEST EVER.
We think they're right!
And there's only one way to get us.

We don't try to be sophisticated. We're not brilliant. We certainly are not empty glitz. We're just plain old hardcore, basic, useful, practical. Which is right on target, because over 95% of street driven hot rods have between 5000 and 10,000 actual dollars invested...and a zillion hours of labor. HRMx is about that.

HRMx is the How-To Magazine.

Lots of other super magazines give you great photos of cars. Good stuff, and the hobby needs them. But, we think the hobby needs us even more! We show how these cars are built, how they are put together. Hot rodding hasn't become a kind of mystical black art, it is still something that happens one bolt at a time.

HRMx is written by the legends of hot rodding. By the pro's. And by the hundreds of thousands of back-yarders who know what it is to save, and scrounge, and invent, and create. HRMx is about everything in hot rodding, just as long as it is fun.

We don't try to dazzle you with dollar signs, and big names. We're for the average rod builder. We cost a bit more, but we're worth it.

YOU GET US ONE WAY ONLY- BY SUBSCRIPTION.

BULLETPROOF PAINT

The start of any really good custom paint job is removal of all old paint. This can be by chemical stripper, blasting, or whatever. Carl Brunson prefers to take the paint down with sanding discs.

When there is to be a complete color change, it is vital that all removable panels be taken off. In this case, the original factory red color was too far different from new Ferrari India Red, so firewall, door jambs, trunk area and flooring was cleaned for new color.

Those of us who are latter-day hot rodders are far more fortunate than our predecessors in a lot of ways that have to do with tools, materials and techniques. One of the most exciting improvements in rod building to come along in recent years has been the two-part paint systems. These are the paint systems that have transformed cars into veritable works of visual art, paints that have a long life and give a wet look that almost defies description.

We first came across the two-part paints in the late '70s, when cars started showing up at rod runs looking as though they had just been dipped in hot wax. The finishes were so smooth they seemed plastic, and according to the car owners they were almost bulletproof.

When it came time to paint the '60 Chrysler, ace painter Carl Brunson suggested the new two-part system. "Makes the car look wet all the time, very shiny, and extremely durable." Wow! Exactly what we wanted. Especially the shiny part and the durable part. There's nothing less fun than cleaning and polishing a car all the time.

Carl had been quietly experimenting with a two-part system paint for some time at his custom shop in Driggs, Idaho, and had perfected the application. In this case, he used the German brand Sikkens, although there are several other brands now available.

Carl painted the Chrysler and the result is superior.

It is highly recommendable, especially to those who want to eliminate routine paint maintenance from their schedule.

We refer to this type of paint as a "system" because it really is. Carl emphasizes that whether he uses imported or domestic paint, he always keeps to the single product system throughout. While it is possible to mix components, the very best results seem to come from consistency within a product line. This means the same product line from initial etching through the final clear coat.

This paint is not inexpensive. Plan on paying upwards of $500 or more just for materials. But the results are so dramatically superior that you'll end up actually saving paint costs over the span of vehicle years. In the case of the Chrysler, the paint has been on for several years now and there are perhaps no more than 3 or 4 rock chips and no scratches. Wash jobs are rare, and we've never added any kind of polish or wax. The paint looks as fresh and wet as it did the day it was applied. During the same period with another car there were 3 paint jobs (because of the trick clear coat) and an almost constant requirement for polish and wax. All that for a finish that couldn't begin to compare in shine and depth.

The first and foremost thing to know about the new urethane type paints is that they can be lethal. Never forget this. It is critical to always use gloves, since the

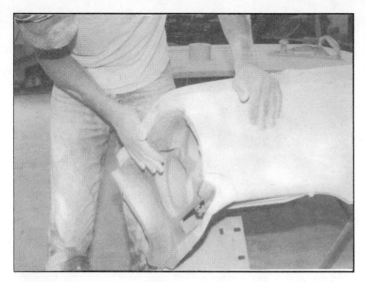

With the front end disassembled it is much easier to fill and sand all the small areas that often are overlooked.

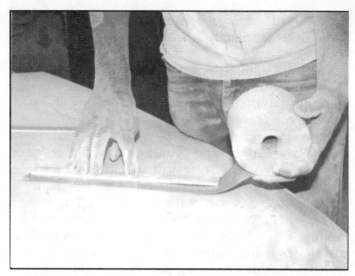

Block sanding the entire body will give the most perfect final finish, here a paint mixing stick is wrapped with sandpaper for long, slightly curved hood area. The flexible stick will conform to surface.

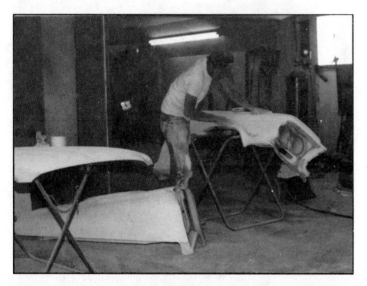

When using the new two-part paints, use the entire system, from bare metal etching primer through clear coats. Prepare every piece of the car the same way.

Perhaps the best known of the imported multi-part paints is Sikkens, but there are some excellent domestic two-parts now available. The American paints are less expensive, as well.

chemicals are absorbed through the skin. Over a period of time this can build into a problem, or it can cause a reaction immediately. Brunson recently experienced an isocyonate reaction that threatened for a time to end his painting career. Keep in mind that this plastic paint gets on everything, and that includes your lungs! Some painters wear a "space suit" for protection when spraying these two-part systems, and there is wisdom in that.

Another caution has to do with your painting equipment. Always clean your equipment immediately after use. If you don't, the paint will kick and ruin the equipment.

Now, to using the systems. The basic truth about any paint job is "the smoother the body surface, the better." This means doing an excellent preparation is imperative if an excellent result is to be obtained. Most professional painters will always advise stripping the paint to bare metal. This might not be entirely necessary on a new car, or reasonably new paint job, but this author's experience has been that when there is any doubt about the current paint surface, remove it. We're especially apprehensive about having any un-sealed old paint under the new urethanes, simply because these new paints make a chemical bond. That is, each layer of paint bites through the preceding layers.

After all body work has been done, it should be finished off with 80-100 grit sandpaper. Do not stop with 36 grit. Brunson prefers to use the ultralight fillers to ensure a perfect surface, but the aluminum type filler material works well, too. Don't reject the plastics out of hand, because this is the way the professionals get the flawless smooth look to large body panels. It should be very thin, however. The two-part primers will fill the rough 36 grit sanding marks, but this causes extra work and costs extra material. So, use the 80-100 paper for bodywork sanding.

There are some two-part putties now available that are great for filling the little imperfections. If you use them, let the car sit overnight so that any trapped solvents can escape.

Now comes the application of the "system". Start with a two-part etching primer (sometimes called a wash primer). The primer actually etches the surface for a maximum bond. In the case of Sikkens paint, a phosphoric acid is part of the thinner/catalyst, one of the reasons to use gloves. There is no reason to use any product such as Met-L-Prep unless there is some surface rust showing. In that case, use the cleaning acid along with a Scotchbrite scouring pad. Be sure to neutralize this cleaner with water, especially in the cracks. Very important.

After the etching primer has been applied, there is no need to sand before going to the filling primer. Again, use the two-part filler (really a surfacer). While this can actually be used without the etching primer base, it won't work as well. The etching primer is good enough to use on an aluminum surface, which tells you how well it works. Let the filling primer (surfacer) dry overnight, although most paint container instructions say that a shorter drying period is possible.

Next, apply a sanding guide coat. This can be a very light coat of lacquer primer/surfacer, usually a grey color since most two-part primers are a different color. Block sand the car, using a block or long board (the latter is for large areas). In this case, Brunson likes to use a paint stirring stick wrapped with sandpaper. It bends to contours, but is longer than most commercial blocks. The long board he uses is about 18 inches long.

The first sanding job is with 150 grit paper, dry. Another light guide coat of lacquer is applied and sanded with 220 grit paper, dry. Now it is time to "cut in" the edges. Meaning putting paint on the door jambs, around the hood edges, etc. This is with the color that you'll be using, and it is a two-part paint. Let this color edging dry thoroughly, then "back tape", which means to tape up around the doors, hood, deck, etc. where you don't want overspray. Sand around the exposed edges of the doors, fenders, etc.

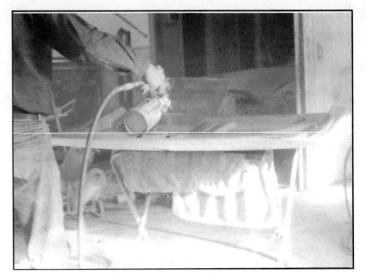

When doing a premium paint job, be sure and spray the underside of hood/deck/inner door panels.

Above- Also "cut in" the door jambs and trunk opening. After spraying these areas, let dry thoroughly before going to rest of the body.

Left- After firewall, door jambs, and similar areas are painted, the front fenders/doors/deck lid can be reinstalled. Some painters like to paint these parts separate, then assemble. Matter of preference.

where there is paint showing.

Use a tack rag to clean the car thoroughly, then spray on the two-part primer sealer. This is necessary to keep the strong solvents of the finish coat from working through to the base materials. Let the sealer dry overnight, then wet sand the sealer with 400 grit. This will give a very smooth surface. Do not sand through the sealer. If you do, spot with more sealer and re-sand.

Now, air and tack the finish. This means to use an air hose while you are using the tack rag. Do each panel separately. Do not rub the tack rag across a crack, since this can leave dust in the crack. A trick here is to drag a thumb or finger along the surface, off the tack rag. If there is any place that is missed, the finger will feel it. Clean hands! No natural oils, another reason for wearing gloves. Brunson tacks the car twice, the top, deck and hood a third time.

Mix the color coat per the can instructions. The air pressure recommended is pressure at the gun, not at the regulator. Never spray this paint in an unvented area. It is essential that some sort of exhaust fan is used. (Editor's Note: When spraying this paint in the home garage, we always raise the garage door a couple of feet and use two floor type house fans for exhaust. It works very well. It also gets paint all over the fans, so you have to buy new ones for the missus!)

The paint is applied much like any enamel, although it will kick very rapidly when it does start to go. Put on the first coat medium and let it dry long enough to get the vapors (solvents) out. If you put the second coat on too soon, the first coat solvents will be trapped and you will end up with trouble. In this respect, it is vital that you check with the paint supply store on the correct reducer to use. Pay particular attention to the spraying environment temperature.

When you can touch the first coat (on a piece of paper or tape) with the finger and you make a print but no paint sticks to the finger (touch the last area sprayed), it is time for the second coat. This can be sprayed wet. The third coat is also wet. It is possible to use additional reducer or a slower reducer to allow the paint to flow out smoother. Be very careful here, because a little bit of reducer goes a long way.

Some of the really dynamite paint jobs have been clear coated. The new two-part paint systems have a clear that does not yellow with age, a common problem with custom paint jobs until recently. You may want to go with two clear coats.

Wait 24 to 48 hours, then color sand the paint job with 1200 ultrafine paper. Carl uses 3M, you can talk to the paint rep about what grit to use and how long to wait. If you wait too long, the paint gets so hard you can't sand it well. When color sanding, use soapy water (liquid Ivory) and a block. Before you color sand, the finish will have a texture, sometimes this will look very grainy. The secret is the color sanding. Do not sand through the clear coats, or the color coats. Finally, buff

with the finest compound you have available. There are some variable buffing pads available that finish with Liquid Ebony. Whatever, this stage is up to you. Brunson tops off his paint jobs with McGuires #7.

One of the greatest benefits to this kind of paint job is that you don't have to pay a lot of attention to the finish. A stop at the local car wash, and the finish sparkles. Even after several years, the Chrysler has never had wax on it. The car cleans up as if the paint was applied just last week. The finish is so smooth that dirt just can adhere well. After hanging around the Bonneville salt flats for a week, we can spray off the underside of the car and notice that where there is traditional paint it is difficult to clean away the salt. Where there is the urethane paint, the salt simply slides off.

Go with the two-part paint. You'll love it.

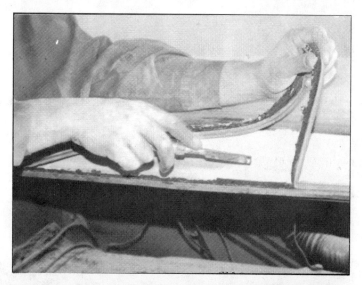

We put this pix out of sequence to make a point. During initial preparation, be sure and remove all weatherstripping and rubber around doors/front end/deck lid. Clean away all old rubber.

Use the best weatherstrip cement available, spread it well, then reinstall rubber. Get new rubber if possible.

POWERTRAIN

1970 440 6-Pack

by Robert Hardy

'A' ENGINES

The small block Mopar, called the 'A' engine by Chrysler, is the Mopar answer to the small block Chevy. A good basic free-breathing engine, it could easily be as popular today as the little Chevy if Chrysler had continued to produce it in quantity. This is especially true considering how little development time the 'A' engine has had, compared to its rival.

The 'A' engine came in four sizes: 273 cu.in., 318 cu.in., 340 and 360 cu.in. Introduced in 1964 as the 273 V8 by Plymouth and Dodge, it quickly became a popular performance choice in the smaller Darts, Valiants, and later on in the Barracudas. In 1967, Chrysler basically bored out the 273 and made the 318 engine. Just a minute, before you write me nasty letters about your father or uncle having a 318 in their 1963 car, let me explain. The 1967 and later 318, (the "A" engine), is a true wedge cylinder head design, with the block being

a modern thin-wall casting. It is related only by size to the earlier 318. The early 318 had a thicker wall casting for the block because thin-wall casting methods had not been perfected yet, but the biggest difference is in the cylinder heads. The early 318 is of a polysphere design. Kind of like a twisted, flattened, hemi design, which proved to be adequate but not particularly good, especially for performance. This early 318 can be recognized by its ripple-sided valve covers. This engine should not even be considered for rodding unless you have a soft spot in your heart for them and are willing to put up with a fair bit of inconvenience hunting for parts.

In 1968, the 340 was introduced. Although it looks much like the 318, and shares the same stroke, it actually uses a different block, with thicker cylinder walls and stronger main webbing.

Lastly, the biggest "A" engine, the 360, was brought out in 1971, using the same block as the 340, but with a smaller bore, longer stroke and larger diameter main bearing.

Interchangeability between the different "A" engines is pretty good, with a few notable exceptions. As noted, due primarily to bore size, the engine blocks are specific to each displacement. All "A" crankshafts, except the 360, are interchangeable. The 273, 318 car engine and the 360 use cast steel cranks, while the 318 truck engines and the 340 use a forged steel crankshaft. Be careful when selecting a forged crank from a 318 truck engine. The light duty truck cranks are OK, but the heavy duty truck cranks have a thicker flywheel flange which rules out using a car flywheel/starter combination.

Cylinder heads are practically a wide open swapping game. Almost any "A" head will fit any "A" engine. The best high-output heads are the 1968-'71 versions of the 340 high-performance model. These heads come with big ports and 2.02" intake valves, and 1.60" exhaust

98

valves. They also have a small 69 c.c. combustion chamber which, when combined with stock pistons, will normally put the compression ratio at 10.5:1, a little high for todays gasoline. The next best head for high-performance, and actually the best head for street use, is the 1972 and later 340/360 heads. These have the same ports as the high-performance 340 heads but use a 1.88" intake valve and a larger chamber which brings the compression ratio down to a more streetable level. If either of these heads are used on a 273 or 318 engine, the cylinder bores may have to be notched to clear the intake valve. Check for clearance before assembly. Also use the 340 intake manifold in order to match the intake port walls as they progress from the intake manifold to the cylinder head. One last point, 1967 and earlier engines use different valve lifters and pushrods.

One 'A' engine variant not talked about so far is the 340 Six-Pack, 340 6-bbl or 340 Trans-Am engine. These three names describe the same engine that initially was released in 1970. This engine uses a different block and cylinder heads than the regular 340. The racing version of the Six-Pack came with four-bolt mains, unavailable on any other 'A' block, while the street version of the Trans-Am block came with two-bolt mains but carried the bosses for the extra two outer bolts, which could easily be installed. This engine is quite rare and fetches a good dollar from those who desire such an animal. Your chances of finding one are slim. Even if you have one, it might be a better deal to sell it off and build a more streetable "A" engine and have some cash left over, but the choice is yours, that's what makes rodding exciting.

'B' & 'RB' ENGINES

In 1958, Chrysler introduced its first series of big block engines, over 350 cu.in., that were not hemi headed. This series of engines were designated 'B' engines, (for big?) and were eventually released in 350, 361, 383 and 400 cubic inch sizes. Out of these, the 383 and the 400 are the most common and popular. In 1959, the 'RB' (raised block) engine was introduced and developed from 383 cu.in. up through 413, 426 and eventually 440 cu.in. You'll notice the duplication of the 383 size. This early 383 RB, built from 1959-'61, used a smaller bore and a longer stroke than the 'B' version and is pretty rare. So any time you see the 383 mentioned, we mean the later 'B' block. The 426 size instantly conjures up visions of Hemi power, but during the early Sixties before the introduction of the late Hemi, this size meant wedge power. Many fearsome Super Stocks and even gas dragsters campaigned the nations dragstrips using Chrysler's Max Wedge for power.

The B and RB engines, besides using different blocks, also use different crankshafts, pistons, connecting rods, intake manifolds and distributors. This somewhat limits interchangeability with the major exception being the cylinder heads. If you have a 1967 or earlier 'B' or 'RB'

block you can use the 1968 and later heads for a bit more power. These heads have better ports and larger exhaust valves and are worth 15-20 hp on an earlier 383 or 413. The 1969 and later heads have an 80 c.c. combustion chamber compared to the earlier heads that have a 73 c.c. chamber. So if you want the better heads and also want to keep the original compression ratio, then use the 1968 heads or use the later heads but have them milled .060" to bring the compression back up, and then mill the intake .075" to realign the ports. Although, with gasoline quality being what it is today, you might just be better off to leave the compression where it is and work around it with better tuning and parts matching.

LATE HEMI

And now ladies and gentlemen let me direct your attention to that expensive, hard to find, big and somewhat heavy, and always impressive looking Chrysler Hemi! Sorry 'bout that, but I couldn't help myself. Seems whenever a street Hemi shows up in a rod, it's like being in a three-ring circus, people crowding around staring wide-eyed and mumbling about outrageous horsepower numbers. Truthfully it's not quite that bad, but pop the hood and that Hemi will draw a crowd anytime.

The original 426 cu.in. or late Hemi was brought out in 1964 as a pure racing engine. It had cast iron cylinder heads and a short ram intake with two Holley four barrels. In 1965 it was updated with a similar looking intake manifold that was now cast of magnesium, and the cylinder heads were now made of aluminum. In 1966 the infamous Street Hemi was co-introduced by Dodge and Plymouth. This street version was quite similar to the racing version but was now built on regular production lines using a modified RB cylinder block. It also came with cast iron cylinder heads, milder cam timing and a dual-plane intake manifold with two AFB Carters mounted inline. The Hemis built from 1970 on used a new design engine block with beefier main bearing webs.

TRANSMSSION POINTERS

A quick pointer on transmissions for these engines. There is one style, or bellhousing pattern, for all 'A' engines, and another style for all 'B' and 'RB' blocks. However keep in mind that the 360 engine uses a specially balanced torque convertor which should not be switched with other convertors.

GENERAL PARTS CHOOSING

Most street rodders use basically a stock engine with changes being limited to the intake and exhaust systems, the camshaft and the ignition system. By limiting modifications only to these areas, the reliability of the stock engine is maintained, and by careful selection of aftermarket components, performance, and many times mileage is enhanced. There are some engines that have been installed in rods that have been modified far in excess of what has been described here, particularly since the advent of pro-street. These power plants are not the mainstream, but rather a fringe of rodding. Your basic, mildly modified engine is still the common choice of most rodders.

Let's start at the top and work our way down. Air filters. Don't even think of running an engine without one, even temporarily. With the amount of air an engine ingests, it would be foolish to think that at least some amount of grit wouldn't be inhaled. Consider how much time and money you have invested under the hood, and now think of dirt going into the engine, wearing out the rings, etc. 'Nuff said.

You will probably want to eliminate the elaborate factory air filtering system. The factory ducts cool air to the engine when it is warm and hot air when the engine is cold. This improves driveability, especially with the lean jetting common to emission engines. You can usually get by without the factory setup but there will usually be some surging and hesitation when the engine is cold. If this happens, running one or two steps richer on the main jets will usually cure the problem.

Choose your aftermarket filter by size. That is, the diameter and height. If you have room for it, a 14" by 3" (diameter X height) is an excellent size, and if your engine makes much over 250 h,p, you will need a filter this big to eliminate the possibility of any air flow restriction. Although most mild small blocks will work fine with smaller filters, such as 14 X 2 or 9 X 2, with very little noticeable difference on the street. A quick way to compare relative flow figures from one filter size to another is to multiply the diameter by the height. For instance, a 9 X 2 filter would flow about the same as a 12 X 1-1/2 filter (9 X 2 = 18, 12 X 1-1/2 = 18). This is a rough comparison and does not take into account the various filtering mediums that do pass air in different amounts. Even similar looking, same-size paper elements from different manufacturers may have flow rates that are quite a bit different from each other.

Another popular filter medium, besides paper, is foam. The foam mushroom and bell types flow about the same as a 14 X 3 paper element. The foam units that are direct replacements for a paper element, naturally flow air according to their various sizes, but all flow more than their equivalent sized paper elements. Many of these units must have their foam oiled before using. Check with the manufacturer. If your unit does require oil, use oil especially made for air filters. Don't use any

other oil, such as motor oil or WD-40. They just won't work as well and there may be a possibility of damaging the foam.

Again, going with the majority of rodders, we will look at the single four barrel carburetor and manifold. Electronic fuel injection is the wave of the future, not only promising, but delivering better fuel mileage and performance. However, that single four barrel comes pretty close to fuel injection and satisfies most rodders' requirements. Besides, not only have they been around forever but they're cheap.

If the carburetor selected is too large for the application, mileage and driveability suffer due to part-throttle mixing problems. This tuning problem is caused by not having enough pressure differential through the carb to properly activate all the circuits. This problem is unsolvable by jet changes. If a carb is too small in size, then there is the possibility that the air-flow through the venturi at high rpm may exceed the speed of sound. If this happens, then the pressure drop across the carb actually diminishes, thereby reducing fuel flow right when the engine needs it the most. The resulting lean condition reduces power output and in extreme situations may even burn a piston. Due to the manner in which most street engines are driven, it is always wiser to go a little smaller on carburetor sizing than a little too big. Remember that street rodding is not racing, and it is not very likely that you could place a carburetor on your engine that would be small enough to present any problems. But due to the fact that there are so many big four-barrels out there, it is a possibility that you could install one that would be big enough to cause a lot of headaches.

There are, of course, variables when sizing a carb. A V6 can handle a carburetor slightly larger than what an equivalent sized V8 could. This is because on a V6 each cylinder would be larger than the V8's cylinder, (1/6 of the total displacement compared to 1/8 for the V8), and therefore imparts a stronger signal to the carburetor. This does primarily apply to wide open throttle conditions, and may or may not be of any consequence to your application.

Since the four barrel used should always be of the vacuum secondary type, for street use, then carburetor sizing for driveability concerns itself only with the primary side of the carburetor. If the primaries are sized properly, then driveability is enhanced and the secondary side of the carburetor could be enlarged to make up for any lost flow, thereby maintaining total power output at higher revs. This type of carb, one that has small primaries and larger secondaries, is called a

---

LATE MOPAR REAR-WHEEL-DRIVE TERMINOLOGY

ENGINE TYPE

Six Cylinder 170, 198, 225

A Engine 273, 318 (1967 and later), 340, 360

B Engine 361, 383, 400

RB Engine 413, 426 Wedge, 440

Hemi 426

---

spreadbore carburetor. Holley has them and, of course, the Rochester Quadrajet is probably the best known example. These carbs can provide very efficient street operation, usually better than the more common square-bore carburetors that have all the venturis the same size.

The intake manifold must deliver air-flow quality as well as quantity. This means that mixtures of equal air/fuel ratios must be delivered to each cylinder. Many stock manifolds deliver richer mixtures to the cylinders closest to the carburetor, and mixtures that get progressively leaner as the cylinder gets farther away from the carb. This is not so much a problem of distance or the length of the runner itself, but the fact that the length has not been properly compensated for during the initial design stage of the manifold.

Most street manifolds are of either single- or dual-plane design. The single-plane intake is one in which all intake runners converge into a single area known as the plenum; this plenum is situated directly under the carburetor. This allows any cylinder to feed directly from the plenum which is supplied by the complete carburetor. On a dual-plane manifold there are two plenums, with one half the cylinders feeding from one plenum and the other plenum serving the rest of the cylinders. Each plenum is fed by one half of the carburetor, that is, one primary and one secondary feeding each plenum. The cylinders are divided so that each plenum is never drawn from by two cylinders consecutively. This allows a small time gap which allows the carb to refill the plenum. For example, on a V8 a typical firing order would be 18436572. Using the firing order you could determine that on a two plane intake, one plenum would feed cylinders 1,4,6 and 7, and the other plenum would feed cylinders 8,3,5 and 2. This is easy to understand just by looking at any stock intake manifold.

Single plane intakes come in many variations, all having the ability to deliver more air-flow to the cylinders than a dual-plane intake. Due to this intake design, stressing flow quantity, there are horsepower increases in the middle and higher rpm ranges. Larger carbs, lumpier cams, bigger valves etc. are usually the rest of the parts combination that go with the single-plane. As can be seen, horsepower, not mileage, is stressed here.

Dual-plane intakes, because each of the two plenums is smaller than the plenum found on a single-plane intake, allows the carburetor to see a much stronger signal. This helps sharpen throttle response and makes for a broad torque curve with strong low to mid-range horsepower, without sacrificing too much off the top end. This make for a good basic street manifold.

Although originally designed as a pure race manifold, the tunnel ram has been used quite a bit on the street so I suppose it deserves some coverage too. The popularity of the tunnel ram is easy to understand. Just by looking at it you can tell it reeks of power. About the only induction system more impressive is a blower.

Tunnel rams can be used on the street successfully and surprisingly their biggest problem lies not in the manifold itself but in the choice of carburetors. For street use, pick a manifold with a small runner, or port, cross-section, and a small plenum. This keeps the signal to the carb strong and the velocity in the intake manifold runners high enough to avoid mixture problems. The best carburetor to use, for two four barrel applications is the 390 c.f.m. Holley with vacuum secondaries. These carbs can be used straight out of the box. Big block engines, over 400 c.i., will sometimes be better off using two of the 550 c.f.m. carbs, but this depends on torque convertor stall speed and rear axle gearing. For carburetors mounted inline with each other, use the side pivot bowls (4160 style), then use the center pivot bowls (4150 style) on sideways mounted carbs. If this sounds confusing, talk to your local speed shop. Carbs mounted sideways have a complicated throttle linkage and their electric chokes may cause clearance problems, depending on the manifold. Also use Holley's Secondary Diaphragm Kit no. 20-28 to equalize vacuum to both carbs. A high-lift, short-duration cam with little overlap also works well with tunnel rams. Some punch can also be put back in the low rpm range by altering the ignition timing. Limit the distributor's mechanical advance to 20 degrees, making sure that the first 10 degrees is all in by 2,000 rpm, and limit the vacuum advance to about 10 degrees. Now, bring the static or initial timing up to about 12 to 14 degrees. This combination works real well with engines that have compression ratios of around 9.5:1 or less, even with todays gasoline.

While we're talking about ignition, we may as well cover that subject. Original equipment manufacture (OEM) single-point distributors can be modified to perform adequately to about 6,000 rpm Above this speed, the dwell time of 30-32 degrees just doesn't allow enough time for the coil to fully saturate and so a weak spark is produced. Dual-point distributors have a total dwell time of 34-36 degrees, thus allowing the coil to produce a healthy spark up to about 8,500 rpm To operate reliably up to these speeds, point type distributors must be modified with special point sets having greater spring tension and even special distributor cam designs, in order to eliminate any point bounce which may occur. Of course, ignition points need continual adjustment during their life to compensate for rubbing block wear.

It is because of these shortcomings that electronic distributors have gained in popularity. Instead of mechanical points, electronic distributors use either a magnetic or optical triggering device which avoids any actual contact between parts, and therefore eliminates any adjustments once the initial setting is made. There is also an electronic system that does use points as a trigger for the coil. This system passes a very small amount of current through the points, allowing them to last an extremely long time, although adjustments must still be made to compensate for rubbing block wear. This does negate one of electronic ignition's strong points (no pun intended).

Despite what type of ignition system you use, it must be properly set up by a professional on a distributor machine, to match your engine/vehicle combination. If the engine and distributor originally came out of a 5,000 lb. highway cruiser with tall gears and an automatic transmission, it certainly would not be set up to work properly in a 2,300 lb. rod with low gears, four speed, improved breathing and a higher compression ratio. The mechanical and vacuum advance must be adjusted; both the total amount of advance and the rate at which it comes in. This can be accomplished by using different weights, springs and advance stop bushings in order to tailor the advance curve. That pro with the distributor machine should be able to tell you exactly what you need.

To go with the newly modified distributor, get a good set of ignition wires. Of the three types of ignition wires, solid-core, carbon suppression and magnetic suppression, only the suppression wires meet government specifications for on-road use. Carbon suppression wires should only be found on stock vehicles. That leaves us with the magnetic suppression wire which uses a solid wire which is wrapped around a core, usually fiberglass, and is covered with insulation. This method of construction allows it to compare favorably with the solid-core wire for strength and conductivity, and yet maintain the no radio static capability of the more fragile carbon-core wires. Two good examples of this premium wire is the MSD Heli Core and the Moroso Spiral Core.

After the induction and ignition systems, the next most changed item on an engine is the exhaust system. In fact, because rodders rarely use an engine in the chassis for which it was originally intended, the exhaust system may be the most changed piece on an engine.

Although stock exhaust manifolds are used many times, no one will admit that the cast iron manifolds are as good as or superior to headers, except for longevity. If you must use the stock manifolds because of cost or clearance problems, then try to make the rest of the exhaust system as free-flowing as possible. Headers come plain, coated, chromed, thick wall etc., as well as many different quality levels. Many headers are made for stock engine/vehicle combinations, and for specific rodding applications, such as Chevy into '34 Ford.

Unfortunately Mopar buffs are a couple of rungs down on the popularity ladder, but call around to the various header manufacturers. They may have a header for you or be able to suggest something that would help. It is also possible to build your own headers, if you are ambitious, from pre-bent 'U' bends, collectors etc. Also you can check the Yellow Pages directory from any large city and you may be able to locate, with the help of a few phone calls, some shop that will build a set of headers for you.

Once you get past the headers, or manifolds, try to keep restriction to a minimum. The pipes from the headers to the mufflers should be 2-1/2", and then the tail-pipes should be 2-1/4" for free flow. These sizes work with most typical street engines, but follow your

VERY GENERAL CAMSHAFT GUIDE

cam duration at .050"
cam lift

up to 230 degrees	good for a heavy car with a small engine or with an automatic transmission, good smooth idle and lots of torque
230-250 degrees	good for a heavy car with a big block engine, or a middle weight car with a small block engine, for combination street and drag racing
250-260 degrees	good for a big block engine in a middle weight car, lots of performance, marginal street use
260-270 degrees	good for a big block engine in a light car, marginal street use

This chart is a rough guide only and there will be exceptions and overlaps to the above numbers. Consult the manufacturers for more detailed recommendations.

Small Block Chevy
Big Block Chevy
Angle Plug Heads
Small Block Ford
Big Block Ford
Ford Cleveland
Ford Y-Block V-8
Flathead Ford
Buick V-6
Chevy 90 V-6
Small Block Dodge
Big Block Dodge
Inside Chassis
Outside Chassis

103

common sense. If the engine is only 200 cu.in., then smaller pipes can be used, and if you have a 500 cu.in. monster, then larger pipes would be the way to go. It is possible to boost low-end power a bit and at the same time mellow out the exhaust by placing an 'H' pipe or crossover, just ahead of the mufflers. The 'H' pipe should be of the same diameter as the head pipes, and because placement is not critical as long as it is upstream of the mufflers, put it where it will fit the chassis best.

All exhaust tubing should be of 14-gauge thickness. This size is about the best compromise between bendability and strength. The standard type of exhaust pipe connection is the male/female slip fit. To keep the exhaust flow as smooth as possible, always fit the upstream pipe into the downstream pipe. Don't forget to paint the exhaust system with a high temperature paint to make it last longer and look better. Stainless steel is an alternative, but keep in mind that there are a couple of different grades of stainless. Most towns and all cities have exhaust shops that can bend up custom exhaust systems. Shop around until you find a shop that has done some rods before, and discuss your needs with them.

Mufflers come in a variety of sizes, shapes and colors, but they can all be lumped into a couple of categories. The original performance muffler was the glasspack. These units are the noisiest of the bunch, don't last too long and restrict the exhaust flow due to turbulence. Not exactly the best choice. Stock design mufflers are also too restrictive, so that leaves us with the last category, turbo mufflers. Originally a Chevrolet design for the turbocharged Corvair, hence its name, this is a free-flowing, baffled design that has a nice deep mellow tone. Don't let its stock appearance fool you, inside it's all performance. A pair of these work quite nicely and because they are usually slightly smaller than stock mufflers, they are easy to place under the vehicle. They are also available in stainless, if that's what you are using.

Two footnotes on exhaust systems. One, don't use header mufflers. They are just too close to the engine and get the exhaust gasses before they have a chance to cool down. This shortens their life too much to make this type of muffler a good choice. Two, if by law or conscience you have decided to use a catalytic converter, use a pair of them mounted directly behind the headers. Converters need the extra heat to function properly and by using two of them, restriction is minimized. Rodders, knowing the limits which factory engineers face, almost always change the camshaft to one more suited for their purpose, even though it involves tearing into the engine. First off, always use a hydraulic lifter camshaft, unless you are a real diehard that actually enjoys adjusting the lifters every month or so to keep the engine in top tune. Choosing that perfect cam is quite complicated. Engine size, compression ratio, induction characteristics, the exhaust system, transmission type, rear axle ratio, tire size, vehicle

weight and its specific use, plus a number of related items, all affect camshaft choice. For this reason it is not wise to pick a cam because a somewhat similar vehicle in a magazine used a such-and-such grind. Nor is it smart to use what a local racer or buddy uses. There are just too many variables. A better way is to use well founded guidelines that have been researched over the years to make an educated choice. This, plus using the cam manufacturers' catalogues, which in themselves are a goldmine of information, will get you very close to the ideal cam for your application. If you are still in doubt, write down everything you know about your car that may affect the choice of camshaft (most catalogues have a form to follow), and give a call to the manufacturer's tech line.

If you are one of those power-hungry rodders that would like every last horse possible, but because your rod will also be driven quite a bit (shouldn't they all?), then consider some of the newer design cams that have come out during the last few years. These cams usually have more valve lift and quicker opening rates than usual, but at the same time have less duration than you would expect. This design has struck a very nice compromise between fuel mileage and power. These cams come under several labels. Competition Cams calls theirs High Energy Cams, Cam Dynamics names theirs the Enforcer Series, and Sig Erson has the TQ Series, just to name a few. All major cam companies have this style of cam. To show you what a difference a cam of this type can make, consider this: a radical, high-powered small-block rod with a 308-degree duration hydraulic camshaft, with an also radical rough idle and eight miles per gallon. This rodder then switched to a cam of this newer style that had only 268 degrees duration. He lost 1/10 of a second at the drag strip, but his mileage increased to 16 mpg. Needless to say a happy customer. Choose that cam carefully!

When it comes time to screw all this stuff together, remember that successful engine construction consists of four things. Number one, attention to detail. Examine everything. Sometimes manufacturers do make mistakes, despite quality-control programs. If you don't think so, drop by sometime and I will show you a brand new spark plug that has no threads on the body. Number two, make sure that everything matches with everything else in the system. In other words don't run a monster cam with stock manifolds. Don't laugh, you would be surprised how easily many people fall into this type of pit. Number three, machining things to precise tolerances. If it calls for a .0025" clearance somewhere then make sure that's what it is, .0035" won't do. Number four, cleanliness. Engines are precision assemblies, don't go putting dirt into it. How many times have you seen someone put together an engine while they're smoking a cigarette, ashes falling into the engine. Use common sense and you will have many happy rodding miles.

EARLY HEMI WHITE PAPER

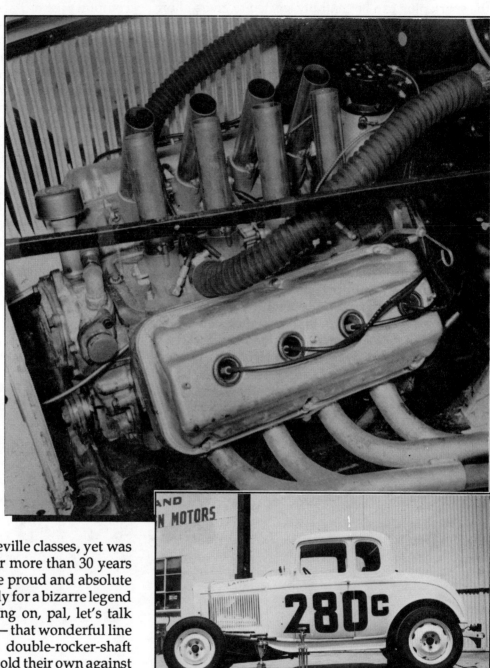

One of the first hot DeSotos to hit the salt flats was in a real barndoor. Bob Johneck turned 154 in the 1932 Ford coupe, straight off the trailer. The 258-inch engine ran straight alcohol. Such easy performances knocked the old Ford flathead V8 stone-cold dead. A modern version of this engine would probably be very similar, but with more cam timing, more porting, forged pistons, better rings and gearing to raise the rev range. Photo from Mark Dees collection.

*by Mark Dees
with special thanks to Al Teague, Barry Kaplan and Ed Donovan*

Do you realize that one of the smoothest, most powerful and most visually exciting engines ever built in America may be waiting in a junkyard for your low-buck hot rod project? Did you know that this engine series won in many of the fastest Bonneville classes, yet was discontinued by its manufacturer more than 30 years ago? Can you remember the once proud and absolute ruler of drag racing? Are you ready for a bizarre legend of corporate craziness? Then hang on, pal, let's talk about the REAL Chrysler hemis — that wonderful line of big, little and medium-sized double-rocker-shaft V8s of 1951 through '58 that still hold their own against the best.

During the 1920s, Walter P. Chrysler's newly-formed auto manufacturing organization earned big profits and a fine engineering reputation with cars that were good looking and very fast for their time. By WWII, that reputation was severely tarnished. After the great Airflow disaster of the mid-'30s, Chrysler Corporation was run by a belt and suspenders type named K.T. Keller, who let the firm coast along making slow, ugly lumps of metal whose only virtues were solid comfort and utter reliability.

Finally, rumors about GM's research into high-performance OHV engines filtered over to Chrysler, and even Keller realized that the firm's inline flathead sixes and eights would have to be replaced. A team headed by James C. Zeder was ordered to come up with "the best engine it is possible to mass-produce." The actual research and design which followed was done by W.E. Drinkard and M.L. Carpentier.

With such a directive, any competent designer will start with the combustion chamber, the heart of the engine, where fuel is converted into heat energy. And the best combustion chamber is the hemispherical. Why? Because it has the best thermal efficiency of any type, due to its low surface-to-volume ratio, meaning less energy loss to the cooling system. This is because the spark plug can be centrally located to give a short, even flame front, and because big valves can be used without shrouding, and because the hemi chamber readily lends itself to big, free-breathing ports. For all these reasons, most of the world's race engine builders have used hemi chambers. A notable exception is the "pent-roof" chamber originated by Peugeot in 1911 and used thereafter by Miller, Offenhauser and Cosworth, to name a few. The pent-roof represents a hemi chamber stretched lengthwise to permit four valves per cylinder. In a race car, the increased breathing ability makes up for a slight loss of thermal efficiency. Any engine without a hemi or pent-roof chamber (or one of the new 5-or-more valve designs) represents at least a theoretical compromise from the ideal.

For reasons of practicality, Zeder's team never thought seriously of the pent-roof chamber. Their first task was to successfully disprove old wives' tales that the hemi chamber had combustion roughness and was sensitive to fuel quality. Probably their work was hastened by the introduction of the sensational '49 Olds and Cad V8s, which promptly wiped out any substantial justification for buying a Chrysler product in their price range.

Most hemi engines (before Chrysler) had used overhead cams for valve actuation, though some used complex pushrod-and-rocker arrangements. Chrysler's engineers settled on a design used in early Talbots and refined by the Arkus-Duntov brothers in the low-production OHV conversions for Ford flathead V8s. It is widely accepted that an Ardun head was perched on the drafting table when the first Chrysler hemi was sketched out. Generally speaking, when high rpm is required, even the best pushrod-and-rocker system is inferior to a system where a large, properly designed cam lobe actuates the valves directly. The reason is that all that monkey-motion is known to flex, break and fail to follow cam contours at high speed. Chevy V8s have been such a success in large part because of light, sturdy and simple pushrod valve gear. The long, heavy exhaust rockers of the Ardun and the various Chrysler hemis are rather scary when viewed as high-speed components, but a lot of empirical work on cam design,

In 1958, Capanna came back to Indy with a 270-inch DeSoto to be driven by Jerry Unser. This engine had a billet crank, needle rocker and cam bearings, special crank supports. Cam was Harman/Collins. Machine was fast, but it also blew. Photo courtesy Indy Motor Speedway.

valve train material and spring pressures have made these complicated set-ups work very well.

Early MoPar hemis — all three sizes of 'em — BREATHE. For their size, they huff and puff as well as, or better than, any production V8 built before or since, with the possible exception of the late, very trick, GM and Ford (and aftermarket) heads. Until very recently, a slightly ported DeSoto head for a 300 cid engine could make a number of ultra-high-buck Chevy small block heads look sad on a flow bench. And since the combustion chamber is better than any Chevy, particularly with alcohol and/or nitro, you can see why the early hemis are the only engines of their era still viable by today's performance standards, notwithstanding a weight handicap and in some cases a lower end strength problem.

The first MoPar hemi was the big Chrysler and Imperial "Firepower" which was revealed in 1950 for the 1951 model year. The scaled down and lightened "Firedome" DeSoto appeared a year later, and in 1953 came the beautiful baby of the bunch, the Dodge "Red Ram." Because of a decentralization program then in effect at Chrysler, each make of engine had little interchangeability with the others and was built on its own line in different plants — even though in many cases actual displacements and power outputs didn't vary that much if at all. This cost be damned design and production approach was sheer management madness from a cost/benefit standpoint. The bean counters (never very influential at Chrysler until Iacocca took over) lay in wait to kill the hemis at the first opportunity.

Meanwhile, Chrysler Corporation wasn't out of the woods. Only the engines were changed in its line of vehicles, either because of limited funds or because Keller still wanted to get into his car without knocking his hat off. In any event, the wonderful new engines were buried in well built but stodgy chassis with horrible brakes. They were usually hooked up to Fluid Drive and its later variants, probably the worst automatic transmission ever built in the country. Even when removed from the prison of the stock chassis, the 1951-'53 Chrysler V8s present some problems to the engine swapper or racer.

From here on out, I use the word "Chrysler" standing alone to refer to the largest series of these engines, with "DeSoto" and "Dodge" used for the smaller versions respectively. "MoPar" refers to all three series.

The early Chryslers are very heavy for their displacement (331 cid) and the blocks incorporate an integral bell housing, overhanging the plane of the flywheel like a '32-'48 Ford V8. Only Offenhauser makes trans adapters for these engines. For racing, a bulky scattershield must be made to surround the stock bell housing.

All Dodges, DeSotos and '54 and later Chryslers have separate bell housings. However, the rear of the block isn't flanged, so the starter and bell housing are hung on a die-cast alloy mounting plate which flush-bolts to the back of the block just forward of the flywheel plane. All early MoPar hemis have the same bolt pattern on the rear of the block, will take the same mounting plates, and thus will take the same transmission adapters. But note that there is more than one thickness of those mounting plates out there, and anyone doing a swap or using a non-standard transmission had better be careful to check the matter of clutch clearance, pilot shaft seating and throwout bearing action before final assembly. Adapter manufacturers (Offenhauser, Wilcap, and Trans-Dapt) can still advise if you talk to the right guy.

Some of the '53 and '54 models shared their oil supply with the loathsome automatic gearbox, which led to immense grief when serviced by dullards who weren't aware of the fact. Dodges and DeSotos were also available with Warner gear three-speed manual boxes with wide ratios (2.57, 1.83, 1.00) and enough strength for a stock engine, but not much more.

In 1955, the entire MoPar line was redesigned, with Virgil Exner doing the styling. The chassis didn't change much, but the solid bodies were considerably lower with flowing lines. The Powerflite two-speed torque converter transmission, which had been used on a few models in '54, was fitted to all lines. It worked well enough, but lacked torque multiplication at low speeds. Another development of 1955 was the first attempt to reduce the Corporation's engine manufacturing costs. For the Dodge and Chrysler lines, there was heavy promotion and sale of engines built on "hemi" blocks, but with more compact single rocker shaft heads, labeled Polysphere. Plymouth's first V8 was a Polysphere version of the original '53 Dodge hemi. These were good engines, which in average use were as satisfactory as the double rocker shaft engines, but the single rocker-shaft configuration necessarily did away with the big straight ports, big valves and the classic hemi chamber. I have never heard of any high-performance or racing use made of Polysphere heads, and for our purpose they're only things you throw away to get a block to be used with true hemi heads.

The most important Polyspheres, from a performance standpoint, are the late '55 Plymouth V8s of 259 cid and the '55 Chrysler Windsor of 300 cid. True hemis never came from the factories in these particular sizes, but as it happens a Plymouth fitted with Dodge hemi heads is nearly ideal for various Bonneville classes with a 260-inch limit. The '55 Windsor with '54-'56 heads is still considered the strongest possible combination for a blown 300 cid fueler. Indeed, at one time, the blown fuel limit at Bonneville was only 300 inches, and a lot of racing Windsors were built. If you could hear a certain spine-chilling tape of Clark Cagle's blown Windsor on a 275-mph pass in Don Allen's old belly tank lakester, you would have some idea of how hard these little Chryslers run.

The news for 1956 was introduction of a fine automatic transmission — the three-speed Torqueflite. Early versions had an iron case. An important change in Dodge and DeSoto blocks took place the same year. Their deck height was raised substantially to gain more displacement. Rod and main bearing diameters were increased. Rods were lengthened, and valve and port sizes were enlarged. Some of these engines were notable in being the only undersquare V8s of the modern era, with a stroke dimension greater than the bore. In 1957, the Chrysler hemis were enlarged in similar fashion.

1957 was the hemi's greatest year from a performance viewpoint, although they were only found in low production, top of the line cars, compared with the cheaper Polysphere models. As a result, they are now rather rare. In that year, the MoPar chassis were at last truly modernized. They featured torsion bar front suspension and ball joints on the control arms. Without question, they were the best handling passenger cars built in this country until that time. Unfortunately, body-chassis quality control had declined, so MoPars tended to shake and rattle badly. And from bitter personal experience, I can tell you the brakes were criminally deficient. But the hemi engines were very fast and amazingly durable, with no weak point in

normal use, unlike Cadillacs of the same era which had unreliable transmissions and crack-prone heads. Most Chrysler engines outlasted the body and chassis in which they came. It is rare to find one in a junkyard which can't be rebuilt.

The street rod builder need only wander through the mud and weeds of his favorite yard, searching for the size best suited for his chassis. If he is lucky enough to find one, all he has to do is rebuild it to factory specs. That's all, and it will run a lot stronger than any Targetmaster 305! Of course, if you need more beans, you can do some hopping up, as described below and in the Chart Notes. There is a problem, however, in getting speed equipment such as manifolds and crankcase girdles for anything but the 392 Chrysler. If you are mounting a hemi in a narrow chassis, you may have to relocate the oil filter with a Milodon alongside the block adapter or an Offenhauser remote mount adapter.

It's my personal opinion that the exquisite little Dodge and the medium size DeSoto are the best choices for the average roadster or early coupe. Even then, the hood panels may have to be bulged out to clear the massive valve covers, but that's one of the hemi's visual appeals. Chryslers are really too big and heavy for the smaller cars and engine compartments, and represent a lot of iron to hang over a beam axle. They work best in fat jobs from the early '50s — Mercs, Hudsons and '53 Studebakers particularly — and are ideal for working pickups.

Turning to the racing scene, the big Chrysler dominated the top classes of drag racing, to the near exclusion of everything else. For several years after their introduction, all three makes (depending upon class displacement limits) were the engines to beat, not only at the drags but at the boat races, the dry lakes and Bonneville. They still are top dogs (sharing glory with big and little Chevys, but hardly anything else) in straightaway competition, where weight is not a handicap. The hemis were highly competitive at road racing and circle track events, but in that type of competition were a bit too heavy and bulky to be invincible.

What did 'em in? Not the Chevy V8. It was Chrysler Corporation. After 1957, they just quit making them,

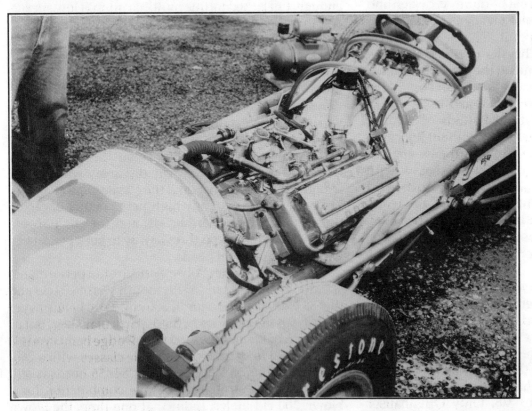

For the 1955 Indianapolis 500, Al Dean installed a Dodge modified by Tony Capanna (Wilcap Company) in the same Kuzma chassis in which Jimmy Bryan had placed 2nd the year before. Bryan (a rodder from Arizona) turned several laps in practice at very competitive speeds, but when Bob Christie tried to qualify the car, the engine's lower end blew. Chet Herbert roller cam was used. Photo courtesy Indy Motor Speedway.

One of the first streamliners ever constructed for Bonneville was the Rudy Heredia machine from northern Calfironia, using a Chrysler hemi with front-mounted Potvin type 6-71 GMC supercharger. Photo from Tex Smith collection.

even Polyspheres, and replaced them with what amounted to two sizes of simple wedge chamber engines. The Chrysler and Imperial hemis of '58 (and a few Dodge Polyspheres) were actually stockpiled '57s. Imagine what the little Dodge V8 would be today if it had been developed over the years as much as was the small block Chevy. It eventually dawned on Chrysler that they'd made a mistake, and a new 426 hemi did appear in 1964, based on the larger "B" series wedge block, but there is virtually no interchange between it and preceding engines. It was hardly better than the earlier hemis upon its debut, except perhaps in sturdiness, but it got a lot more racing development from its parent.

The ultimate "early" hemi isn't a Chrysler product at all. Years ago, Ed Donovan brought out his famous 417 as a sleeved alloy block of nominal 392 internal and external dimensions to take Chrysler heads, cranks, cams and other components. At the present time, everything for the engine can be supplied by Donovan

without using a single Chrysler part. Alloy heads with shallower valve angle, needle bearing rocker arms, gear drives, stainless valves, hard-chromed billet crankshaft, blower manifold, roller cams, special pushrods and forged pistons — most of which fit (or can be made to fit) 392 Chryslers as well.

Getting back to MoPar iron engines, never before and never after did brute horsepower come so cheap. They lent themselves to the most incredible simplicity of modification, even in the case of blown fuelers. In the early '60s, I kibitzed often on the activities of such hemi proponents as Don Alderson, Boyd Pennington and Gary Cagle. These fellows would go to the junkyard, buy an old '54 or later Chrysler and tear it apart. Nothing in the lower end would be replaced except the rings — and those were Grants because they got them free. Even the stock lead babbit inserts would go back, on the theory that 60 or 80 thousand miles of street use opened the clearances just the right amount for racing use. Grind the valves and replace the springs. Reassemble everything and slip in a Racer Brown cam. Bolt on a 6-71 with injector and drop in an old Vertex. Add alcohol and a splash of nitro and stand back. Go 200 in a hiboy '32, 275 in a tank, or terrorize Long Beach in a rail job — cast pistons, stock rods and all. But they

The accompanying chart lists all the major early MoPar hemi variations. Pay close attention to the Chart Notes, which contain important interchange rules.

MOPAR 1951 to 1958 HEMISPHERICAL CHAMBER V8 ENGINES DIMENSIONAL AND INTERCHANGE CHART

	Bore	Stroke	Cubic Inch Disp.	Main Brg. Diam.	Rod Brg. Diam.	Rod Length (C to C) Diam.	Int. Valve Diam.	Ex. Valve Diam.
"DODGE" ENGINE GROUP								
A. Low Block Hemis:								
'53-'54 Dodge V8s -	3.475	3.25	241	2.375	1.9375	5.9375	1.75	1.41
'55 Dodge Custom Royal -	3.625	"	270	"				
B. Low Block Single Rocker Shaft Engines:								
'55 Plymouth V8s -	3.475	"	241	"	"	"	"	"
Some '56 Plymouth V8s*	3.56		259					
'55 Dodge Coronet V8, Royal	3.625	"	270	"	"	"	"	"
'56 Dodge Coronet V8								
*NOT '56-'57 Plymouth 277, 301.303, 318, V8s								
A. Tall Block Hemis:								
'56 Dodge D-500 -	3.625	3.80	315	2.500	2.250	6.62	1.87	1.53
'57 Dodge D-500 -	3.69	"	325	"	"	"	"	"
B. Tall Block Single Rocker Shaft Engines:								
'56 all Dodge V8 exc D-500 & Coronet	3.625	"	315	"	"	"	"	"
'57 all Dodge V8 exc D-500								
'57 DeSoto Firesweep S-27	3.69	"	325	"	"	"	"	"
'58 Dodge Royal, Coronet V8								
"DESOTO" ENGINE GROUP								
A. Low Block Hemis:								
'52-'54 DeSoto V8 -	3.625	3.344	276	2.375	2.0625	6.0625	1.84	1.50
'55 DeSoto -	3.72	"	291	"	"	"	"	
B. Low Block Single Rocker Shaft Engines: NONE								
A. Tall Block Hemis:								
'56 DeSoto Firedome, Fireflite	3.72	3.80	330	2.500	2.250	6.62	1.94	1.75
'56 Adventurer	3.78	"	341	"	"	"	"	"
'57 Firedome, Fireflite								
'57 Adventurer	3.80	"	345	"	"	"	"	"
"CHRYSLER" Engines								
A. Low Block Hemis:								
'51-'53 Chrysler V8s* -	3.81	3.63	331	2.500	2.375	6.125	1.81	1.50
'54 Chrysler V8s	"	"	"	"	"	"	"	"
'55 Chrysler exc Windsor -	"	"	"	"	"	"	1.94	1.75
'56 New Yorker, 300B Imp								
'57 Dodge D-500-1 (police engine)	3.9375	"	354	"	"	"	"	"
*'51 to '53 blocks have integral bell housing flange								
B. Low Block Single Rocker Shaft Engines								
'55 Windsor -	3.63	"	301	"	"	"		
'56 Windsor, Saratoga -	3.81	"	331	"	"	"		
'57 Windsor, Saratoga -	3.9375	"	354	"	"	"		
A. Tall Block Hemis:								
'57-'58 New Yorker, 300C, 300D, Imperial -	4.00	3.90	392	2.625	2.375	6.95	2.0	1.75
Donovan 417	4.00 to 4.3125	3.50 to 4.90	351 to 572					
B. Tall Block Single Rocker Shaft Engines: NONE								

CHART NOTES:

High performance, truck, marine, and industrial variations (mainly in valve gear, cam, carburetion) not shown.

In spite of similarity of bore, stroke and other dimensions which may appear on the chart, major components WILL NOT interchange BETWEEN groups except as follows:

Distributors, oil pumps, and bell housing/starter mounting flange plates will interchange (except for '51-'53 Chrysler blocks with integral rear flange) however these flange plates vary in thickness depending on the transmission model.
'51-'55 Chrysler front cover will fit all DeSotos
'56-'58 Chrysler front cover will fit all Dodges
Dodge tall block and DeSoto tall block rods will interchange.
Valve stem diameter (3/8") is the same in all engines, and overall length is quite close, so valves from larger engines can be used as oversizes fit smaller ones.

Certain major components WILL interchange WITHIN groups as follows:

Low block and tall block heads will interchange, and the single rocker shaft (Polysphere) heads may be replaced by hemi heads, but be advised: 392 Chrysler heads are wider than earlier heads so that the earlier intake manifolds may be used; thus must use spacer plates when using early manifolds AND hemi heads on a 392 block. Conversely, only a custom narrow manifold can be fitted when 392 heads are used with an earlier block. '57-58 heads may be best in stock form, but ported, big valve '54-'56 heads are considered superior to later heads because of better port angles. On DeSotos and Dodges the later hemi heads are the same width as earlier heads, so the width of the manifold to be used depends on the year of the block.
Camshafts WILL NOT interchange between low and tall blocks in any group because the angle of the lifter bores differs. '51-'55 Chrysler cams will not fit in a '56 block without special Isky sprocket adapter.
Main journals of tall block crankshafts in each group can be ground down to fit low blocks of the same group, and a stroke increase can be accomplished by grinding the rod journals of the later crank off-center and using earlier rods. (BUT NOTE - Longer than stock Chryslers tend to push the rods through the cylinder walls)

were never turned past 6000 rpm. As Don "Muldoon" Alderson put it, "Low budget racers hold the revs down." Gary Cagle, to run his dragster-beating Windsor-powered modified roadster 180 in the mid-8s (that was in the early '60s), had to turn his mill much faster, so the specs got a little more exotic.

Alderson, former kingpin of Milodon Engineering, a firm founded on specialized Chrysler racing parts, moved on to a higher stratum of racing where everything could be (and was) done to the highest standards possible. But one can still build up a strong street, Bonneville or nostalgia drag engine with less outlay than any other engine, although I don't guarantee it'll live forever.

Here are a couple of examples: Al Teague is breaking international records now with a KB version of the 426 hemi, but he once went nearly 270 mph in a hiboy '29 A on '32 rails with an iron 354 built according to the standards mentioned here. The 6-71 blower was driven 8% over with 28 degrees lead in the mag and a good dose of pop in the methanol. This car still holds the A and AA fuel roadster records at Bonneville and El Mirage.

The Mike Steward-Don Riepe team set the Bonneville E Fuel Roadster record in '78 with a 248 cid unblown Dodge, and it still stands. This little engine had a stock early Dodge crank, stock rods massaged by Childs & Albert, '56 heads ported by Riepe, stock '56 valves, adjustable rockers, 13.4:1 Jahns pistons, an old Isky 550 cam, Cloyes chain, and a '56 Chrysler oil pump. With the exception of the Vertex and Hilborns, the entire engine was built (then) for less than $400. What did it do? Well, on 40% nitro and 40 degrees lead (terrifying combination with that compression, perhaps possible only because of Bonneville's altitude and 1 ounce per gallon of toluene as an anti-detonant) this econo motor wheeled Stewart's barn door '29 hiboy back and forth across the Bonneville "short" course at an average speed of 205 mph. And yes, the Dodge crankshaft was so webbed with cracks it never ran again. But it proves you don't need a 417, or even a 392 to go fast.

In that connection, sometimes it isn't realized that when running a 6-71 or larger blower at the limits of its efficiency there is little if any difference between a 354 and a 392 Chrysler (or even a Donovan 417) horsepower wise, and even a 300 cid Windsor set-up isn't far behind. The point is that the blower can only pass so much air and fuel, and generally speaking a given amount of fuel and air is going to produce only so much power no matter how big or how small an engine it's burned in. An example of this is presented by another famous hot little hemi — in this case the Markley Brothers famous 6-71 blown 259 cid Plymouth with Dodge heads, which for years made their lakesters the fastest open-wheel cars in the world, with speeds over 290 mph. That was faster at the time than any Chrysler, regardless of displacement in a similar chassis.

Here are some qualitative comments concerning the use of various components.

HEADS

All but the 1956 heads have a feature which is both good and bad, depending upon the application, namely that the exhaust valves are seated in the head itself, not on removeable seats. In an unblown engine or highly nitrated unblown engine, the seat must come out for better exhaust valve cooling and to avoid the unpleasant consequences of coming out on its own. But the hole left by its removal required you to use an exhaust valve larger than is desirable. In a Chrysler, it means a 2-1/8" exhaust valve, which is probably too big for a heavily boosted engine. For this reason, and those stated in the Chart Notes, the '56 head is the best to use in any hemi.

Stock head capscrews work fine. Studs are, of course, better and are available from Donovan and others. O-ring grooves are also a must for racing, and some fellows cut a "receiver" groove to match in head or block as the case may be. Isky's O-ring grooving tool works so well that there is hardly an excuse not to use it.

It's hard to advise on head gaskets because everyone seems to use something different. I have been told that the Victor 3125 composite gasket works well in all but the nasty blown Chrysler, which may require solid copper gaskets and double O-ring grooves. The Stewart-Riepe team used FelPro composite gaskets in the fierce unblown Dodge, without O-rings, and they state flatly that it's the only gasket that will do the job.

CAMS AND VALVE GEAR

It's true that the early Chryslers first started to run well with Chet Herbert's famous roller cams (the Herbert #70 roller was the standard for years), but all the major grinders ground cams for hemis. Most of the guys I knew on the west coast in the '60s ran Herbert, Racer Brown, Engle or Iskenderian cams, while Harvey Crane was supplying knowledgeable east coast racers. Now, of course, simply consult your favorite cam source for grind and valve spring recommendations. Today's springs are far superior to what we had in the old days. Rocker arm angles become very acute beyond .590" lift. Donovan makes gear drives, but a lot of fellows just use a Cloyes chain.

Chrysler cams may be available from the grinders' shops, but for a Dodge or DeSoto I'm sure you'll have to supply your own core.

Since Dodge and Chrysler hemis also saw marine, truck and industrial service, adjustable rocker arms were once available for the high-performance versions of these engines. Not so for the DeSoto. Late model MoPar slant-six adjustment screws improve these adjustable arms. Of course, adjustable pushrods are available for all models, and may make for a lighter valve train. Most Chrysler racers use Donovan's investment-cast non-adjustable intake and exhaust rocker arms. These have needle bearings, which require little lubrication other than an oil mist. If stock rockers are used, it's advisable to hard-chrome the rocker shafts to prevent sticking and galling. Hone the bores in the arms to give about .0015" clearance. The pushrod seats must be well lubricated or they will pound out in a hurry.

BLOCKS

Don't get carried away with the boring bar. Hemis need all the wall thickness they can get. In the Dodges and DeSotos, the big-bore version of each category ('55 and '57) is simply an overbore of the original casting, so the bigger the bore the thinner the wall. Even in Chryslers, hold the overbore to .030". A big-bore dry block may work at the drags, but you can't get away with it at Bonneville. Milodon and Wilcap used to make 4-bolt main caps for Chryslers, and Offenhauser still catalogs main cap reinforcements for all sizes of early hemi. Milodon once manufactured a steel main bearing girdle, and the alloy girdle from the Donovan 417 can be made to fit a 392 Chrysler.

RODS

Boxed stock rods used to be the hot set-up, but it was found that they were too stiff and heavy for high rpm and detonation-prone situations. Alloy rods or custom steel rods give very good results at Bonneville and the drags, and in an unblown engine magnafluxed, shot-peened, bushed, and aligned stock rods work well enough. Consult the rod manufacturer when setting deck height, as alloy rods can stretch at high rpm. Big-end side clearance is critical to allow full oil flow past the inserts. In a race hemi, my cohorts would not run less than .050", even 1/8" is not unheard of.

PISTONS

Forged pistons are available from all the major manufacturers. It's no trick to get very high compression in a hemi without flame travel or breathing problems. Suggested ratios: 7.5:1 blown, 9.5:1 street, up to 13.5:1 in unblown racing engines depending upon fuel. The usual blower piston, which needs mass in the piston head, presents too heavy a casting for an unblown engine. I have heard good reports on the Jahns lightweight high-dome piston in unblown engines.

CRANKS

Stock cranks are the weak point of Dodges, some-what less so with DeSotos, but aren't such a problem with Chryslers. Some guys add counterweights to the center throws and/or weld radii at the ends of journals. In fuel engines, hard-chroming seems to work better than Tufftriding. The chrome is nearly indestructible and lets detonation, fuel dilution and dirt do their number on the inserts rather than the crankshaft. Cranks that flunk Magnafluxing may still be OK to run. Experts judge by hitting them with a hammer and listening to the ring. If they get a thunk, it's junk.

BEARINGS

Stock replacement lead-babbitt inserts are fine unless you intend to run on the ragged edge of detonation, in which case they will be pounded out. Then you will want aluminum-backed TRWs or Clevites. Clearances for a competition engine should be .003" on rods and mains.

OILING SYSTEM

The best stock pump for any hemi is the '56 Chrysler because it puts the pickup deeper in the pan and will accept Wilcap and Milodon special pickup assemblies. I understand that the special Howard Barnes second stage pump, which bolts to a 392 pump to convert it to a dry-sump unit, will also fit the '56 pump with some alteration. Milodon offers a plug to reduce the flow of oil to the lifter bores where it's wasted unless hydraulic lifters are being used. It's also advisable to restrict the flow of oil to the rocker arms — say with a pan and a crankshaft baffle. Al Teague and others of the ultra-banzai school finally had to use a dry-sump to hold their bearings, which I admit gets us away from all this economy talk.

MANIFOLDS

As it happens, Chrysler manifolds of whatever type interchange through all the years of manufacture, or can be made to do so easily by using spacers. Single and dual four-barrel manifolds were made by the factory, and ram-log manifolds were once available from Edelbrock and others. Offenhauser still offers dual quad and triplet manifolds for the bigger (315/325) Dodges and multi-carb log manifolds for the Chryslers. With Dodges and DeSotos, one sometimes has to find a manifold meant for the block height of the engine in question, but single and dual four-barrel manifolds were a factory item for both heights. They are now very hard to find. Fuel injector systems are still available for Chrysler and once were made for Dodge and DeSoto, though they were rather small in port diameter by modern standard. It isn't difficult to fabricate manifolds for hemis because of the fact that the manifold assembly is completely separate from the valley cover.

STREET HEMI USER'S GUIDE

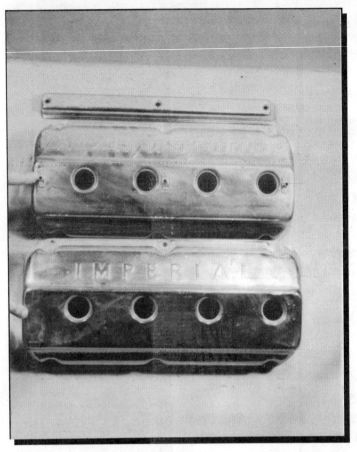

Chromed (chrome is not a stock item) Chrysler Fire Power cover and a 1958 Imperial valve cover. Note that someone has cut off the stanchions that are used to anchor the spark plug tube covers. If you plan to drive an open-motored car, you'll want the covers for foul weather driving. Spark plug tube cover is at top.

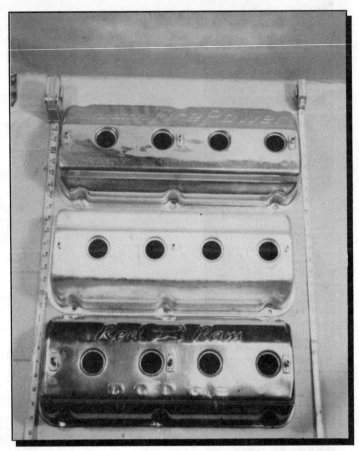

Note the differing lengths in the Chrysler valve cover on the top, DeSoto in the middle and Dodge Red Ram on the bottom. Red Ram covers will have either a decal or an embossed valve cover.

by Skip Readio   photos by Skip Readio & Dennis O'Brien

Early Chrysler hemi engines were built in various displacements between 1951 and 1958. Almost everyone has seen the familiar "Chrysler Fire-Power" rocker arm covers at one time or another. Most of us know what one looks like, but few can tell the difference between the various configurations.

All Chrysler Fire-Power passenger car hemi engines of that era (as opposed to Dodge and DeSoto automotive applications) used the same distinctive valve cover. There are a couple of exceptions, and one is the '58 Imperial. That motor had the word "Imperial" stamped on the cover instead of "Chrysler Fire-Power". Marine and industrial engines may also have distinctive markings depending on their vintage. The 300 series of engines had a special valve cover that had bumps on it to clear the valve train used on those solid-lifter engines. These valve covers are all interchangeable. However, you can't substitute any other covers on the 300 series

motors unless you change the valve gear. The Dodge and DeSoto valve covers are not interchangeable with the larger Chrysler covers or even between Dodge and DeSoto.

The Chrysler hemi was a behemoth. It weighed in at 760 pounds, or thereabout. The DeSoto was a tad smaller and the Dodge was even smaller than that.

Dodge engines were designated "Red Ram" while DeSotos were either Fire Dome or Fire Flite, usually depending upon whether there was a 4-barrel or a 2-barrel carburetor.

Few parts are interchangeable between the three families. Fans, some pulleys, some bolts and nuts, and possibly the oil filter housings are all that will swap around. Many Dodge parts are interchangeable with other Dodge motors and the same goes for the DeSoto line.

The Chrysler Fire-Power motor is the only one of the

three that had an appreciable amount of speed equipment produced for it. This is the motor you will find in many '60s slingshot dragsters, Bonneville race cars, drag boats and the like.

You can spend a lot of money and make a lot of horsepower with a hemi motor. The combustion chamber design, while expensive to produce, provides a very efficient means of getting the air/fuel mixture in and the exhaust out. The hemispherical design of the combustion chamber reduces the tendency to ping when you advance the spark lead. This is a plus with today's poor fuels.

The motor is so big that a 671 GMC blower is dwarfed on top when you compare it to a blown small block Chevy with the same blower arrangement. Speaking of Chevys, the small block Chevy actually required a wider motor mount stance than does a Chrysler hemi. I remember that from our fuel dragster days when the team switched to a small block and had to widen the frame to get it in.

The Chrysler hemi first arrived in 1951, with a displacement of 331 cid. The motor was produced for three years with little change. The carburetor was a water-heated 2-barrel and the block had an integral cast extension on the rear that housed the fluid coupling unit for the fluid drive. Exhaust ports were round in shape and not too big in comparison to later years. Intake ports left a lot to be desired.

With the advent of the automatic transmission in the 1954 model, this block extension was no longer present. The manifolds and heads were redesigned as well. Gone was the water-heated 2-barrel and in its place was a Carter WCFB. Intake and exhaust manifold remained the same. There was a water temperature sender between cylinders 5 and 7 and a heater pipe threaded into the hole between cylinders 6 and 8. Between cylinders 1 and 3, and 2 and 4 there was a common passage that lead to a thermostat housing and radiator hose gooseneck in the front of the manifold. The generator bracket also bolted to the intake manifold.

The water pump was housed in a casting that served as the timing cover as well as the fuel pump mount. To remove this cover, it is necessary to first remove the water pump, as there's one more bolt inside the water pump.

1955 saw a dramatic change in the cooling system design. The bore and stroke remained the same, but water jacketing was altered slightly, causing a slight mis-alignment if you try to use earlier head gaskets. Externally, the changes were more apparent. The thermostat was no longer housed in the intake manifold. This eliminated the significant preheating of the air/ fuel mixture in cylinders 1-4 by eliminating the water passage that previously fed the thermostat/radiator hose gooseneck. Coolant was now routed out through diamond-shaped holes on the front of the head (new this year) and into a cast connector passage that also

Note the long extension in the rear of the block on this 1952 Chrysler. This was used for the three years 1951 - '53. That's a stock dual-point distributor. All hemis came stock with dual points that take the same points and condenser as a later model 340. The cap and rotor are the same as a Mallory YL cap and rotor.

The serial number is right under that homemade "Y" pipe. This "Y" pipe is necessary because of the later model intake manifold being used. This manifold has no thermostat housing.

held the thermostat housing and radiator hose gooseneck. This design was to continue right on through 1958. Using one of these manifolds on a '51 - '54 motor requires that you add a remote thermostat housing to gather the coolant from both heads via the passages between cylinders 1 and 3, and 2 and 4, and send it out to the radiator.

Another significant change to come with these new heads was a wider deck. Pushrod holes in the gasket will be teardrop shaped as opposed to the earlier round hole. While this is of little concern with the 331 motor,

Here's a '54 manifold (with the thermostat) and heads on a '53 block.

The large timing cover is a '51 - '54 cast job with the water pump housing in the cover. The smaller cover is typical of the '55 - '58 stamped steel timing covers. The fuel pump bolts to the timing cover.

Notice the small round exhaust ports from a '51 - '53 motor, and the large oval ports of the '54 - '58 motor. The head on the left has the typical water outlet that is common to '55 - '58 motors with the thermostat above the water pump instead of in the intake.

it becomes significantly more important with the following year's design.

In 1956, the bore was increased from the previous diameter of 3-13/16" out to 3-15/16". This produced the 354 cid motor. The gasket significance lies in the fact that when you bore any of the older motors to their limit of .125" (Note: Mark Dees comments on bore maximums. - ed.), the sealing lip of the head gasket falls into the cylinder instead of being compressed by the head/block contact. The head will still contact it on the top, but the cylinder is missing 1/16" of stock that would normally squeeze the gasket. A good seal in this case is nearly impossible. The way to get around this is to obtain Fitzgerald 0559-SR head gaskets. Another way around it is to use '56 head gaskets. They have the correct bore size but the dowel pin on a '56 is smaller. You'll have to open up the dowel pin hole a few thousandths of an inch. The water passages will align closed enough to not cause serious problems.

A third solution is to contact Tom Hannaford at Antique Auto Parts Cellar, P.O. Box 3, South Weymouth, MA 02190, (617) 335-1579. Tom has an asbestos substitute developed by Armstrong for high heat/high flange pressure applications. That's just the ticket for head gaskets. Put a bunch of mold-release on the gasket (copper coat or Teflon works, too) and torque the head down. Let it sit overnight and re-torque it the next day. Fire up the motor and re-torque it again. The stuff is great, but if you don't put plenty of mold-release on first, you'll never get the head back off afterwards. I had to remove the rocker shaft assembly on the way to Oklahoma City a few years ago to change a rocker arm. I took it off again to fix it after arriving in Oklahoma City, then again in Driggs, Idaho to do it right (I'll explain why later on). The 10 bolts that secure the rocker arm assembly also serve as the head bolts. The head gasket never blew, and I've got 12.5:1 compression pistons in that motor. Tom can duplicate any head gasket, new or used, that you send him. If there is a sufficient demand, he will have a die made and stock these gaskets. He currently stocks the overbore gaskets for '51 to '54 Chryslers. They're designed for a maximum overbore and they DO work.

The camshaft, timing gears and chain from a '56 will fit any earlier block, but you have to use everything. The earlier cams have a snout on them that's not on a '56. Most aftermarket cams that are available for these motors will be for the '56 block. If you want to use an earlier cam gear, you'll have to machine a spacer for the front of the cam to hold the gear and the fuel pump eccentric in place. The spacer routine will work. I've had that arrangement in my '34 since the winter of '64-'65 when I built the motor. It was cheaper for me to make a spacer than to buy another new timing gear.

I have a roller cam in my motor (one of Crower's Imperial cams with roller journals and roller tappets) and it doesn't need as much oil to the lifters as the stock hydraulic cam would. What you do in this case is drill and tap the oil passages in the lifter bores and put a 10x32 Allen screw with a .050" hole in it as needed, especially if you're running serious valve spring pressures.

I've got triple springs on my motor and one of the problems I've run into is galled rocker arms. The slightest drop in oil volume will result in galling if you've got substantial valve spring pressure. Revving up a hemi motor when it's cold will do the same thing. Keep the revs down until you've got plenty of oil up in the rocker shafts.

The oil to the rocker shafts is metered through a set of holes drilled in the camshaft. Oil will flow to the rockers only when the holes are aligned. As soon as the cam rotates beyond this hole alignment, the oil is shut off until they realign. Oil feeds are on the 2nd and 4th cam bearings and feed the rockers through passages that continue up through the head and into the rocker arm assembly via the rocker arm stanchions. Sloppy cam bearings will reduce the amount of oil getting to the top, as will low oil pressure from the pump sucking air bubbles due to low lubricant level in the pan. Gall the rockers and you'll have to disturb the head gasket seal when you remove the rockers for repair.

Iskenderian used to have an exchange program that allowed people to send in their old shafts as cores, and they'd send back a set that had been machined and hard-chromed. They don't do that anymore, so you'll have to find a machine shop that'll do it for you. It ran me upwards of $450 last time I had it done (1986). I'd just done a valve job and had replaced all the valve springs as well. When I flipped the rocker assembly over to install it on the head, enough of the oil ran out of the intake shaft that when I fired the motor up again, the intake rockers on the right side galled. Of course this didn't show up until we'd driven for six hours and were in East Nowhere, Pennsylvania on the way to Oklahoma City. When you gall a rocker, it puts tremendous strain on the pushrod, and the pushrod wears itself into a point extending into the rocker arm lubrication hole. The rocker arm and shaft are swollen from all the extra heat, and this doesn't help get the oil out to the pushrod either. A new end on the adjustable pushrod (I don't have adjustable rockers like those that are found on the marine and industrial engines or on the Chrysler 300 solid-lifter cammed engines) will usually get you a few hundred more miles. I ate up half a dozen pushrod ends getting to Oklahoma City. I didn't have any place to fix the motor in the motel parking lot, so I cleaned up the rocker shafts as well as possible and replaced three of the four rockers with ones that I'd had air mailed from home. That patch got us to Driggs, Idaho where I completely disassembled the rocker shaft and polished the shafts with emery paper so that they wouldn't gall the replacement rockers.

When you put a set of these rocker arms on your

Notice that neither of these motors have provisions for getting water out of the front of the heads. It must come out between the intake ports, and requires modification to the intake manifolds as seen on the left motor.

The head on the left is a '57 head, while the one on the right is a '55 head. Notice that the bottom edge of the intake manifold face is nearly even with the bottom of the head on the left, but quite a ways above the block surface on the right head.

Another feature is the slightly lower placement of the water outlet. These heads are the same on either end, so they can be swapped from side to side. There is no right or left head.

Dodge intake rocker arms need to have a bevel on them to clear the spark plug tube because the motor is so short.

This intake rocker arm has a fair amount of galling inside. It made the 2500+ mile trip back home, but I don't think I would trust it for much longer, especially now that I've got newly chromed rocker shafts on the motor.

motor, invert them and fill both shafts with oil through the common feed hole next to the head bolt on the first stanchion in from the right. When the shafts are full of oil, poke in a plug of chassis grease. This will hold the oil in the shafts until you can get them torqued against the heads. When you're putting this assembly together, you have to lay it on top of the already-installed pushrods. This causes the assembly to sit above the head a bit, instead of right on it. Without some grease holding the oil in the intake shaft (that one is directly in line with the feed hole), the intake shaft will drain before you can get the shaft assembly torqued down. I ruined a good set of Isky shafts trying to cut corners. It was cold, the oil was thick and I thought I could re-torque the head fast enough. Don't take chances. Fill the shafts and grease the feed holes.

If you're scouring the flea markets for rocker arm assemblies, be careful of what you're buying. There are three distinct sizes of rocker arm assemblies out there

for Dodge, DeSoto and Chrysler. Your prime interest in flea market rocker arms will be getting usable arms and shafts. The majority of the arms you'll find will be junk. Unless you have the attachment for your valve grinding machine that can reface the valve stem contact surface, you won't be able to use the rockers. If the motor was run with low oil pressure or had any other problems that would either starve the rocker tip and/or cause a lifter to collapse, the result will be a pounding away of the tip of the rocker arm. This indention will have to be ground off so that it doesn't grab the new valve stem and pull the valve sideways as it opens.

The other problem you'll see will be rockers that are rusted to the shafts. Getting rusted rockers off is a tedious job and usually doesn't yield usable rockers in the end anyway. Soak them forever in penetrating oil or you'll ruin the bores or, worse yet, break them trying to get them off.

The Dodge motor, being the smallest of the three, needs to have a special chamber cut on the pushrod end of the intake rocker arm so that the arm will clear the spark plug tube. The overall length of the Dodge intake rocker is 3-3/8".

Both the DeSoto and Chrysler use an intake rocker with a length of 3-1/4". The Chrysler, however, will have a casting number of 353 on the valve stem arm of the rocker. Exhaust rockers for all three motors are easier to identify. The Dodge is 3-7/8" long, the DeSoto is 4-3/16" long and the Chrysler is 4-5/8" long.

The rocker arm shaft lengths are also different for all three motors. The Dodge is 17-3/16" long, the DeSoto is 18-15/16" long and the Chrysler is 19-5/16" long.

The Chrysler motor has the head bolts on the same side of the intake and exhaust rocker shafts while the Dodge and DeSoto motors have the rocker arm shafts between the two rows of head bolts.

Rocker arm assemblies for the solid-lifter 300 engines (some marine and industrial applications as well) are quite sought after as they eliminate the need for hard-to-adjust adjustable pushrods. These can be recognized by their adjustment ball and locknut on the pushrod end. A solid-lifter-equipped motor will also have 4 clearance bumps between the spark plug holes in the rocker arm covers so that the exhaust rocker arm adjustment stud doesn't hit the valve cover. If you want to run adjustable rockers, you will need a set of these covers or a set of aftermarket aluminum covers in order to get the clearance.

Punch out the 5/8" Welch plugs in the ends of the rocker shafts and clean out the insides. You may find the little rubber plugs that Chrysler used to keep the oil from draining out during assembly. These plugs fit loosely in the oil inlet and are blown into the rocker shafts when the oil pressure comes up for the first time.

Most of what I've covered up to now has pertained to the short-stroke Chrysler hemis. In 1957, the bore and stroke were increased to 4.00" x 3.90" resulting in a displacement of 392 cubic inches. The deck height caused the heads to be spaced wider apart than the earlier motors. To compensate for this, Chrysler added stock to the intake side of the cylinder head so that the manifold surface ended up in the same relative position as the earlier motors. This kept the manifold bolt patterns the same as in previous years.

If the thermostat isn't a primary concern, a 392 manifold can be used on a 331-cid motor from 1951. As mentioned earlier, all you need to to is fabricate a remote thermostat and coolant junction housing.

The '57 motor had a 9.25:1 compression ratio, and the '58 motor saw the ratio raised to 10.0:1. 1957 and '58 heads can be recognized by their longer intake manifold extension. If you lay an older head flat, the bottom edge of the intake manifold flange is 11/16" above the block surface plane. The 392 heads are nearly even with the block plane. If you have the heads off the motor and on a flat surface, the difference becomes quite apparent (see the accompanying photos). All Chrysler heads will have a head gasket length of 19-3/16". If your heads or block are appreciably shorter than that, you've got a Dodge of DeSoto block or heads.

Many internal parts for the 392 motors are still being stocked by both speed equipment manufacturers and aftermarket suppliers like TRW, Sealed-Power, etc. The earlier 331 and 354 motors aren't as well covered and, in most cases, parts haven't been carried on the books for twenty years or more. Such things as early valves and guides certainly have to be made, unless you can find someone with a set still on the shelf. The big factory warehouses have scrapped everything they had.

Pistons are pretty easy to find for 392 applications, as are valves and guides. Cams are getting a bit scarce, but the major cam grinders will still grind you one if your particular grind isn't available.

Dodge and DeSoto motors were impossible to find speed parts for in the '60s. They're even worse to find speed parts for today. Almost everything for one will have to be made or modified from something else. There are no aftermarket off-the-shelf parts available other than rings and bearings, and rings won't fix a motor that really needs to be bored and fitted with a new set of pistons.

The serial number for all Chrysler hemis will tell you what year motor you are dealing with. The serial number can be found on a pad on the block right in front of the stamped steel cover under the intake manifold. From 1951 to 1956, the Chrysler passenger car serial numbers started with the letter "C". The second and third digits denote the year of manufacture. In 1957, Chrysler went to a different serial number scheme wherein the beginning letter referenced the particular application for which the motor was destined. The second letter, "E", simply means "engine". The following two digits will represent the year of

Rocker Arm Oil Feed

The three rocker arm assemblies pictured here are Chrysler (the longest), DeSoto, and Dodge (the shortest). Note the placement of the ten headbolt holes, outside the shafts on the Dodge and DeSoto and on the same side of each shaft on the Chrysler assembly. Although they don't show in this photo, the second stanchion from the right in each one of these assemblies is different from the other two "center" stanchions in that it has an oil feed passage adjacent to the head bolt on the intake shaft. If you disassemble an assembly, make sure it goes back in the same spot. The light-colored spots on the left ends of the shaft assemblies are the dowel pins that hold the shafts onto the left stanchion. The right end is held in place with cotter pins.

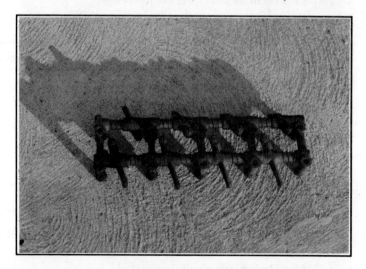

Note the beefier construction of the rocker arms and the adjustment ball and locknut on the 300 rocker arm assembly.

manufacture. WE is a Windsor engine, and should not show up as a hemi, as Windsors came with 354 polyspherical combustion chambered engines that year. LE is Saratoga, NE is New Yorker and 300, and CE is Imperial.

Industrial/marine engines will have an "I" or "IND" prefix and truck engines will have a "T" prefix. You may also find an "M" for marine.

Hopefully, this information and these photos will help you spot the right hemi. Don't pay a lot of money for one if you don't know what's been done to it. You may wind up doubling the price of the motor by fixing someone's negligence. Be careful of what you're buying and you may end up with a motor that'll last 20 years or more. Mine has.

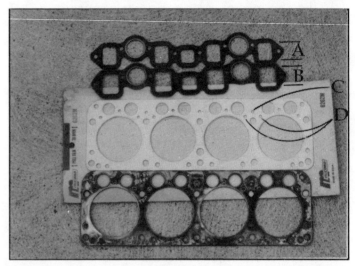

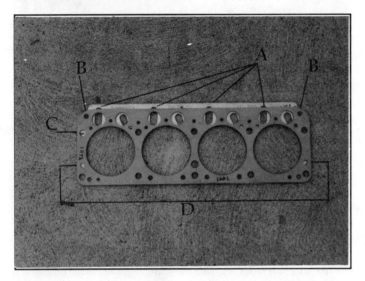

The top gasket is an overbore gasket for the '51 - '54 motor. The gasket below it has the same bore size but fits the '56 block. Notice how the lower gasket extends beyond the edge of the top gasket. Oil can escape at point "A". Silastic can cure leaks here in a pinch. The dowel pin holes ("B") in the bottom gasket are smaller. Hole "C" is only punched into one end of the '56 gasket because it has a top and bottom side due to gasket manufacturer's design preference. Holes "D" are misaligned and are barely visible in the lower left and lower right.

Dimension "A" is noticeably smaller than dimension "B". The former is a '51 - '53 intake manifold gasket, while the latter is a '54 - '58 intake manifold gasket. The light-colored head gasket is a stock bore (3-13/16") head gasket for a '51 - '53 motor. The lower, darker (used) gasket is an overbore Fitzgerald gasket for the same motor. Hole "C" is the rocker arm oil feed hole. There is a similar hole in the opposite end of the gasket. This gasket can be put on either side up. Holes "D" are the coolant passage holes. The fourth hole in the group is the cylinder headbolt hole. The close proximity of these four holes, along with the two adjacent cylinder holes, causes problems when a steel/asbestos/steel gasket is used because the gasket won't squash properly with all the beads around the holes. Invariably, one of the coolant holes ("D") will sprout a leak as soon as coolant is put into the block. Fresh, soft aviation gasket cement is the only cure for this problem.

COARSE ROCKER ARM ASSEMBLY DIMENSIONS

	Chrysler	DeSoto	Dodge
Height of rocker stanchion on exhaust side, less hollow dowell	2 13/16"	2 1/2"2	11/16"
Height of rocker stanchion on intake	2 1/16 "	2 3/16"	2 1/4"
Center to center head bolt spacing end to end	18 1/4"	17 3/8"	16 3/4"
Center to center head bolt spacing between intake row and exhaust row.	3 1/2"	3 7/16"	4 5/16"
Rocker arm shaft diameter	7/8"	7/8"	7/8"
Intake rocker length	3 1/4"	3 1/4"	3 3/8"
Exhaust rocker length	4 5/8"	4 3/16"	3 7/8"
Rocker arm shaft	19 5/16"	18 5/16"	17 3/16"

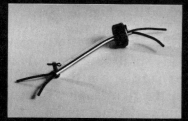
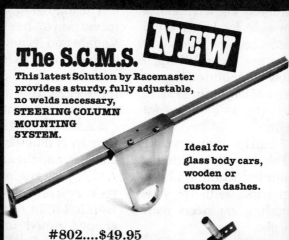

SLANT SIX HOP-UP

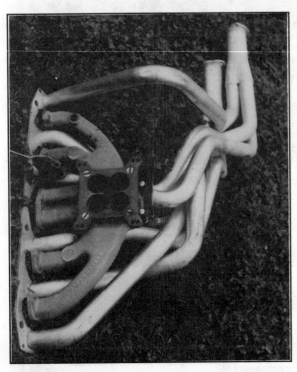

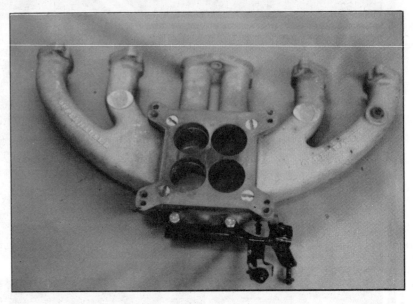

The Offenhauser four-barrel manifold is the only aftermarket design known and is very similar to Chrysler's. Clifford Research has carried them, and they've been in the MoPar Performance catalog in recent years.

Rare, but possibly more plentiful than the genuine MoPar slant six Hyper-Pack, is an aftermarket set-up like this one of Norm Kyhn.

by John Lee

As heavily as Chrysler Corporation was into performance and racing in the late 1950s and early 1960s, it was no surprise that interest carried over to the new generation of six-cylinder engines introduced for 1960. It was the first overhead valve six and the first new six for Chrysler since 1929, replacing the reliable, but outdated, flathead six.

The slant six, as it was immediately known because of being laid over to the right side for lower hood clearance, has lasted 30 years and become legendary for its durability. In 170 cu. in. form rated at 101 hp, it was the powerplant for the new Plymouth compact Valiant in 1960 and Dodge's spin-off Lancer in 1961. In the large 225 cu. in. size, it was the base engine for Plymouth and Dodge full-size lines.

Chrysler wouldn't drop a V-8 into its compacts until 1964, a year behind Ford's Falcon. But with the development going on with ram induction, multiple carburetion and other hop-up tricks with the new wedge V8s, Chrysler's hot rodding engineers were bound to try tweaking the new six.

In fact, at the Daytona Speed Weeks in 1960, a modified Valiant was a runaway winner of the compact race on the sports car course and turned a top speed of 128 mph on the 2-1/2 mile banked oval! A Chrysler engineer disclosed that the 170-cube six was turning out about 195 horses, compared with the stock 101 hp. A less potent version of this set-up was offered to Valiant owners in 1960 at a fairly stiff $400 price. The Hyper-Pack, as it was known, included a four-barrel carb and manifold, high-performance cam, 10.5:1 compression pistons and exhaust headers. It was rated at 148 hp.

The following year, Chrysler offered the larger, 225-in. version of the slant six, at 145 hp, as an option for the Valiant and its new stable mate, Lancer. For both drag strip racing, (where the MoPars dominated their stock classes), and for the street, the Hyper-Pack was available for the 225. This boosted the rated horsepower to 195, although some estimated it as high as 275!

Each new engine Detroit introduced brought aftermarket manufacturers into the picture with hop-up goodies, and the already hot slant six was no exception. As Chrysler engineers had discovered, laying the valve rockers over against the right engine compartment wall left a lot of room on the left for long, rainbow-shaped tuned intake manifold runners and large, tubular headers. Companies like Offenhauser were soon on the market with their own versions of four-barrel and multi-carb manifolds, cams and headers.

If you have a Hyper-Pack or any of the aftermarket goodies for your angled inline, consider yourself fortun-

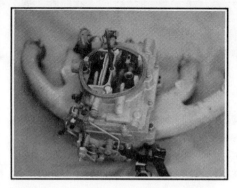

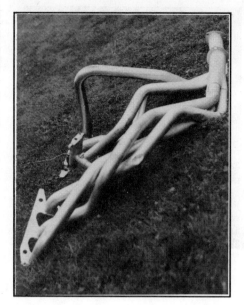

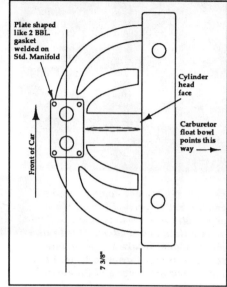

Four-barrel carb recommended for the slant six is the Carter AFB as used in 273 V8 Formula S applications.

Right- Tubular headers are aftermarket and, although these are unmarked, Norm Kyhn said they are identical to a set he had with Hedman's I.D. stamped on them. The design is similar to the Hyper-Pack headers.

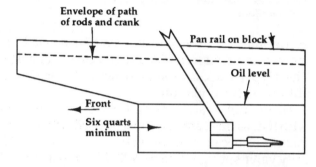

ate. If you're looking, here are some things to keep in mind.

Kuhl Enterprises, a developmental engineering firm in Mt. Clemens, Michigan, in the early 1960s may have worked closely with the Ramchargers engineers at Chrysler. They offered the Hyper "6" Performance System of optional equipment and parts, along with a bulletin discussing recommended use and combinations, under a banner reading: "ATTENTION: Draggers — The new NHRA E/MP class is a snap for Slant 6 wins!" We obtained a copy of this rare piece from MoPar enthusiasts Norm Kyhn and Jerry Grubb of Longmont, Colorado. Herewith some of Kuhl's slant six tips for street and drag engines.

Carburetion: Any 170 cu. in. six having a standard BBS carburetor (1-1/4" dia. venturi) will realize about 5% more power with the 225 cu. in. BBS carburetor (1-11/32" dia. venturi). These two carburetors can be identified by measuring their throttle bore diameter. The larger carburetor has a 1-11/16" dia. throttle bore. All 170 engines with manual transmission, and the 1960 and 1961 170s with automatic, have the smaller carburetor.

A two-barrel set-up as used on the 225 in. marine engine is available from MoPar as follows: carburetor part no. 2463849; manifold, E8467 M; and air cleaner, 2465310.

The two-barrel from an 318 V8 engine (without CAP package) can be used as shown in Fig. 1. The larger two-barrel from a 361 or 383 can be installed in the same manner. However, low speed driveability in cold weather may be unsatisfactory on the street.

The AFB from the 273 power pack, Carter model 3854-S, gives proper fuel mixture and distribution characteristics for the six-cylinder engine using a Hyper-Pack intake manifold or a modified standard intake manifold. The four-barrel bores must be centered

upon the standard six cylinder inlet manifold's plenum chamber. The following modifications are required:
• Replace the metering rods with No. 16-177 rods (.067 .065.055" dia.)
• Replace the throttle side secondary jets with No. 120-181 jets (.049" dia.).
• Replace the choke side secondary jets with No. 120-226 jets (.065" dia.).
• Replace the primary venturi clusters with cluster No. 48-464S.
• Fabricate a throttle linkage to match the installation.

Compression Ratio: Up to .090" can be removed from the slant six cylinder head, which has an especially thick lower deck surface. Removal of .090" will raise the compression ratio of a 225 engine from 8:1 up to 9.5:1 and of a 170 engine from 8:1 up to 10:1.
It is advisable to use the stainless steel head gasket from the 225 marine engine after milling the head. Also, the valve-to-piston clearance should be checked if the milled head is used in conjunction with a high lift camshaft.

Spark Advance: For street use, the total spark advance at engine speeds over 3000 rpm should be 30-32 degrees (check with the vacuum advance disconnected).

Valve Gear: Marine engine camshaft #E7885M is the best all around street cam. It has 244 degrees duration with .405" lift and 26 degrees overlap. The standard six cam has 232 degrees duration with only eight degrees overlap.

Hyper-Pack cam #2205620 (276 degrees duration) is

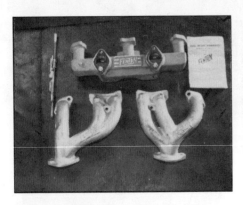

The first step toward hopping up the plentiful, but sluggish, Plymouth and Dodge flathead sixes was adding a dual-carb manifold and headers. This Fenton aluminum dual intake accommodates two single-throat Carter carbs that were factory issue on Dodge and Plymouth sixes. The Fenton cast iron headers scavenge exhaust more efficiently than a split manifold.

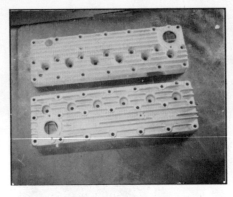

Edmunds and Fenton were two high compression heads made for Plymouth and Dodge sixes. Both are aluminum. The Fenton 8.5:1 appears to be a better finished product.

Flathead six hop-up goodies include (from left) Fenton 8.5:1 head, dual intake manifold and headers and Edmunds high-comp head.

borderline for driveability even when used with a manual transmission and a high numerical axle ratio. The Hyper-Pack cam should never be used with an automatic transmission.

Heavy duty valve spring #1944554 should be used with the marine cam and must be used with the Hyper-Pack cam because of the valve lift involved. Heavy duty valve spring retainers #2202546 must be used any time engine speeds over 5000 rpm are attempted. Both cam E7885M and cam 2205620 use standard tappets.

Exhaust System: The best street exhaust manifold combination includes the front three cylinders from the standard manifold combined with the rear Hyper-Pack header manifold. This allows the front three cylinders to provide carburetor heat, which is necessary below 50 degrees ambient air temperature. The back three cylinders exhaust through the Hyper-Pack header #2129900 and the Hyper-Pack exhaust pipe and muffler #2208350 can easily be modified to fit this combination. The Hyper-Pack pipe and muffler assembly #2208350 fits the Valiant and Lancer through and including the 1961 model. This is a 2-1/2" diameter exhaust pipe and a "B" engine size muffler and offers several percent gain in output over the standard system. On the '62 and later 170 slant six, the rear pipe must be modified for clearance to back geared starter. The assembly will clear the starter on all 225s.

DRAG RACING MODIFICATIONS

The basic Hyper-Pack can be improved upon for modified drag racing as follows:

Carburetion: Three Weber dual carburetors 48 IDA will improve engine output nicely compared to the Hyper-Pack intake manifold and carburetor. Obviously, a hand-fabricated manifold would be required, with one Weber bore per cylinder.

Compression Ratio: Compression ratios of 12:1 to 13:1 should perform satisfactorily on the drag strip. "West Coast" pistons would be required to attain ratios this high.

Step-seat "Dykes" top piston rings should also be used because they lower engine friction at high speeds. "Slug" pistons should be fitted at .008" to .010" clearance.

Valve Gear: It appears that either the Racer Brown ST12 or the Iskenderian 1012B should perform well in fully modified engines. Obviously, push rods, retainers and springs made to work with these cams should be used. These cams have produced power very well in the Chrysler wedge head V8s.

Exhaust System: Cylinders 1, 2 and 3 should exhaust through 1-5/8" or 1-3/4" o.d. pipes about 40 inches long into a cloverleaf collector and then through a 2-1/2" o.d. outlet pipe much like factory sponsored super stock practice. Cylinders 4, 5 and 6 should have a duplicate system.

Big Valves: The standard six-cylinder valves are 1.62" dia. intake and 1.36" dia. exhaust. The 1-3/4" dia. exhaust valve, #163744, from the 1957-58 Chrysler 392 hemi V8 can be made into a .130" oversize intake valve. However, it is necessary to reduce its length by .270" and cut three new lock grooves down the stem. No bore notch is required for clearance.

The 1957 Dodge V8 exhaust valve #1827958 makes a very convenient oversize valve for the slant six. The head diameter is 1-1/2", or .140" oversize, and the length is satisfactory. It is necessary to provide a clearance notch at the top of the bore.

Engine Oiling: The high-speed, fully modified engines must be provided with more oil flow through main bearings to the rod bearings. One way to achieve this is to groove the crankshaft (which, unfortunately, can result in crank breakage). A better way is to use upper main bearing shells in the main caps. It will be necessary to file down the locating tabs to allow the grooves to align. These tabs merely locate the bearings. They do not prevent rotation; the inserts are "crushed" by the cap to prevent rotation.

The oil sump should be greatly enlarged so that the oil level is at least six inches below the crankshaft's path. At least six quarts capacity is necessary (see Fig. 2).

<u>Durability:</u> The truck 225 crankshaft, which is shot peened and not cold straightened, should be used for fully modified 225 slant sixes.

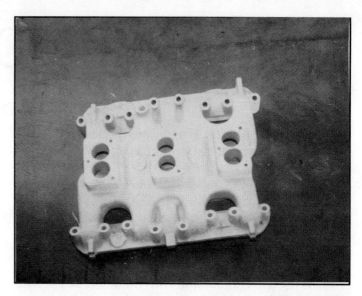

Offenhauser aluminum triple two-barrel manifold is for a '56-'57 Dodge 315 or 325 hemi or poly V8.

MoPar Hyper-Pack Components

Part No.	Item
2205620	Camshaft assembly
1944554	Valve spring and damper assembly
2129619	Valve pushrod assembly
2129898	Intake manifold
2129900	Exhaust manifold - front
2129881	Carburetor assembly
2121952	Carburetor flange gasket
2129992	Air cleaner assembly
1821170	Air cleaner gasket
2201223	Clutch cover & pressure plate assembly
2201219	Clutch driving disc assembly
1636570	Exhaust pipe flange gasket
2298350	Muffler and exhaust pipe assembly

Aluminum dual-quad cross-ram manifold topped the 426 race hemi in '64 Dodges and Plymouths. The '65 model was cast from magnesium for lighter weight.

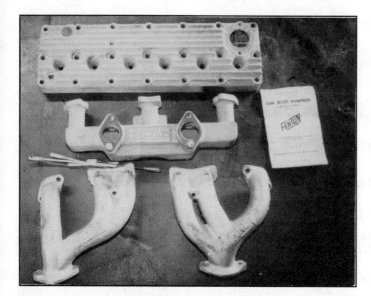

A complete Fenton hop-up kit: 8.5:1 head, dual intake and exhaust headers, along with an instruction manual. Norm Kyhn has it planned for his '47 Plymouth convertible project.

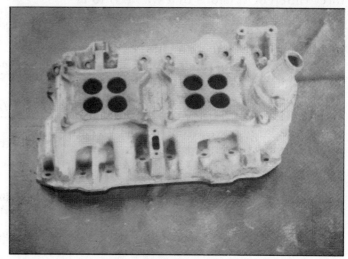

Manifold for early MoPar 318s used dual Carter AFB four-barrels.

TRANSMISSION OVERVIEW

MANUAL TRANSMISSIONS

Chrysler Corporation's modern 3-speed and 4-speed manual transmissions are strong and reliable, and they are excellent for use in street rods.

The 3-speed that was in use in 1964 was model 745, which was replaced by model A-903 until models A-230 and A-250 were introduced. Model A-903 was employed through 1972 in applications with 6-cylinder engines. In 1973, model A-250 superceded the A-903 and is used only with the 198 and 225 engines. Model A-230 is used in conjunction with the small V8 engines (318, 340, 360), and is also used with some 6-cylinder applications.

Gear ratios for these 3-speed units are as follows:			
Transmission	1st	2nd	3rd
A-903	2.95	1.83	1.00
	3.22	1.84	1.00
A-250	3.18	1.83	1.00
A-230	2.55	1.49	1.00
	3.08	1.70	1.00

In 1964, Chrysler Corporation introduced their basic 4-speed manual transmission, which is designated by model number A-833. Since that time, this transmission has been through several different versions, updates and modifications. There are two different overall lengths (the A/F-body is short, and the B/E-body is long), there are four different production ratios (as well as several different special ratios), and there are both fine- and coarse-pitch gears.

As far as interchangeability goes, there are three different versions that we need to be concerned with; there is a small spline (23-tooth), large spline (18-tooth), and overdrive. In addition to that, there are three different drive pinion bearing retainer pilot sizes. As an example, in 1970 and '71 the 340 V8 engine had a small spline and small pilot; the 440 and 426 Hemi for those years had the large spline and large pilot; while the 383 V8 had a small spline and large pilot.

The large pilot bearing wasn't introduced until 1968. Transmissions from 1964 to '67 were equipped with small pilots, and the 4-speed overdrive model came out in 1975 with a small spline but a large pilot retainer with an outside diameter of 5.125".

Model A-833 transmissions have been made with two different types of shifting mechanisms and side covers. A double-lever interlock side cover assembly came out in 1970 for the 340-6-bbl Trans-Am Barracuda and Challenger. Prior to that, a ball-and-detente unit was employed on all 4-speeds since 1964.

A different transmission mounting pad position was used on the 4-speed for the '70-'74 E-body (Barracuda and Challenger) and on the '71-'74 Coronet, Charger, Satellite and Road Runner. The newer mounting position is farther forward and lower than on the older model transmissions.

Changes to the A-833 since its introduction include the synchronizers. The synchronizer in the '71-'72 model years performs best and can be installed in the earlier transmissions, reducing shift effort and eliminating gear clash. The part number for the 1-2 synchronizer assembly is 3515470, and the number for the 3-4 unit is 3515469. For ordering the springs, the part number is 3515468, and the rings are 3515023. The snap rings have a number of 6024131.

Gear ratios for the A-833 transmissions with fine-pitch gears are as follows:				
Model	1st	2nd	3rd	4th
Small spline ('70 & earlier)	2.66	1.91	1.39	1.00
Small spline ('70 Trans-Am and '71-'74)	2.47	1.77	1.34	1.00
'65 6-cylinder & '74-'75 318	3.09	1.92	1.40	1.00
'75-'80 O/D	3.09	1.67	1.00	0.73

Gear ratios for the A-833 transmissions with coarse-pitch gears are as follows:				
Model	1st	2nd	3rd	4th
Large spline ('70 & earlier)	2.65	1.93	1.39	1.00
Large spline ('71-'74)	2.44	1.77	1.34	1.00
Race Red Stripe	2.65	1.64	1.19	1.00

AUTOMATIC TRANSMISSIONS

The modern Chrysler Corporation 3-speed automatic transmission is called the Torqueflite, but there are several different versions of the same basic transmission. Model A-727 is the longest and heaviest of the group, and is the only automatic that was ever intended for use with the 426 Hemi. Models A-904, A-998, and A-999 are shorter versions that were designed for use with the 6-cylinder and smaller V8s.

Model A-904 came along in 1960 and was used with the slant six engine. A-727 was introduced in 1962. Changes have taken place over the years. The '62-'64 units had a flanged output shaft, while the '65-'82 models feature a slip spline output shaft. The earlier transmission had a two-cable shift mechanism (one for the pushbutton gear selector).

Three different levels exist for the A-727 transmission torque capacity — standard, heavy duty, and extra heavy duty. Heavy duty was available for the 340, 383 4-bbl, 400 4-bbl HP, and the 440 4-bbl HP. The extra heavy duty unit was available only with the 426 Hemi or the 440 6-bbl engines. Difference between these versions of the 727 transmission is in the automatic upshift speed and shift harshness — all of which can be adjusted for any transmission anyway.

There are three different transmission cases for the 727, permitting it to be mated with either the 6-cylinder, the A engines (273, 318, 340, 360), or the B-RB engines (383, 400, 440, and 426 Hemi).

Features of model A-904 are identical to the 727, but it is a smaller and lighter transmission. This model also comes with three different capacity levels that are designated A-904, A-998, and A-999. Model A-904 is the Torqueflite designed for use with the 6-cylinder, the 273 and the 318 engines. Model A-998 was specifically intended for use with the 318. In 1974, model A-999 was introduced for the 360.

TRANSMISSION DIMENSIONS

When planning the installation of drivetrain components, it is real handy to have the dimensions of the transmission at your fingertips so you can calculate exactly where the crossmember needs to go, and how long the driveshaft is going to be. Stuff like that. So, here is just about everything you are going to need to know to get you successfully through this aspect of the installation planning.

MANUAL TRANSMISSION LENGTHS

Trans	Body/Engine	A	B	C	D	E	Yoke
A250	A-body 6-cyl	7.38	19.75	22.66	30.58	33.77	1.08 p.d.
A230	A & F body	7.38	19.83	22.66	30.58	33.77	1.08 p.d.
A230	B & E body	7.38	19.83	22.66	34.39	37.89	1.25 p.d.
						38.13	1.25 p.d.
A833	A & F body	7.38	19.75	22.66	30.58	34.08	1.25 p.d.
A833	B & E body	7.38	19.75	22.66	34.39	38.13	1.25 p.d.
						37.89	

AUTOMATIC TRANSMISSION LENGTHS

Trans	A	B	C	D	Yoke
A-727	20.41	22.66	34.39	38.13	1.25 p.d.
A-904	20.41	22.66	30.58	34.12	1.08 p.d.
A-998	20.41	22.66	30.58	34.12	1.08 p.d.
A-999	20.41	22.66	30.58	34.12	1.08 p.d.

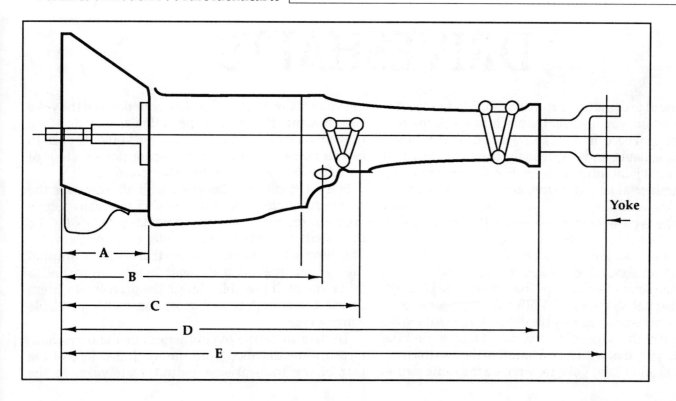

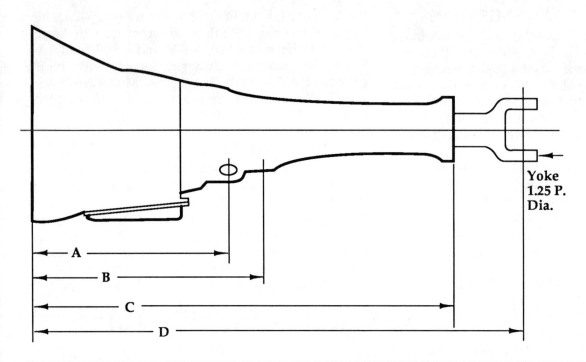

Yoke
1.25 P.
Dia.

A

B

C

D

LATE MOPAR REAR-WHEEL-DRIVE TERMINOLOGY	
TRANSMISSION TYPE	
A-833	Chrysler 4-speed manual, 1964 to 1974
A-727	Chrysler 3-speed Torqueflite, mated with 340, 360, 383, 400, 440 and 426 Hemi engines from 1962 to 1974
A-904	Chrysler 3-speed Torqueflite, mated with 6-cylinder engines and the 273, 318 V8s
A-745, A-250	Chrysler 3-speed manual transmissions

DRIVESHAFTS

You need to come up with a driveshaft to fit your hot rod, but before you head for the machine shop, do some measuring. There is a huge selection of driveshaft lengths available, and surprisingly, there is a great deal of universal joint interchangeability. For example, the Volvo universal joint is a standard Chevrolet item.

You know the type of rearend you have, and you know the type of transmission. At the transmission output shaft and at the pinion, there are yokes that secure the U-joints in place. The critical bits of information about these yokes are the measurements across the semi-circular cups that receive the U-joints. They area not all the same. With a steel tape or a set of calipers, measure carefully the distance across the yoke cup right at the edge of the machined face, to find the size of U-joint that will fit. Be aware that the transmission output shaft U-joint yoke may not be the same size as

the yoke at the pinion. The ideal situation is if the yoke cups measure the same at the pinion as they do at the transmission output shaft. This way, you only need to carry one extra U-joint in the spare-parts section of your tool box, and it can fit either position.

Some U-joints are designed with all four cups the same size, while others have two different sizes of cups on the same unit. You may have larger cups for the driveshaft attachment and smaller ones for the yoke. The thing to keep in mind here is that the more unusual the U-joint, the more difficult it may be to find a replacement. If possible, design the driveshaft system to use the strongest and most commonly available components.

To determine the overall length of the driveshaft, measure the distance from the machined face of the rear of the transmission output shaft yoke, to the machined face at the front of the pinion yoke. These machined faces represent the centerline points of the U-joint cups. This will get you close to the overall shaft length you need. Now shop the junkyards. Pay close attention to the U-joint sizes. If in doubt, ask what universal joint might interchange with the shaft and rearend that you have.

As you're measuring, keep in mind the slip and spline joint which allows the driveshaft to lengthen and shorten as the rear suspension works up and down. Although the slip and spline has a built-in travel of several inches, it should ride just about in the center of its travel when the driveshaft is installed between the transmission and rearend, and the full weight of the car is resting on the ground. Take care to avoid inadvertently measuring the driveshaft length with the slip joint either pushed in or pulled out beyond its center of travel, otherwise you may end up with a slip joint that destroys itself when the suspension gets real active. If you are lucky, you'll find a shaft that fits. Sometimes it's a drop-in.

Be aware that MoPar transmissions have two different output shaft spline sizes. There are, therefore, two different slip and spline yoke sizes for the front of the driveshaft.

If you must have a shaft made, plan on it costing from $60 to $150. Most communities have machine shops that will make driveshafts. They will cut and fit the tube, or install a new tube (using the measurements you supply), with a yoke that will fit the rearend. Have the shaft balanced while you are at it.

You do not cut a driveshaft in two and butt-weld the pieces to the length you need! This might be ok for a dune buggy, but it doesn't cut it on a street-drive vehicle.

If you are building a car with lots of horsepower, be sure to use the larger Universal joints and a large diameter driveshaft tube. A good driveshaft shop will be able to advise you regarding the recommended tube diameter and U-joint size as it relates to your engine's horsepower.

"I HEAR ERNIE'S GOT SOME NEW SUPER FAT TIRES FOR HIS ROADSTER."

129

A CASE IN POINT

MAKING EARLY MOPAR CRUISERS
Wherein we look at building both a Plymouth and a Chrysler

The 1934 Plymouth used independent front suspension, which is one reason the frame is so beefy. The large X-member is far enough aft to clear most auto trans combinations. The front end gives a very good ride if all bushings and bearings are replaced. As with most contemporary rod building projects, this one includes taking the frame completely apart during rebuild, again later for painting.

While it would seem that there are MoPar hot rods under every bush, such is not at all the case. At the NSRA Street Rod Nats, the annual MoPar Country gathering has an abundance of Chrysler products on display. But, this large gathering is just a smattering of the 12,000 or so registered participants, and they have been gleaned from all corners of the U.S. and Canada.

By comparison, go to any street machine event for post-1948 cars, and a very large percentage will be MoPar. The reason is simply that more Ford and Chevy cars from the 1920-'30s have survived than other makes. Not that more cars of these two builders were built originally.

So, tracking down the very good MoPar machines with a camera always seems to be a subject of frustration for journalists. Even more difficult is the problem of finding builders who have documented their efforts.

Incidentally, since this is book one of an ongoing series, if you have a good record of your Chrysler product hot rod, any year, give us a call.

During our search for good examples of Chrysler-made vehicles for this first MoPar book, we discovered Jerry Mattson, who just happens to have a business called Mopar Street Rods, 608 N.W. Third Ave, Aledo, Illinois 61231. Jerry has kept a record of his projects, and we selected a 1934 Plymouth PE model as well as a 1933 Chrysler CT. These are great representatives of the early MoPars, that are so popular with rod builders. They are medium size and big size, respectively, and have full metal bodies with the front-opening "suicide" doors that contemporary rodders find so appealing, and Jerry has gone the full Chrysler product swap series on both. Follow along to see how the cars were built.

Vehicles: 1933 Chrysler CT and 1934 Plymouth PE   Owner: Jerry Mattson, Aledo, Illinois

Peculiar to early IFS practice, upper A-arm is only about half as long as lower arm. Here, the upper A-arm also actuates a double piston shock absorber. This absorber can be rebuilt, but the option is to add a tubing shock between lower A-arm and frame.

Neat trick to verify where ride height will be is to use a turnbuckle to hold the A-arm and spring in ride position during building. Disc Brakes off a 1971 Duster with front-mounted calipers bolt to the 1934 spindles. Duster outside bearing is same as stock '34, inside Duster bearing is shimmed from base of spindle bolt with spacer made on a lathe.

Stock '34 Plymouth has center-point idler arm so that tie rods pivot at the same point as lower A-arms. Here, a 1967 Chevy power steering gearbox is adapted and connects to the center-point idler via a short drag link.

The large Mopar 8-3/4-inch rearend can be made to fit the early cars (with this disc brake setup), but some machine work is needed. Here, the more common 8-1/4-inch 1971 Duster rearend has been fitted with 1975 Chrysler Imperial discs (a direct bolt-on). All these rearends area a direct bolt-on to the Thirties era springs.

Left- The Imperial disc brakes include small internal expanding shoes for parking brakes, cables from these are run forward to any convenient parking brake handle.

Proof that you can build a hot rod with whatever power you want is the fact that Mattson chose a 1978 Plymouth arrow 4-cylinder engine, 2600 cc's with small Torqueflite transmission. This engine was adapted to the frame using two mid-point engine mounts off either frame rail. The front springs were made by a spring shop to drop the front end 2-1/2 inches. Jerry reports that the resulting ride is excellent. After all the chassis work was completed, the frame was stripped and painted, then everything was reassembled.

After the car was on the road a while, Mattson decided that twin spares were needed in the front fenders. A 1955 Chevrolet spare tire well (from the trunk) was found to be the correct size. A pattern of this well was made in cardboard, transferred to the Plymouth fenders, then a hole cut in the fenders.

Right- Jerry MIG welded the spare well to the fender, then worked out minor warpage with hammer and dolly.

Steering column holder was made from a cut-down small-block Chevy V8 connecting rod. Underseat heater came from a 1940 Pontiac.

The Chevy spare tire well was trimmed around the edges to fit the contour of the Plymouth fender. The lip was cut away.

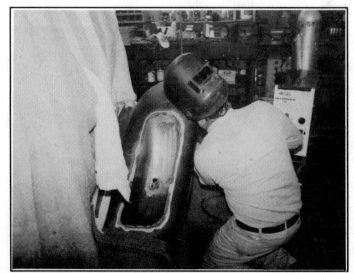

During the fender reworking, this photo was taken of a tube shock setup that had been added to the front end.

Brake pedal from a 1967 Dart was almost a bolt-in. Stock instruments were retained.

This is part of the reason early Thirties MoPars are so popular with family rodders. Spacious interiors. This one is reupholstered in period styling, and garnish moldings are woodgrained.

The 4-cylinder Arrow engine was turbocharged with a unit from a 1978 Buick. Air conditioning was added. Result is a good highway performer.

A 1933 Chrysler CT caught Mattson's eye as something for personal transportation, so it came into the garage for an extended renovation. Meaning, it got the basics and continues to be worked on through the years, while Jerry drives it to rod runs everywhere in the country.

Rearend from a 1977 Dodge wagon (8-1/4-inch version) was bolted to the stock Chrysler springs, and disc brakes from a 1975 Imperial added.

The Chrysler originally used a beam axle with a semi-Elliot end (meaning the axle ends cupped the steering knuckle inside, unlike more traditional Ford/Chevy practice).

Torsion bar front end (complete) from a 1979 Cordoba was selected to replace the stock Chrysler beam axle. All mounting brackets were cut off the Cordoba unit.

The frame horns are cut from the Cordoba front crossmember, then dropped center section is cut away. This 17-1/2 inch section is replaced by rectangular heavy-wall tubing. The tubing and crossmember ends are held clamped to a heavy I-beam during this cutting/welding to make sure the front end stays in perfect alignment. Cutting away the dropped crossmember center means that there is more clearance and the new front end is not visible to curious spectators.

Ribber top from a 1964 Dart wagon was installed in the Chrysler. The Dart transplant has been mounted backwards, a slight V-shape cut in the middle for better fit.

Left- You're likely to see Jerry Mattson at a rod run anywhere in the U.S. or Canada. His unfinished 1933 Chrysler does all the road work just fine, thank you!

UPDATING A
MIDDLE-AGE MOPAR

With the sheetmetal removed, it's pretty obvious why MoPars were never popular for engine swaps. While the steering box posed no problem for the original flathead six, it's right smack in the way of a V8. There have been swaps done by repositioning the steering box or by switching to another box altogether, but we were looking for an easy swap, one in which we could retain as much of the original steering as possible.

by Eric Pierce
courtesy Street Rod Action magazine

Building a low-buck '39 to '48 Plymouth or Dodge can be a tricky proposition that demands a lot of tape measuring, head scratching and trial and error fabricating. Such was the case with this '47 Plymouth project, but with some careful planning all the right components were able to be installed without too much pain and anguish.

One of the early steps was an engine swap to a '72 Dodge 318 V8. We had heard that the nicely maintained and low mileage '72 Dodge Dart Swinger belonging to the mother of a couple of long time friends, Ed and Al Newton, had been totaled and was available for a very "right" price. The engine, a two-barrel 318, along with the matching automatic transmission had survived unscathed — in fact, the car could still be driven even though the radiator and front end were history. Being firm believers in divine providence, we committed to the purchase of the car even though we had no idea how well (or even if) the engine would fit in our coupe.

We were somewhat worried when the car first arrived because a quick walk around with a tape measure disclosed that some of the lumps on the engine would

encounter some of the lumps on the chassis. The biggest problem is the intrusion of the steering box deep into the space that needs to be occupied by the engine.

While there are any number of ways around this problem, we had hoped to retain the original steering box in the original location. These old MoPars drive very nicely with very low steering effort in stock form. We didn't want to use tubular headers except as a last resort. We wanted to perform an engine swap that would allow us to retain as much of the original vehicle as possible to keep the cost down — and because these cars do not need steering or suspension improvements. All they really need is more power.

Because the steering box in the Dart makes exactly the same excursion into the engine compartment as the '40s MoPar units, only more so, the factory was forced to make some concessions for the use of the 318 in these cars. The first was to install the engine 2-3/4 inches closer to the right side of the car than the left, a 1-3/8 inch offset from center. The second was to design a left side exhaust manifold specifically to clear the steering column in these mid-sized cars. If we could mount the

Vehicle: 1947 Plymouth Coupe   Owner: Eric Pierce, Canoga Park, California

mount the 318 in the coupe in the same way it had been mounted in the Dart, it just might fit. It appeared that with the engine mounted where it must go to clear the front crossmember and the firewall, the left exhaust manifold would wrap around the coupe's steering column with the same grace as it had the Dart's.

The tape measure said it would work, but the only way to know for sure would be to try it. We pulled the engine out, cleaned and degreased everything, and slid the 318 into the coupe's engine bay just far enough to know that our theory was correct. Then we contacted Manny Martinez of Mr. Street Rod (888 Chambers Lane, Simi Valley, CA 93065; 805-526-1800) to see if he'd build a set of prototype motor mounts for the car, which he could then add to his growing mail order street rod product line.

Once in the Mr. Street Rod shop, the car was relieved of the original transmission crossmember and the engine lowered and blocked into place. The fit was tight until the engine was positioned exactly in the right spot. The firewall required a light massage for passenger side valve cover clearance, but with that done the engine fit as pretty as you please. The left side manifold clears the steering column perfectly with the engine exactly one inch offset to the right of center. The crankshaft centerline is an inch or so higher than was that of the original six-cylinder, but this is of no consequence and allows some very necessary clearance at the steering column and crankshaft pulley. The right exhaust manifold tucks inward enough to clear the rails, but we'd recommend a 90-degree oil filter adapter (available from MoPar Performance, part number P3690884) to ease oil changes if your engine is not already so equipped. MoPar Performance also has a fuel pump block-off plate (part number P4349626) which may be of interest to those who prefer a more exotic fuel delivery system.

There is only one engine location where everything fits and clears as it should. Manny built his engine and transmission mounts (Mr. Street Rod part number MOP39-48 sold as a set at $129.95). They are used in conjunction with two front motor mounts (Borg Warner #31-2266) and the original transmission mount and drop-out section from the '72 Dart. It is also necessary to replace the original oil pan and pickup tube/screen with units from a '78 Dodge 4x4 pickup truck (available at Chrysler/Plymouth dealers — pan is part number 04387606, tube/screen is part number 03462337). You'll also need the matching dipstick (part number 03496960) and dipstick tube (part number 03496959). This allows the engine to clear the stock Plymouth/Dodge steering arms with room to spare.

We found it easiest to bolt the mounts to the engine and then lower the engine back into place to correctly position the mounts. The engine is positioned with the crankshaft plane slightly above and parallel to the original six-cylinder's plane, it is one inch offset to the

Having access to a donor car like this '72 Dodge Dart Swinger makes the swap easier because it has small items such as wiring, linkages, throttle assembly, steering column, brake parts, A/C components as well as the engine, transmission and driveshaft. Here, Jerry Johnson helps clear the way to pull the motor out.

Hopefully, this'll be the last time the old coupe ever sees the leisure end of a trailer. Seemed strange not to be driving the coupe, it having served as daily driver ever since we got the old flathead running again.

passenger side, level from side to side, and with a finger's thickness clearance between the inside curve of the exhaust manifold and the outside curve of the steering column mast jacket. At this point, the right valve cover just kisses the unmodified Plymouth firewall. Because all car frames, Plymouth included, vary from unit to unit, the Mr. Street Rod engine and transmission mounts may require a bit of grinding to fit your frame perfectly. Once they've been precision fitted to your frame, just weld them on and you're finished with the heavy portion of the MoPar-to-MoPar swap.

While we were swapping things, we decided to swap a Ford 9-inch rearend into the Plymouth. The 9-inch Ford has become the standard of the street rod building world in recent years, and not without good reason. They are simple, easy to service, feature easy-

A couple of eager teenagers helping Dad by cleaning the motor with Gunk S-C. Building street rods is seldom glamorous, it is far more often just plain old hard work, dirty clothes and skinned knuckles.

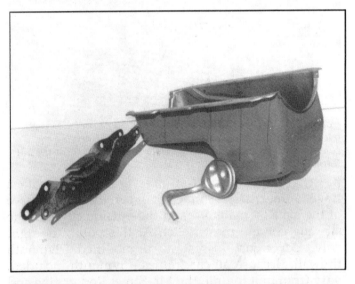

Among the parts needed to perform this swap are the center "drop-out" from the '72 Dodge Dart Swinger with attached transmission mount, the oil pan and matching pickup tube and strainer from a '78 Dodge 318 4x4. You'll also need the dipstick and dipstick tube from this same engine. They're available from your local Chrylser/Plymouth dealer.

to-change drop-out center sections that facilitate ratio changes, have large bearings and are virtually unbreakable with street tires. These venerable rearends have proven themselves very dependable since the later '50s in both passenger cars and light trucks, with a wide variety of gear ratios available in both open and positive traction styles. Axle housing widths, spring perch arrangements, pumpkin shapes and offsets are as diverse as the applications, making the basic 9-inch axle versatile enough to fit just about any street rod application. Combine this wide array of physical dimensions with the unit's innate strength and the result is an ideal street and strip rear axle assembly.

Selecting a 9-inch Ford rear axle for a street rod isn't as difficult as one might think. For most street rodders, there are four basic criteria: width, gear ratio, posi or open, and overall condition. Sometimes the shape of the pumpkin, its positioning in relation to center, and the presence or lack of a drain plug are critical, but for most of us these are of secondary importance. Likewise, the original spring mounts are not of any real significance as they will be removed during the installation process anyway. For the purpose of obtaining service parts, it's good to know exactly what year/make/model the unit came from, and if possible what engine the car or truck had. And it's good to consider only units that are complete right down to the last cotter pin. Even if some of the parts are worn out, you'll have examples that can be matched with new ones.

Unless you have a specific reason to do otherwise, your best bet is to select an axle that is equal to or not more than an inch narrower than the original axle's width. It is almost never good to go wider than the original axle for cosmetic reasons. Conversely, one must be careful not to go too narrow. You'll need to allow sufficient room for the backing plates to clear such obstructions as the frame rails and the leaf springs, especially on lowered cars. Use of deeply reversed wheels will not solve brake drum-to-frame or backing plate-to-spring clearance problems.

If yours is a special case, a pro-street car for example, most cities have at least one machine shop that is capable of narrowing a housing to your specs.

Select a gear ratio that is appropriate to the way you drive your car most of the time. If your street rod is used for drag racing most of the time, then select a high number ratio. If you don't use the car for drag racing most of the time, don't select one of the high numerical ratios because they will cause the engine to turn too fast at highway speeds, making street driving a noisy and unpleasant matter.

A common mistake is to assume that a lower numerical ratio such as a 2.6, 2.7 or 2.9:1 will give better fuel economy than would a 3.0 to 3.5:1. While this may be true under steady state cruise conditions on level ground, a ratio that is too low numerically will rob the engine of its performance potential while preventing it from running efficiently. Mileage may suffer and make the climbing of hills a chore. Mild small-block V8s do their best cruising at 2200 to 2500 rpm at 55-60 mph. V6s

" I TOLD YOU NOT TO LET THAT KID PLAY WITH THE CHAIN SAW ! "

Above- Manny Martinez, aka Mr. Street Rod, made short work of the original transmission crossmember, knocking the rivets off with an air chisel. A cold chisel and small sledge will get the job done. Then he pried the assembly loose.

Left- A trial fit of the engine came next. Notice that we first tried it with all the bolt on stuff in place. As we went along, however, we removed the fuel pump, oil filter and starter so as not to damage them as we wrestled the engine around in search of the perfect mounting location.

Because the engine and transmission were offset in the '72 Dart, the drop-out is not symmetrical. To allow it to sit properly in the coupe and fit the Mr. Street Rod mounts, it must be trimmed just slightly in the area shown. This is easily accomplished with a cut-off saw, but a hacksaw will do the job in a pinch.

spin a bit faster while big-blocks generally are best a bit slower. Heavily modified engines are generally more efficient turning somewhat faster than stock or mild ones.

On the question of posi vs. open differential, there is nothing to be lost by the use of a positive traction rearend as long as it is in good condition. Ford positraction units are quiet, strong, dependable and ideal for extreme service and racing applications. They do, however, require some special service and lubrication as well as an occasional opportunity to stretch their legs in order to operate properly and live long lives. Wrecking yard posis are often in less than perfect shape due to high mileage, lack of proper maintenance, the use of improper lubricants and, surprisingly, lack of exercise. Buying a posi unit from a private party is risky because they've often been abused or serviced by individuals who know little about rearend set-up procedures.

Often as not, there is little to be gained by using a posi unit in a street rod. Few of us ever use our cars hard enough to cause the posi to operate, much less do us any good. Non-posi rearends are considerably less expensive and are at less risk of being bad when purchased used.

No matter how good they look, it's a good idea to rebuild the brakes before putting the new rearend into service. Replace the brake return springs while you're at it.

Keeping all the aforementioned items in mind will help you make the best purchase decisions when it comes time to swap engines and rearends into your middle age MoPar.

With the engine blocked correctly in place and leveled to the chassis, the drop-out is bolted to the transmission using the original bolts. It is checked for level in the flat pad area as shown, and the stubs bolted to it so they fit to the frame as shown here. Each is then tacked into place.

The driver's side stub mount should fit just to the rear of the original master cylinder frame bracket, if so equipped, and uses it as part of the weld surface. This dimension may vary from car to car. Be certain the brake lines which exit the rear of the master cylinder will clear the stub mount before welding it in place.

Finally, this is how the completed transmission mount should look. It's plenty stout and allows the transmission to be easily removed for service without the need to remove the engine.

On the passenger side, everything clears as well, including the transmission dipstick and the exhaust manifold.

With the engine in place, note that the driver's side exhaust manifold wraps around the steering column like it was made for it. There's plenty of room for the distributor, starter and even the stock kick-down linkage.

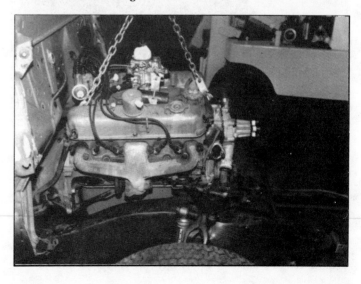

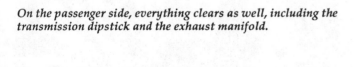

In the final installation, we moved the engine rearward ever so slightly so that the right valve cover just kissed the firewall. This portion of the firewall was massaged to allow ample clearance for the valve cover. Note the right angle adapter for the oil filter, giving clearance to the filter even though the engine was offset to the passenger side.

Right- Direct Connection parts used for this swap include a right angle oil filter adapter, fuel pump block-off plate and spray cans of engine enamel.

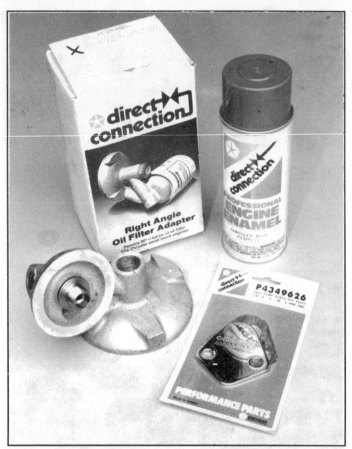

The engine mounts may require slight trimming to fit snugly since no two frames are exactly alike. Be sure to mount your crankshaft pulley before welding, to be sure you have the engine mounted high enough for it to clear and allow a belt to be installed. Also double-check the clearance around the left exhaust manifold as well as the overall level of the engine. It's a good idea to tack the mounts in place and slack the tension on the hoist to allow the engine weight to settle on the mounts and again check clearances. If you're satisfied, then weld 'em up.

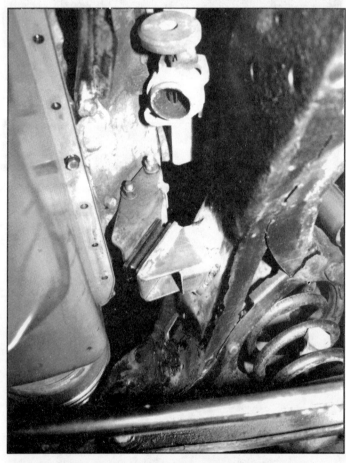

This is how the passenger side mount should look from the bottom. Note that there's plenty of clearance for the exhaust manifold and exhaust pipe.

This is the driver's side mount as seen from the bottom. All components should have plenty of clearance for the engine to torque without fear of hitting. A finger's thickness of clearance at the exhaust manifold should be plenty.

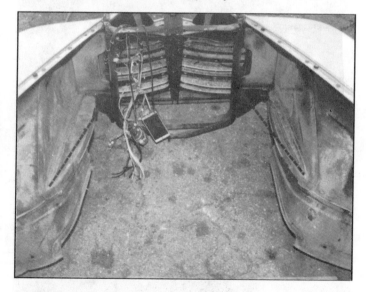

As the dotted lines indicate, it was necessary to modify the inner fender panels to allow the wider V8 to fit between them. This was accomplished by making a cut along what is now the weld seam and pulling the lower sections outward until they are in the positions shown here. You'll need to fabricate the two roughly triangular pieces that help support the radiator housing. You'll also have to trim the lower panels for upper control arm clearance. Carefully finish all edges and fabricate some rubber flaps to control the water around the control arms, like late models, and you're home free.

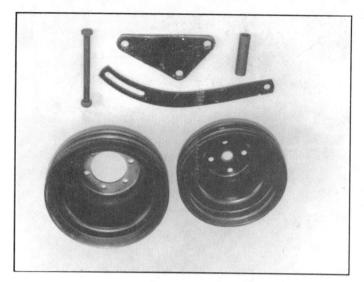

If your engine came with an air conditioner pump and power steering and you'd like to do away with them, you can search the wrecking yard for engine with the non-air, non-power steering pulleys and brackets. Or, you can do what we did — nothing. More Accurately, we retained all the original pulleys and brackets but used different belts in different places to drive different things. The alternator belt is no problem as it passes around the crank pulley and is tensioned by the alternator. The water pump, however, presented a major problem because we were unable to find a pulley with the correct grooves in the correct places to allow it to be tensioned by the alternator as well. Our final solution was to use a belt (Gates XL #7335 in our case) which tensions into place as the water pump pulley is bolted into position.

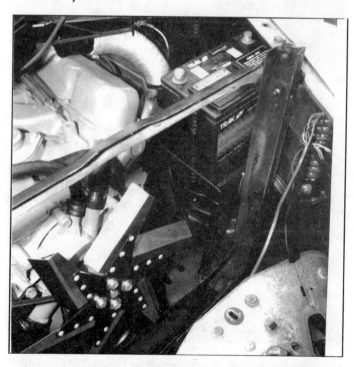

After considering a number of alternatives, we found that one of the new mini high-amp batteries would fit neatly in the front corner of the engine compartment. This puts the negative terminal close to the engine block and allows the positive cable from the Dart to be recycled into this car. The battery body is fabricated from angle iron and sits on what's left of the inner fender shelf. A single support leg was fabricated to support the inner section of the box, a leg which bolts to the frame through an existing hole.

In order to allow enough space for the somewhat long 318 water pump, it was necessary to space the radiator forward. Fortunately, we were aware that some Plymouths and Dodges exported to other countries were equipped with DeSoto and Chrysler flathead sixes. To accommodate these longer engines, the factory simply turned the radiator support around front-to-back. This allows the stock radiator to mount to the front of the support instead of the back, effectively moving it two inches forward with no changes other than the removal of one brace. This is what we did, and it worked perfectly.

We installed a separate transmission cooler to relieve the heat load from the engine's cooling system. We used a MoPar Performance Heavy Duty Transmission Cooler (P4349197) which is manufactured for Chrysler Corporation by Hayden. Note also the use of a Jacobs Energy Pak ignition microprocessor and Energy Coil to augment the Plymouths point-type ignition system. These are available from Jacobs Electronics, 3327 Verdugo Road, Los Angeles, CA 90065; (800) 627-8000.

We called Ron Francis (Ron Francis Wire Works, 167 Keystone Rd., Chester, PA 19013; 215-485-1937) to explain our needs regarding the engine swap electrical system (engine, starting, alternator systems). Several days later, we received a box containing all the pieces we'd need to rework our harness to work with the new components, along with specific instruction about how the modifications should be carried out. Major components were a new starter relay and new electronic voltage regulator. Following directions, we wired 'er up and fired 'er up without problem.

We used the Dart throttle cable, linkage and pedal in our Plymouth because it fit almost perfectly. The pedal mount needed to be recontoured slightly to fit the firewall shape and the mounting rod needed to be heated and bent in a couple of spots to hang at the right angle and allow full throttle before touching the floor. It fits and operates just fine, and it was free.

Typical of used 9-inch Ford rearends, this housing was a third hand pass along unit of uncertain parentage and condition. It was also missing both brake drums. A classic example of what not to buy.

On the plus side, however, was the fact that this unit was complete with ratio tag naming it as a 3.0:1 non-posi axle and giving a good indication that the unit has never been apart or mistreated.

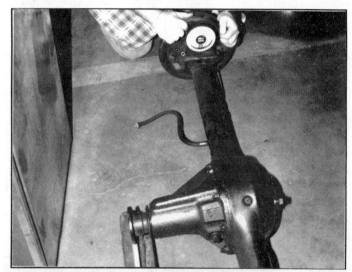

Above- Encrusted with dirt and minor surface rust, the housing was free of evidence of fluid leaks. Though we'd not recommend buying a housing without emergency brake cables, replacing them is no big deal.

Upper Right- The new 9-inch was the correct width to replace the existing rearend. It was decided to duplicate the original pinion angle. A magnetic protractor is used for this task. The angle is determined by blocking the pinion flange at zero degrees and then reading the angle on the spring perch which results. It's usually something like six degrees.

Right- The original spring mounting pads and shock mounts are removed with a torch. Care was taken not to cut through the axle tube and to prevent the buildup of heat in the area, which can warp the housing.

The axle tubes were then ground smooth and the new pads from Mr. Street Rod set into place. The correct placement is determined from the original rearend housing and transferred to the 9-inch by careful measuring.

Below- The protractor is used to duplicate the pinion angle on the new rearend housing. The pads are tacked into place and all measurements taken again to ensure the correctness of the final position.

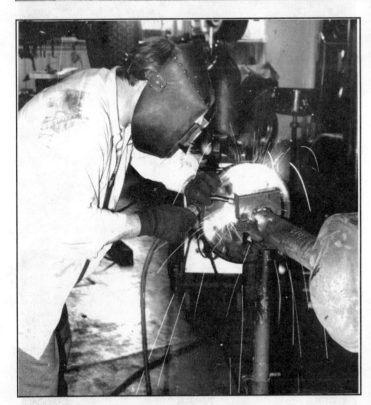

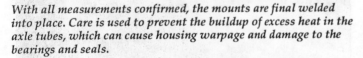

With all measurements confirmed, the mounts are final welded into place. Care is used to prevent the buildup of excess heat in the axle tubes, which can cause housing warpage and damage to the bearings and seals.

Right- The axle is then ready to bolt in place. Note that the Mr. Street Rod mounting pad is also a lowering block, giving a drop of approximately one inch. They are center drilled to index with the spring bolt, but can be redrilled to suit.

146

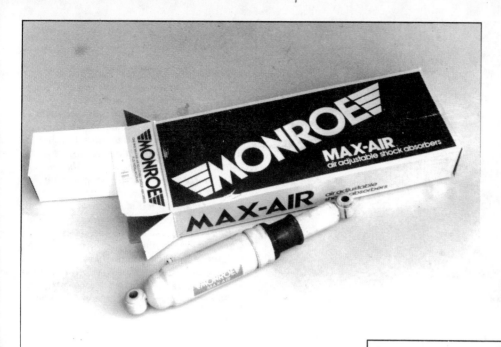

If you have decided to use lowering blocks, your car may look and ride great when it's empty, but a weekend worth of luggage, a full cooler and a tank of gas may put you right down on the snubbers. Monroe Auto Equipment Company has Max-Air adjustable shocks to fit just about any street rod or custom car application. They can be adjusted to maintain the car's profile while also giving extra load capacity to maintain the smooth ride at the same time.

Below- The Fat Fendered Street Rod Shop (13664 Whittram, Fontana, CA 92335; 714-357-2700) supplies this emergency brake cable kit to replace damaged or missing original cables. It comes complete with support brackets, connectors, equalizer and an adjustable length cable that's ideal for street rods.

Below- We tried to use as much of the original Plymouth equipment as possible, including, in this case, the emergency brake mechanism. We also employed the mount which used to bolt to the side of the transmission, which supported the rear of the cable casing. By re-routing the cable slightly, we were able to position the original rear mount on the driver's side frame rail just ahead of the master cylinder. By welding the mount to the frame at this point, the end of the cable itself was in the perfect place to mate with the Fat Fendered Street Rod Shop emergency brake cable kit. The pull angle is correct and the completed system works better than the stock one did. It was simple, and it was free.

We had the driveshaft modified to fit after the engine swap. We utilized the Dart driveshaft and had a local driveshaft shop cut the tube and install a Ford rear U-joint. However, we found that the U-joint still wouldn't mate with our pinion yoke. It was the correct width, but the cups were too big. Rather than go to the trouble and expense of having the shaft re-cut and another U-joint carrier installed, we visited our local parts store. Using calipers, we were quickly able to find a U-joint with the correct cups that would interchange with the cups on the joint in our driveshaft. By exchanging the cups, we got our shaft to fit and ended up with a spare U-joint with two large and two small cups for an emergency spare.

A complete custom exhaust system was fabricated to fit the new engine/chassis configuration. Although stainless steel has become popular and custom milled brackets common on street rods in recent years, our car is a driver and needed a serviceable, attractive and affordable exhaust system. The '72 Dart 318 exhaust manifolds fit our engine installation perfectly and because we prefer cast iron manifolds over headers, we decided to retain them permanently. We elected to use Thrush Super Sonic II mufflers because we like their throaty tone. MoPars of this vintage present a problem at the rear because the layout of the gas tank, springs and spare tire well combine to eliminate graceful routes for a matched set of tailpipes. We decided to massage the spare tire well slightly to give access to the rear on the passenger side. The result was pipes in a perfect mirror image of each other.

"HEY, MAN, THIS IS THE MIDWEST... YOU DON'T REALIZE
HOW HARD IT IS TO FIND A GOOD STEEL BODY."

EXAMPLES

1917 DODGE ROADSTER

The '49 Mercury rearend has '56 Ford pickup 4.27:1 gears inside. The spring mounts, shock mounts, and trailing arm brackets were all added. Spring mounts were cut from pre-1949 Ford rearend and installed.

Model T rear spring flexes between N50-15 tires on 15x10 wheels. The Model T taillight is a bit of nostalgia rodding not often seen nowadays. Paint for this exoticar-killer is Porsche Bahama yellow lacquer.

by Russ Young

Some rods hit the street in finished form with everything completed and just right. Not much room for improvement in an on-the-trailer pro-built high-dollar car! However, most of us have limitations, certainly bucks, maybe time, maybe skill, certainly experience. In the worst case, the car doesn't get completed or is discarded shortly after it is. Usually, the rod starts out attractive, functional, reasonably safe and a complete kick in the pants. And it just gets better with more money, time, skill and experience.

John Millar's Dodge Brothers hiboy roadster is such a car. That is, such a hot rod. Over the years, it has gotten more power, more safe, more good looking and more Dodge.

John has owned the car since 1971 and has been able to trace the history back to the original builder/owner, a fellow nicknamed Hemi Henry. The car literally hit the streets of San Jose, California in 1961, powered by

an earlier hemi coupled to a Packard stick shift transmission. Henry either knew how to make his hemis run or at least how to pop the clutch. When the weight of the hemi brought the car back to earth, it didn't stop at the tires! An early improvement was to heavily reinforce the front suicide spring mount.

The second owner added the shortened Ford pickup bed, the current hemi motor and a Torqueflite transmission. John bought the car from the third owner and has completely gone through everything mechanical, including the motor, transmission, rearend, brakes and steering. He also upgrades to original Dodge Brothers parts when he finds them.

This hot rod was built before someone decided that all roadsters should be Ford-bodied and Chevy-powered. Although it no longer terrorizes the streets of San Jose, it is driven regularly and improved occasionally.

Vehicle: 1917 Dodge Roadster   Owner: John Millar, Santa Clara, California

Left-
Roadsters are made as often as they are born. This one started life as a touring. The rear body portion was abandoned in favor of a molded-on, shortened T pickup bed.

Right- Millar replaced a Model T grille shell with one from a Dodge product, lending more authenticity to the roadster. Tubing crossmember between frame rails positions beefy suicide spring. Axle is dropped '32 Ford item, front brakes are '48 Ford, shocks are Monroe. The tie rod mounts ahead of the axle, which has a strange effect on the Ackerman steering principle. Front wheels are 15x6 with 165SR15 tires.

When he got the car, Millar found the steering shaft "floated" without support. He has added a dash support below the wood-rimmed wheel. The steering gearbox is from a '56 Ford and does an excellent job of directing the 94-inch wheelbase road rocket. Original MoPar pushbuttons on the dash command the '57 Chrysler Torqueflite, prepped by Joe White of Ad-Tech.

John had custom headers fabricated to tuck inside the frame. Motor mounts are Hurst, bolting to stubs off frame rails.

151

THE DODGE GANG

Out here in "Hole In The Wall" country, famed outlaws Butch Cassidy and the Sundance Kid made history holding up stage coaches and robbing banks. Their reign of treachery began in the late 1800's and ran into the new century, a time filled with all kinds of new-fangled gadgets. Local rumor has it that Butch didn't really die in that shootout in South America, but returned to Utah and lived in quiet solitude until his death in the late Thirties. It's even possible he had the chance to ride in an automobile, perhaps like these two early Dodges owned by Bob and Louise Eames.

by Burly Burlile

1916 DODGE SCREENSIDE DELIVERY

Together, the Eames head up the Dodge Gang, a pair of very rare and unique street rods. On Bob's side of the street is his 1916 Dodge Screenside Delivery, a commercial truck which found great popularity in the rural state of Utah. He originally paid $300 for the truck and in the ensuing years has spent $3500 restoring it to the present condition.

To start, Bob and friend Dick Hall cherried out the existing body shell and located replacement sheetmetal where metalwork could not save it. The frames on early Dodges were boxed and are very sturdy, so no

modifications were necessary. It was simply prepped and painted black. At the front, a '56 Ford half-ton axle was dropped six inches by Mordrop for a definite in-the-weeds stance. The spindles and brakes were altered to accept '49 Chevy pieces and the steering box changed to a reversed Chevy II unit.

The rear axle, a '67 Chevy II assembly, was attached to the stock quarter elliptic leaf springs and Monroe shock absorbers. Rotation from the '65 Torqueflite transmission was provided by a driveshaft that was shortened 18 inches, fabricated out of a MoPar front and a Chevrolet rear section. Power comes from a later

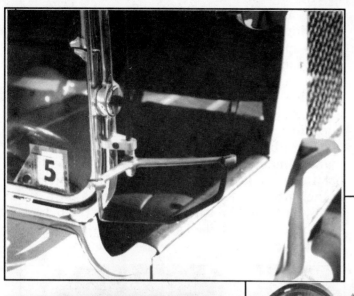

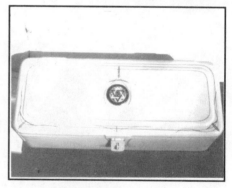

Dodge product, a 225 cu.in. slant six engine of stock dimensions. The carburetor is a Holley Economaster and ignition is by Accel. A Hayden transmission cooler keeps the ATF at the proper temperature. Many of these components have been chrome plated for the "show" as well as the "go" modes.

All the custom woodwork came from the hands of Fred Christiansen, who fabricated the many bows and runners from Philippine Mahogany. Interior appointments were the craft of M.B.'s Upholstery and were done in deep saddle brown Naugahyde, and deep pile carpeting. Stewart Warner gauges and wiring

were installed by Dennis Williams.

Dick Hall applied the special effects R.M. yellow lacquer that gives a definite glow to the Screenside's appearance. This helps to highlight the original 1916 Dodge accessories, such as the running board tool box and side vent wings. The taillight and headlights are stock '16 items, but the wheels once graced a rare Buick Skylark. Even the starter crank is original, but with the low stance, it would never be able to make one full revolution.

1920 DODGE TOURING

Louise's 1920 Dodge Touring model is a little bit more practical than Bob's Screenside. To begin with, it doesn't even have a crank. Also, when it rains, as it has a tendency to do at many of the mountain-west runs, she can zip in the practically invisible side curtains that M.B's designed especially for this car. In may other areas, the touring is similar to hubby's wheels.

The motor is a slant six Dodge of 225 cu.in. and is topped off by a Holley Economaster carburetor. A Torqueflite automatic transmission has been converted form the original pushbutton design to a pull-shift set-up, and transmits energy to a Chevy II rear axle, shocked by Monroe. A small change up front involved the use of a 1937 Plymouth swoopy-style tube front axle and brakes. Steering is from a Ford Econoline. The shocks are '41 Ford, and Skylark wheels are mounted inside BF Goodrich radial tires.

A lady requires more comfort and consideration, so M.B. saw to it that she was treated like a queen. A square tufted pattern was followed throughout the interior with deep saddle brown Naugahyde and lush carpeting. Although no heater is installed, those invisible side curtains (look closely at some of the photos) attached to the beige nylon top help keep wind and rain from Milady's bouffant. And when exiting the car, the Philippine Mahogany running boards and aluminum Dodge step plates provide safe footing.

Reproduction Moto-meter and Stewart Warner gauges supply information about the motor's operating condition, while other details help add the final touches to this special Dodge. A deflated BFGoodrich instant spare hangs above a simulated fuel tank in the rear, which in reality is a storage container for waxes, polishing cloths and numerous other items. Norris Robbins gets the nod for this as well as the aluminum hood and dash.

All in all, these two Dodge rods have been executed in the grandest of fashion, with particular attention to obtaining that just-right appearance. Next time you're in their neighborhood give a wave and a flash of the lights, and don't be surprised if you're invited in for some rod talk. With the Dodge Gang, friendship goes with the territory.

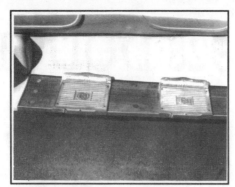

1928 DODGE

by Burly Burlile

If you're a Henry man who hasn't looked around too much lately, take notice of the great amount of non-FoMoCo tin that is flushing out the rod runs. In the mountain west region of Utah and Idaho, Dodges and Plymouths are running a very close second in quantity, and sometimes surpassing in quality, the ever popular Fords.

A prime example is the 1928 Dodge Brothers coupe owned and assembled by Steve and Betty Bangerter and family from Woods Cross, Utah. This fabulous Datsun-blue Dodge took the Bangerter family two years and a lot of nickles to put together after a to-the-frame teardown, modification and restoration. About the only problems they encountered (besides the numerous little headachy ones we all experience) were locating the genuine Dodge pieces to complete the project. When it got down to the nitty gritty of create or not finish, Steve put his many talents in gear and hand-fabricated the window frames and engineered power window set-ups to replace the missing and non-locatable stock window regulators.

Along the way, owner-built motor mounts and shock mounts were added to the already sturdy frame that Steve boxed, and a MAS tube axle featuring a six-inch drop was placed under the springs. Fifty Chevy front brakes and a '57 rear axle housing provided a mounting location for the Corvette Rally wheels and Goodyear rubber. Steering is accomplished by a '56 Ford truck box and is controlled with an anti-sway bar and steering damper.

The always-popular Chevy mouse was elected to power the Dodge and was helped along with fueler heads and cam and a .020 overbore. Hydraulic lifters help keep things quiet while a Holley 650 cfm double pumper atop a Holley Street Dominator intake manifold swallows the Arabian gold. Doug Thorley's Number

Vehicle: 1928 Dodge Coupe   Owner: Steve Bangerter, Woods Cross, Utah

One headers see that the spent gasses get away as quickly as possible. To assist in giving the coupe a driving range of over 650 miles, a 25-gallon gas tank was installed.

M.B.'s Upholstery and the House of Customs share honors for the stitching with M.B. Bessire doing the light silver blue nylon velvet interior and John Kennedy laying in the fully-upholstered trunk. The steering wheel is original stock that has been modified to fit the Ford truck column. Power windows and antenna add a feel of luxury to the early Dodge.

Stewart Warner gauges keep the driver informed of the important happenings under the hood, and all electrical circuits have breaker systems installed for insurance against short circuits. The stock headlights have been altered to accept Yamaha quartz-halogen headlight bulbs, which provide excellent lighting on night rides. The etched rear-view mirror was done by Betty's friend and fellow rodder, Marie Zaversnik.

Steve and Betty are some of the most active and nicest folks involved in street rodding today, being active members of the Rocky Mountain Auto Association and co-editors of The Mountain West Street News.

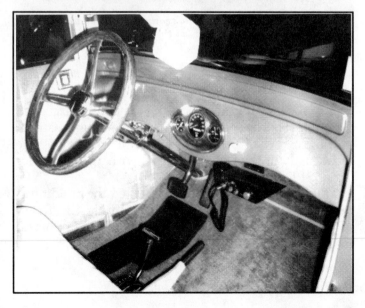

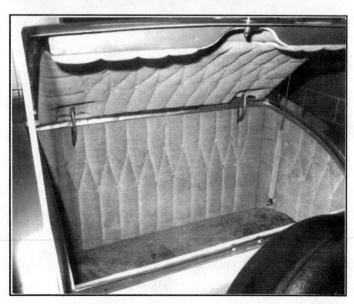

1929 DODGE

There's hardly anything nicer to look at than a chassis in the preparing stages. This body-off resto-rod build-up is a choice piece of work. The stock '29 Dodge frame had a couple of extra crossmembers added for strength.

Steering is handled by a Mustang gearbox that is mounted below the left-side frame rail just behind the spring perch. The pitman arm points skyward, and a drag link runs forward to the steering knuckle.

If a late Twenties MoPar resto-rod is your cup of brew, Tom Peterson's 1929 Dodge will certainly turn your head. The neat thing about it is that Tom found this car (in very good condition) almost in his backyard. Neater yet was the price: $850. Of course, during the 3-1/2 years of construction Tom put another $15,000 into the project, but look at what he got, and then think of what $15,000 will buy you at a new-car store these days.

This is truly a rare car. Although factory production numbers are unavailable for the 1929 Dodges, Tom figures the total for this model could not have exceeded 500 units. He has found only 3 others still in existence in the U.S. When the car was new, it was among the most costly of the Dodge models, with a factory price tag of $1025.

The way Tom planned and executed the building of this rod retained almost all of the original styling flavor of this beautiful car, yet updated all the important mechanical areas in best resto-rod tradition.

Vehicle: 1929 Dodge DA Vicky   Owner: Tom Peterson, Brigham City, Utah

A stock front axle is employed, and suspension is damped by Monroe hydraulic shocks that run between the axle and a homemade frame mount. Stock spindles were machined to receive the 1977 Dodge Aspen disc brakes which are powered by a '76 Chevy master cylinder.

As Tom was going through all the work of putting this '29 Dodge on the road in cherry condition, one of the first steps was to pull the body off the frame so it could be worked on inside and out, top to bottom.

As things were starting to come together, the dashboard was modified by Tom to accept his concept of an instrument panel. The tilt steering column was rescued out of a '79 Pontiac Gran Prix, and the steering wheel is Vega stuff.

The finished interior was kept very simple and totally functional. Only the basic instrumentation was included. Mustang II front seats provide good support for front passengers, and are covered in grey mohair and leather. An overhead console houses the radio and interior lights.

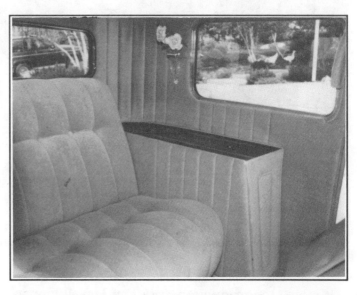

The rear seat is stock, and a storage console to the side narrows the seat to a 2-passenger capacity. Note the rose vase on the rear quarter — a touch of class from the past.

Left- A '71 Dodge contributed the rear axle and brakes. Stock '29 Dodge leaf springs were modified by removing alternate leaves to soften the ride. Twin pipes make mellow exhaust notes.

Left- Upgraded power is in the form of a 1971 Dodge 318 V8, which turns a 904 series Torqueflite transmission of the same vintage. Gear selection is via a Pinto shifter. Cooling for the trans is through a Hayden unit, and an Eskimo radiator does the job for the engine coolant.

1931 PLYMOUTH

photos by Bill Temsey

It wasn't too many years back that Lowell Ehman and his wife, Helen, spent a year and $5000 to build what you see here. With a little luck and a lot of ingenuity, the same job could be done again today for not too much more outlay.

Here is a car that you have to look at twice to discover what it really is. This '31 Plymouth 4-door has an almost-restored appearance to it. The stock-height roof, original headlights, taillights and bumpers, dual side-mounts and trunk add to this flavor. But spend a little time looking the car over carefully and it doesn't take long to discover that this is a rod pure and simple.

For example, lift the hood and feast eyeballs on the '70 Chevy 307 V8, backed up by a turbo 400 automatic transmission, all resting on homemade engine/tranny mounts. Listen to the dual exhaust and glass-pack mufflers, play with the '66 Cougar trans shifter. This is hot rod stuff.

When you're done with that, crawl around underneath and admire the homemade tube front axle with '40 Ford spindles, '66 Chevy control arms and '66 Ambassador disc brakes. Power steering is out of a '66 Chevy. The rear end is '67 Ford Mustang with chromed leaf springs that have had the Teflon treatment to smooth out the bumps. Wheels are wires off of a '54 Chrysler, and tires are 9.00x15 all around.

Interior retains the original seats, with upholstered material in complementary colors of toast and teak brown. The dashboard was custom-built by Lowell himself, and the tilt steering column makes long hauls a bit easier on the driving posture. Tunes come from an AM/FM stereo system, and an onboard CB keeps the crew in touch with the outside world. Vent window glass was etched with delicate patterns.

If a radical rod is not your kind of car, consider how nice it can be to go the subtle rod route the way Lowell Ehman did. A hot rod with a semi-restored appearance may attract twice the attention as folks look once and then look again when they discover what the car really is.

Vehicle: 1931 Plymouth 4-door   Owner: Lowell Ehman, Andalusia, Illinois

1933 PLYMOUTH

photos by Rick Eccli & Bill Brutsman

It all began when this car was found by accident in a garage, it wasn't for sale, yet Tony Castaneda lucked out and ended up with it anyway. It happened like this: Tony's brother-in-law went to look at a motorcycle at a friend's house. In the garage, he spied this old car sitting in the corner. Asked about selling the car, the owner said he hadn't really thought about it, but he might. And that's how Tony got the car for a grand total of $470. Thirty-five hundred dollars and seven months later, the bright orange '33 Plymouth hot rod was complete. Now, is that a hot rod Cinderella story or what?

Bright orange is one of the right hot rod colors, the '33 Plymouth coupe has all the right shapes (especially with the half hood that shows off the engine), and what Tony did to finish the car made it one dynamite rod.

Under that half hood rides a '65 Chevy 327 powerplant, filled with TRW 11-1/2:1 pistons that wear Grant rings. A Corvette 30-30 cam kit works TRW valves that live in the .010 milled head. Intake is via a Holley 780 carburetor atop an Offenhauser tunnel ram manifold. Mallory makes the sparks, and a custom exhaust system with Mitchell mufflers takes care of the fumes.

A custom aluminum firewall was fabricated to allow room for the engine and turbo 400 automatic transmission. Engine and transmission mounts were homemade.

Chassis work includes a dropped '33 Plymouth front axle, Ford spindles and control arms. A '67 Mustang contributed the steering gearbox. Tony made his own steering shaft and U-joint. Stock '33 Plymouth front leaf springs and '57 Chevy rear leafs control the bumps. Volvo front disc brakes and '57 Chevy rear drums do the stopping. The rearend is a '57 Chevy unit with 3.36:1 gearing. The chassis rides on Rocket wheels (7"

Vehicle: 1933 Plymouth Coupe   Owner: Tony Castaneda, Wellington, Colorado

front, 8" rear) all around, shod with radial T/As.

Tony left the body pretty much alone, but an aluminum floor was installed. Front and rear bumpers are '32 Ford pieces and headlights are custom by Dertz, while taillights are '64 Chevy. Imron orange paint was applied, then dressed up with flames and stripes.

Interior stuff includes '73 Pinto bucket seats, upholstered in brown Naugahyde. The dashboard is stock, but Sun gauges have replaced original units. Mustang pedals give Tony's feet what to do, while Pioneer AM/FM stereo cassette and CB keep his ears busy.

So, what do you do with that extra $470 that's burning a hole in your pocket? Take a look at what Tony Castaneda did. Give you any ideas?

SEDUCED '34 PLYMOUTH

After spending years working on street rods belonging to friends, Frederick Pulliam decided it was time he had one of his own. He knew he wanted an early model sedan with suicide doors, something that would enable him to take his family along with him to various shows. It was 1985 before he found what he wanted.

The car is a 1934 Plymouth 2-door sedan PE model. When Frederick got it, the thing was painted what he termed "an extremely ugly shade of forest green." The interior was in shreds. His first move was to get a yellow paint job sprayed on it because he "didn't want to be seen driving anything that was painted that ghastly shade of forest green."

An early priority was installation of a 1976 Chrysler Cordoba steering column. This gave the car a short column with a shift indicator, but it also gave Frederick a MoPar ignition key.

Next step was crafting a dashboard out of 1-inch cherry wood, and then fitting it with gauges from Classic Instruments, ordered through Wabbits Woodworks.

Original front seats were located in Carlisle,

Pennsylvania, and an original rear seat was found in a small backwater town in West Virginia. Jim Conner, owner of American and Foreign Upholstery, covered them (along with a set of Mercedes Benz armrests) in tan cloth. After all the bodywork was completed, Jim finished off the interior in matching tan tones.

The drivetrain consists of a blown Chevy 327 and turbo 400 automatic transmission. A custom-built firewall (made by Frederick) adds sparkle to the engine compartment. The differential is out of a 1966 Chevy II with coil overs. The front suspension was ordered from Independent Chassis in Canada, and Frederick did the installation.

The body was gently massaged and a 1971 Volkswagen sunroof was added to fill the cloth roof. Fenders from Anderson Industries replaced battered originals, and steel running boards were ordered from Buckeye Rubber. Flames were added later by Glendale Custom Auto, and the exhaust system was custom bent by Benny Woo.

After years of working on street rods belonging to friends, finally, Frederick Pulliam has one of his own.

Vehicle: 1934 Plymouth 2-door sedan   Owner: Frederick L. Pulliam, Silver Spring, Maryland

1937 PLYMOUTH

Above- Slick body work includes shaved doors, no bumpers, rolled rear pan, filler panels below the doors and smooth running boards.

Right- The Coyote says it all. Terry Joker's '37 Plymouth is still Under Construction, but a lot of the work has already been done, and a closer look is revealing.

Poised fearlessly on the trunk lid of Terry Joker's 1937 Plymouth is a portrait of the Coyote (of TV's Road Runner cartoon fame), Acme torch in hand, and lettering which accurately describes the car's condition- Under Construction.

It's a fair guess that most of the street rods in America (nay, the world) today are still under construction. Even after they're "finished," they seem to never really be finished because something else always comes along and begs to be installed or modified or played with.

So it goes with Terry's ride. This is an almost totally owner-built car. The only thing that was done in a pro shop (The Hot Rod Shop in Fort Wayne, Indiana) was the rear end and suspension. Terry has done the rest himself.

What we have here is a nice example of a '37 Plymouth with '40 Chevy headlights, Gennie parking lights, tunneled '39 Ford taillights, and smooth running boards. Smooth exterior work includes a filler panel below the doors, rolled rear pan, no bumpers, and smooth side panels on the custom-made (louvered) hood. The car rides on '80 Mirada wheels with knock-offs from Springfield Street Rods. Shaved doors are operated via electric screwmotors from Ball's Hot Rod Parts. In order to keep the dash clean and simple, Terry installed the stereo system in the glove box.

We'd say that's a good start on a car that still Under Construction.

Vehicle: 1937 Plymouth   Owner: Terry Joker, Fort Wayne, Indiana

A set of '39 Ford taillights have been nicely tunneled into the rear fenders.

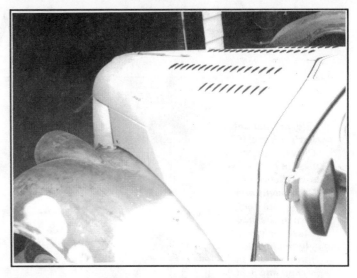

The engine compartment is covered by louvers on the top of the hood, and smooth hood side panels. 1940 Chevrolet headlights have been molded into the front fenders.

Above- Work is progressing up front where the '80 Mirada wheels are surrounded by the Plymouth's big wrap-around fenders. Knock-offs were supplied by Springfield Street Rods.

Right- A nice LeCarra steering wheel attached to a GM tilt column makes life easier on the driver. The stereo system has been installed in the glove box to keep the dash clean and simple.

SHANE'S SWAMP BUGGY

Big, fat and ugly; that's what a 1938 Chrysler Imperial was. In fact, when Shane Gilchrist first thought about restoring this one, he was dissuaded because the car was so ugly in stock form. But after a 3-inch chop and 3-inch channel, plus some other custom tricks, this car looks pretty neat.

You never want to overlook the stuff that lives in a swamp. It may turn out to be some kind of treasure. Shane Gilchrist discovered his 1938 Chrysler Imperial completely overgrown in a swamp near Wynnum on the Queensland coast in Australia. Of course, when Shane first found the car, it wasn't exactly in the condition you see it here. Trees had grown completely through the body, and the bottom 4 inches (including the floor) were shot. But an enterprising hot rodder like Shane can work wonders, especially when the raw materials can be obtained for free.

The components that Shane used in the build-up of his rod are not commonly found in the United States, so some of the names may sound a little strange to our U.S. readers, but the folks down under will recognize them immediately.

To get things started, Shane stripped the body and contemplated the possibilities of building a resto-rod. However, he soon decided that the body style was too ugly to simply restore, and shifted his emphasis to building a custom rod instead. The top was chopped 3 inches. To compensate for the lower profile, the windshield and rear window were laid down. Then, the body was channeled 3 inches to get it down closer to the weeds without a loss of suspension travel.

Rain gutters were filled and the trunk hinges hidden to give the body a smoother appearance. Molded and recessed into the trunk lid is the license plate. Shane made the running boards from sheetmetal and widened the rear fenders 1-1/2 inches. Front fenders and the grille shell were molded into a single piece. The hood was modified so that it can open from either side, or be removed entirely if desired. The stock headlights were replaced by flip-out units filled with Holden Statesman lamps that emerge from the sides of the hood when the sun goes down. Control of the headlights is by cable. All of the car's chrome was removed. The rear bumper was replaced with a shortened and sectioned version of an HQ Holden bumper, and then it was molded into the Chrysler's body.

When all the outside work was completed, Shane had a coat of Chrome Yellow shot over the whole thing and then "Fat Attack" (the car's name) graphics applied.

The interior was trimmed with Front Runner silver cloth. Seating is stock up front but a custom rear bench seat, complete with arm rests, was made. Floor covering is a darker grey loop pile carpeting. The dash is done in yellow to match the car's exterior, and a set of VDO gauges keep Shane in touch with engine functions. The speedometer was a HQ Holden item before it found its new home here. The steering wheel and column is a stock XY Falcon item, directing the Commodore rack and pinion system.

Power comes from a Holden 308 V8 engine which

Vehicle: 1938 Chrysler Imperial   Owner: Shane Gilchrist, Wynnum, Queensland, Australia has been outfittted with twin 465 cfm Holley carburetors on a Cain twin tunnel ram intake manifold. A dual-point distributor provides the spark. All this turns a Celica 5-speed transmission, and finally works its way back to the Jaguar XJS/XJ6 combination rearend and 3.77:1 limited slip gears. Stopping power is derived from 4-wheel disc brakes, a HT Holden dual reservoir master cylinder and VH40 booster.

Tires and wheels are Riken 235x60x14 and Hankook 275x60x15 (front and rear respectively) mounted on a set of CSA Magnum Eliminator 5-slot mags that measure 14x7 and 15x10 respectively.

Shane worked 6-1/2 years and spent $9000 on this project, from digging it out of the swamp to hitting the rod runs. And in all that time, he hasn't encountered another rod quite like this one. Our bet is that he isn't likely to — ever.

Below- Stock headlights were removed and replaced with flip-out units that hide inside the hoodline when not in use. Front bumper was removed and fenders and hood molded into a single piece.

A Holden rear bumper was shortened and sectioned and then molded into the tail of the Chrysler. Rear fenders were widened, and the running boards were fabricated of steel. When the top was chopped, both the windshield and rear glass were laid down rather than being cut.

Left- The swamp did its damage, eating away the bottom 4 inches of the Chrysler, so all that needed to be reconstructed. Here, the car rests on its firewall, giving us a clear view of the new floorpan.

The view from the pavement leaves little room for crawling around. Visible are the Jag rearend and a portion of the X-member. With the car channeled 3 inches, it gets right down to the weeds without losing suspension travel.

The chassis consists of original frame rails with a welded in HT Holden front member. A modified X-member was fabricated to allow fit for the transmission. The rearend consists of a combination of Jaguar XJS and XJ6 pieces. Power is provided by a Holden 308 V8 with a pair of Holley 465 cfm carbs on a twin tunnel ram manifold.

No, this photo hasn't been flopped. That's the way the steering wheel is positioned down under. Simple dash has been adorned with VDO gauges and a speedometer from a Holden. Stock XY Falcon steering wheel and column were employed.

A stock Chrysler front bench seat is combined with a custom-built rear bench (complete with arm rests) for passenger comfort. Upholstered in Front Runner silver cloth and carpeted with a grey loop pile carpet, the interior of Fat Attack is comfy.

ORV ELGIE'S PLYMVETTE

Typical of Elgie's work, many minor modifications add up to a radical rod. The two-piece hood is stock, but vents just forward of the cowl have been filled, as have the bumper-iron holes. The windshield posts were laid back one inch when the top was chopped.

by Geoff Carter   photos by Rich Overstreet, courtesy Hot Line News

To those whose only contact with California hot rodding is through the pages of the west coast magazines, reality may be just a bit shaded. We are here to assure you that many of the cars you see featured are actually built at home, and are driven often. Orv Elgie and his projects are outstanding among that number.

You may find it hard to believe that someone who turns out the sort of machinery he does every three years or so can be doing it in the garage behind his house, with very little specialized equipment, and almost no professional help. Believe us, it's true.

His latest, the '40 "Plymvette" you see here, has wheelcovers machined at Boyd Coddington's shop, an over-the-counter air cleaner and air conditioner brackets from Fat Jack, upholstery work by Collins Trim Shop, a driveshaft built by Jerry's Transmissions, and pinstriping by Billy B. He took the stripped body to Doc's Hot Rod Welding to get the top cut two inches, then finished the welding at home. Everything else was

done solo, unless extra hands were needed. Sometimes he drafted a friend or two who just happened to be standing around, but most often, wife Shirley or son Miles were "volunteered".

Orv stopped in the middle of building this one and spend six months building a new garage, but it's too nice to work in, so he paints all his cars sitting out in the driveway. "Just scatter 'em all out and get the paint going," is how he describes the process.

The wiring he made from scratch, "I just go down and buy a spool of every color I can find and then I start from scratch," he explains.

So, Orv, you must make several test runs around the neighborhood, just to make sure all your ideas are going to work. Right?

Wrong. "I took it down to Palm Springs (about 250-miles round trip) first time I had it out."

There's no way to put a value on experience.

Vehicle: 1940 Plymouth   Owner: Orv Elgie, Norwalk, California

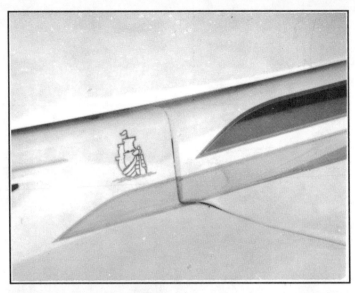

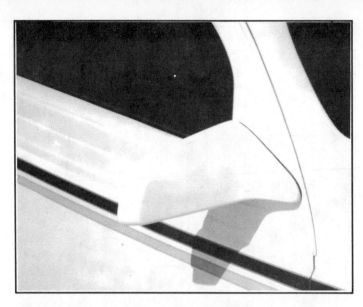

Vanilla paint, accented with plum and peach graphics by Billy B, make this a sundae driver ... groan!

Orv deleted the windwings and added a subtle fillet that mounts '86 Buick electric remote control mirrors.

The taillights are frenched '39 Plymouth, slightly below the original location. The panel below the deck lid is new, filling the gap left when the bumper was removed.

The only non-factory dress-up item on the engine is a Fat Jack air cleaner. Understated and subtle is an Elgie trademark.

Left- Orv is caught in the act of modifying the non-folding 4-door '86 Cadillac Cimmaron seats. He added the side mechanism off an '82 and newer Camaro, then notched the piece of Cimmaron plastic that covers it for a perfect fit.

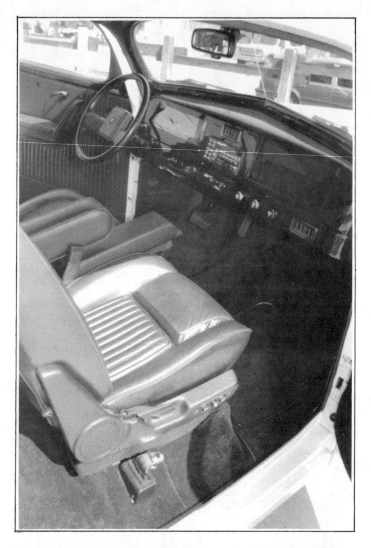

Above- The original dash contains '84 Cutlass instruments and an '87 Trans Am radio. The control knobs — all black with international insignia — come from the Lighthouse in Los Angeles. Orv added a 2-3/4" panel below the dash and made the glovebox door from a piece of aluminum. The latch is a push-to-open/push-to-close cabinet item. The brake and gas pedals are Corvette, and the emergency brake pedal is from an S-10 pickup.

Left- The mechanism for the 6-way power seat is all attached to the seat. The only wiring required is one hot wire and a ground.

The original rear seat, with Cimmaron armrest added, is covered with material from the same '86 Cadillac Cimmaron that donated the front seats, saving hundreds of dollars for new leather trim.

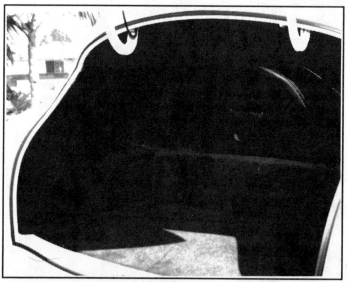

The late-model GM inflatable spare came with jack and tools inside and makes a compact unit. Because of the Z'd chassis and wide wheels, the new floor is five inches higher and three inches narrower than stock.

THE BUILDING OF THE "PLYMVETTE"

Now that you've had a look at Orv's finished car, here's how it all came together. The car is called a "Plymvette" because of the '86 Corvette front suspension cradle/crossmember which is bolted to the frame. The only suspension components welded to the frame are the shock towers.

Orv made new motor mounts because, in the Corvette, the motor is about 2-1/2" lower than he wanted it to be. As he explains, "This thing sits so low I didn't want anything to ever drag."

The rear suspension also unbolts in Corvette style. Orv doesn't believe in reinventing the wheel. "The GM engineers went to so much trouble to engineer everything to fit and to work properly," is the way he looks at it. And it works.

The complete front suspension unbolts a'la '86 Corvette. New motor mounts raise the engine 2-1/2 inches to prevent pan dragging. After everything is tacked together, Orv sends the frame out for stripping and sandblasting to ease welding.

The seven-blade flex fan is off a late Cadillac. It will draw a ton of air at idle, but out on the highway the blades straighten up and run free. According to Orv, you'll never have a cooling problem with it.

The exhaust manifolds are stock ram's horns off a '68-'72 Chevy truck. The left side manifold turns in and back, giving better clearance for the steering.

Notice the heater hose exiting the back of the cylinder head (arrow). Orv eliminates that ugly hose running all the way back from the intake manifold by using the hole that corresponds with the water temperature gauge on the left head. It's already tapped (make sure it's drilled all the way into the water jacket); put a fitting in it and clamp the hose to it.

Orv Z'd the frame five inches by making cardboard patterns of the new section, having them transferred to steel at a friend's metal shop, then welding the pieces together himself. The emergency brake cable is a late-model unit that runs from the pedal to the rear crossmember. There, it attaches to a bellcrank Orv fabricated, eliminating the need for a yoke on the center crossmember, and a long cable to each wheel.

That's the original rear crossmember between the homemade rail sections. The rear suspension unbolts just like in the '86 Corvette.

Orv puts the '78 and newer Cadillac Level-Ride system (arrow) in all his street rods. A solid link connects it to the suspension. When an extra load lowers the chassis, its electric sensing device starts the pump, inflating the air shocks. With the body on, it would ride in the middle position.

Orv uses all rubber-isolated factory-type exhaust mounts (arrow) so it's drone doesn't transfer inside the car. Welding the brackets to the pipes gives the whole system a much cleaner look than the typical hanging clamp arrangement. Notice that the exhaust is inside the frame. If your car is low, run the exhaust as high as you can or you'll drag it. Also, don't forget to make your transmission-mounting crossmember removable so you don't have to pull the engine to get at the transmission.

Far Left- This is the Level-Ride pump (arrow). If you build a car or truck with enough spring to handle a load in back, it will ride like a log when you're alone. With the Level-Ride you put in a spring that's going to ride nice, then when you get three or four people in back the air shocks do the work automatically. Also notice the transmission cooler, located away from the heat of the radiator.

Left- After mounting the Sankyo air conditioning compressor on Fat Jack brackets, Orv made an idler (arrow) from a timing belt tensioner off a late-model Ford OHC 4-cylinder.

"...BUT NOT <u>EVERY</u> STREET!"

1941 DODGE

by Dan Allison

The first day at its new home, the '41 Dodge 3-window business coupe looked to be in surprisingly good condition, with all pieces present and accounted for. For $700, this wasn't a bad purchase.

Some folks would never know from looking at a 1941 Dodge 3-window business coupe that it could make a neat rod. But then Dan Allison isn't just "some folks". Actually, the real credit for this car becoming what it is today belongs to Dan's wife, Anne. She's the one who took an initial interest in the car and urged Dan to consider it for his project. But we'll let Dan tell the story.

"In May of 1986, I had spotted four cars sitting on a major highway in the Spokane Valley. A '67 Nova, a '49 Chevy coupe, a '69 Fairlane hardtop, and the ugliest, longest-trunked coupe I had ever seen — a '41 Dodge 3-window business coupe.

"After work one night, I took my wife, Anne, over to look at the '49 Chevy coupe. Instead, she started looking at the Dodge. I wouldn't even look at it. We went back a second night to look at the Chevy again. This time, she pressured me to look at the '41 Dodge. I couldn't believe how odd looking it was. After a closer check, I noticed it was in extremely good shape, no rust and very complete except for motor and transmission. It only had 62,000 miles on it.

"My wife was right, it was ugly, odd and the first one I'd ever seen. So, I decided to check into it. It took 2 months to locate the owner. He wanted $1200. I offered him $500. He was offended and that looked like the end

of it. I went out and bought another car — a '50 Olds 2-door sedan.

"After about a month had passed, he called me on a Sunday night and told me he would sell the car for $700. I had 15 minutes to get to his house before he left for jail. If I wanted the car, it had to be right now. I went right over and bought it. Two weeks later, I brought it home.

"I lined up a motor and transmission and got it running. We decided to build the car stock except for wheels and tires. A good friend of mine, Phil Cunningham, is an excellent body and paint man. We trade out work all the time. I'm a sheetmetal worker who has done a few drag car interiors in aluminum and stainless steel. So, we worked out a trade.

"As we started taking everything off for paint, the ugly Dodge started to look a little better. I decided to heck with stock! Let's shave it, louver it, lower it, and fill in the cavity below the trunk where the bumper had been.

"After the Deltron special mix red paint job, the Ken Fuher fine line brush pin stripes, and leaving off the

Vehicle: '41 Dodge 3-window Business Coupe   *Owner: Dan Allison, Spokane, Washington*

As the car was stripped, it started to look a little better, although the long, humpy rear deck and tiny turret top give it a unique visual quality (that's how we say "ugly" in a nice way).

Phil Cunningham did the body and paint-prep work in his shop. Note that the trunk has already received one of its stainless steel walls. These business coupes featured small interior area because passenger space wasn't a consideration, and large trunks to allow salesmen to carry a load of samples.

After removing the rear bumper, a custom trunk apron was fabricated, complete with a sunken licence plate area. Taillight openings have been made to accept Yugo side marker lights to serve as stoplights.

After installation of the trunk apron, the rear of the Dodge tucks under nicely at the back and flows smoothly around from the fenders resulting in a natural body line that looks as if it had come that way from the factory. The Yugo side marker lights look perfectly at home as taillights for the Dodge.

bumpers, it was a unique street rod.

"We drove it for a year with the six and fluid drive. It was fun but very slow. In November of 1988, I jerked the six out and put in a warmed '74 Dodge 360 V8 and a rebuilt 727 Torqueflite, a bigger radiator by Jerry's Radiator of Spokane, KMC wheels, '87 Mazda truck A/C and heater, a '40 Plymouth dashboard that I cut the center out of and put in the A/C controls. I also installed an Alpine stereo, Pentron gauges, tach and speedometer, along with a '78 Dodge tilt steering column and wheel.

"In the engine compartment, I took out all the inner fender aprons and cut the center of the firewall out to accept the 360. Everything I put back in is stainless steel with a brushed finish. I couldn't find an air filter

housing that would match the rest of the stainless steel, so I built one.

"The gas tank is 16-gauge stainless, and the trunk is 22-gauge stainless. The car has a Mustang steering box so as to clear the exhaust manifolds. A Chevy V8 would have dropped right in, but it's not a Chevy car — it's a Mopar, so a Mopar V8 was the only choice.

"Pricewise, I'm into the car from the time I bought it and including the purchase price, tax, licence, everything — $4700. It's a budget rod. In area car shows, I have grabbed four First Place trophies, and that was when it was a six and fluid drive.

"It's fun and different and I wouldn't trade it for any of the current fad rods."

The hood received a louver job, being ventilated 102 times by Gary Harms. Note the trim clip holes along the lower edge of the hood, indicating that the finished car is intended to retain its trim.

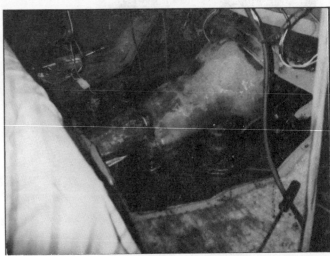

When it was time to replace the fluid drive, a 727 Torqueflite was chosen. Some firewall work was necessary to allow the transmission and V8 engine to fit, and the transmission was rebuilt before final installation.

With the entire front of the body removed, plans could be made for shoehorning a big Dodge V8 into the under-hood area. A Chevy engine would have just dropped in, but this is a Mopar, and a Mopar V8 was what Dan wanted, even if it meant more work to make it fit.

Special motor mounts were fabricated to support the 1974 Dodge 360 cid V8. In addition to the engine mounts, Dan had to make a special transmission crossmember to hold things up out back.

The engine was trial-fit to see if any more modifications had to be made to the under-hood area. Once everything was properly positioned, the engine came back out for rebuilding. Then an Edelbrock intake system and cam went in to warm things up a bit.

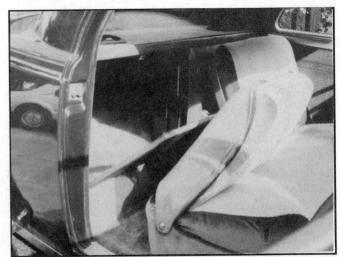

With no rear seat, a storage compartment is located behind the front seat and concealed by the package deck and a compartment door. Between the compartment and the cavernous trunk, Dan and Anne can haul a lot of trophies home from the car shows.

178

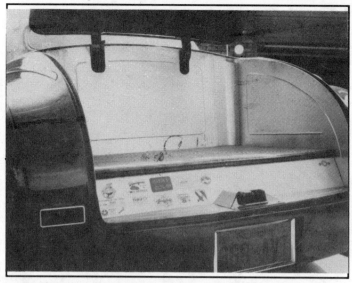

Being a sheetmetal man has its benefits. Stainless steel was used for fabricating the trunk walls and floor. Carpeting was then installed on the floor.

A 1940 Plymouth dashboard was installed. Dan cut out the center section so he could install the heater and air conditioner controls. Climate control is handled by an '87 Mazda heater/air conditioner unit. The tilt steering column is out of a '78 Chrysler Cordoba.

Dressed up with a custom-made brushed stainless steel air filter housing to match the firewall and fender apron material, the Dodge 360 engine is a tight fit. Cooling is handled by a copper "Life Liner" radiator.

No, the stock '41 Dodge didn't sit quite this low to the ground. Front suspension was lowered 4 inches, and the rear was brought down 2-1/2 inches. KMC wheels are a nice touch on this car.

TEX'S 48

Tex Smith here, talking about a 1948 Chrysler 7-passenger sedan I built as a genuine hot rod in 1974. Not at all in agreement with the emerging idea that hot rods had to be 1948 or older manufacture, I was looking for something to build (for the family with 4 kids), when I spotted this car in Montana. It had been one of 8 special VIP cars used by Yellowstone Park. Anyway, I worked on it, got it running, and drove to California. Then a few months before the '74 Street Rod Nats in St. Paul, I started an updating program.

The body was in excellent condition, so it got some slight massaging and a 1971 Ford maroon paint job. Stock brakes were rebuilt, and wide white tires installed. The interior was completely redone in Cadillac velour-type material, similar to the stock motif.

The six-cylinder engine was removed and a rebuilt 1954 version installed, complete with an Edmunds finned aluminum head found at a swap meet. This upped compression, and helped me claim that this was a hot rod because it had a finned head and was pre-1949! The car had come originally with a standard clutch and 4.30:1 rearend gears because of the mountains of Yellowstone. We added a Plymouth overdrive to the trans, which dropped the final gear ratio to a bit over 3, which allows the car to hum along at 75 mph at very low engine rpm.

This was one of the finest rods I've ever had, when considered as a road car. Skip Readio in the Boston area now has the car, and uses it for long-distance cruising same as I did. It is not uncommon to get 21 mpg from the car. Yes, it can get a late model MoPar OHV engine, and better brakes/steering. But then a lot of the original charm would be lost. Besides, everywhere the car goes, it is considered a hot rod rather than a restoration.

Vehicle: 1948 Chrysler 7-passenger sedan   Owner: Tex Smith

'50 CHRYSLER LIMO

by John Lee

Chrysler established itself in the luxury car field early in its history. The first Imperial seven-passenger sedans and limousines appeared in 1926, the company's third year of production. Seven- and eight-passenger models on extended wheelbases were in the Chrysler line all the way through the first half of the '60s, when Crown Imperials were custom-built by Ghia of Italy. At over $18,000 a copy, production was fewer than a dozen a year, and Chrysler abandoned the market for a few years. Then, in the early '80s, with the advent of front-wheel-drive, long wheelbase Executive sedans and limousines returned to the line.

Except for an occasional maverick like Tex Smith, no one has paid any attention to these huge and heavy cruisers as rodding material. We do remember seeing one in the '60s being put to good use as a combination tow vehicle for a drag car and Pullman sleeper for the two-man crew.

Now, Mike Houck of Independence, Kansas knew it was going to take something pretty special to keep his wife happy going to car cruises with him. See, Dawn's daddy is Gary Mundy, and she'd been riding in a variety of his custom creations throughout her young life. When Mike found a '50 Chrysler limousine for a mere $400, he figured with the right combination of modification it could be a ride they'd both enjoy.

With dad-in-law Mundy's assistance, the first order of business was to get the land yacht down out of the wind with a 6-1/2-inch top chop. The front portion was cut out ala town car with removable tinted Lexan T-tops for weather protection. The rest of the top was eventually padded and covered with silver vinyl.

Headlight doors from a '76 Cordoba tunnel the headlight lenses, with dual turn signal lenses tunneled below. All extraneous chrome trim was removed and all four doors converted to electric solenoid operation.

Vehicle: 1950 Chrysler Limo   Owner: Mike and Dawn Houck, Independence, Kansas

An exposed spare tire carrier and extended rear bumper add a classic touch. The fenders were extended with '55 Chevy taillight housings and Lee Plastics lenses. Frenched housings were built for triple-cap lakes pipes and a power antenna.

Dave Bellm at Cherry Body Shop in Independence sprayed the limo in candy apple red urethane over a charcoal base, with underlaid flames. John Freeman added lavender and coral pinstriping. TruSpoke wire wheels and Sears wide whitewalls are right in character.

The cavernous interior has room for an entire entertainment center with 9-inch TV, VCR, phone, wet bar with an overhead wine rack, stereo and built-in CB. If she wants to get away and relax with a little TV, Dawn can shut off the rear compartment with a power divider window. The

chauffeurs compartment is anything but utilitarian, with under-dash air conditioning, '68 Cad tilt-tele steering, '74 Nova pedals and a console flanked by captain's chairs from a van. Dave Shepard upholstered everything in silver and burgundy velour.

Weighing in at over two tons, the custom limo's underpinnings consist of a '74 Nova front clip spliced to the stock frame with hydraulic lifts at all four corners for adjustable ride height. Power comes from an internally stock 350 Chevy with a 600 cfm Holley four-barrel, Weiand manifold and Mallory ignition. The transmission is a 350 Turbo, connected to a '75 Monte Carlo rear with 3.88:1 gears.

Mike's goal was to build a car the likes of which he'd likely never see. Needless to say, so far he hasn't.

183

1951 CHRYSLER

by Al Drake

Buzz and JoAnn Magnuson are long-time Chevy people and currently own a pair of '41 coupes, one restored and the other a street rod. But when Buzz saw a 1951 Chrysler New Yorker hardtop near his hometown of Richfield, Minnesota, he became fascinated with it. It was a big boat of a car, with huge expanses of metal and loads of chrome, but Buzz instantly saw the possibilities for a very different street machine.

After purchasing it, Buzz pulled out the original running gear and turned the car over to fellow MSRA member, Carl Zechbauer, who cut away the front part of the frame and welded in a '72 Chevy Nova subframe. He also installed the rear end, transmission and 400 cu.in. V8 from a '74 Chrysler. These changes dropped the car and made it into a modern, reliable runner. Many owners would have stopped there and called the car a resto-rod. Not Buzz. He wanted to bring out the beauty of those expanses of metal, and so he had Carl remove the boat anchor emblems on the hood and trunk, the stone guards and the wide chrome strips around the windshield, and fill in the holes. The door handles were removed, and the doors now open via an electric set-up Buzz made using heavy-duty solenoids from an airplane. The trunk opens via an electric switch borrowed from the trunk of a 1983 Chrysler.

That's one hulluva hood! Looks better without the anchor-shaped emblem and big bird. Thick chrome around the windshield is also gone. Entire grille and front sheetmetal from Windsor model were adapted to the New Yorker, resulting in a cleaner appearance.

Buzz still wasn't satisfied with the car as a mild custom, so he had it chopped. The operation was simple. The top was removed, the windshield and rear corners cut 3 inches, the top was moved forward 3 inches and welded in place. The rear window was then slanted to meet the new roofline. The center portion of the rear window is stock glass and the two end pieces were shaped from 1/4-inch Lexan plastic.

The most difficult part of getting this boat out of dry dock was one of those subtle changes that most of us never notice. The New Yorker front end is very busy, with chrome bars, large parking lights and a vertical center bar with a big medallion. Rather than try to clean up the front end, Carl replaced it with one from a Windsor model. This required a great deal of shaping and fitting, but the clean two-bar grille, using stock back-up lights for parking lights, is aesthetically perfect on this massive machine.

Another problem was what to do with the wheels. One day, Buzz found a 1980 Cordoba wheel cover in the street and decided this was what he wanted on his

Vehicle: 1951 Chrysler New Yorker   Owner: Buzz and JoAnn Magnuson, Richfield, Minnesota

Chrysler. For weeks, he searched in junkyards without success, and finally he had to buy three new wheel covers at $60 apiece. However, they look more pleasing on the car than mag, spoke or even stock wheels would.

The entire car was rewired and updated with a 12-volt system. Then it was driven to the paint shop and shot with two gallons of black acrylic enamel which emphasized the ripple-free metal work.

Chryslers of the '50s are known for their well-appointed interiors, and this top-of-the-line New Yorker is beautiful. Everything was left stock except for the '69 Buick tilt wheel. The upholstery was recovered with '85 GM burgundy material by another MSRA member,

Mark Milbrandt.

Now, when Buzz and JoAnn head for the rod runs, the Chevy coupes are left at home because the big boat is so comfortable, reliable and unique. They chart a course for every rod run, near and far, and the voyage is always smooth sailing.

Below- Top has been chopped 3 inches, moved forward 3 inches, and the rear window slanted to meet the new roofline. Although cut was moderate, the result is dramatic.

Bottom- Chryslers of the '40s and '50s were busy with chrome, especially the '51 models with the first V8. Removal of trunk trim, door handles and stone guards cleans up the car and emphasizes its good lines.

1957 DESOTO FIREFLITE

Custom cars are, by nature, unique. Each has its own personality, borrowed from the builder or owner who designed it. But some customs are more unique than others by their very rarity, and here's a prime example. How many 1957 DeSoto customs have you seen lately? In the many years that George Kasternakis has owned this one, he has never seen another.

This '57 FireFlite was chopped 6-1/2 inches and lowered 4 inches, which made an already long body style appear to grow by a mile. The car was dechromed, although there are hints of brightwork remaining in just the right places. A '78 Monza hatchback rear window was installed, taillights were frenched and exhaust tips were removed from the rear bumper. The bright-shiny consists of an '88 GM garnet metallic red with candy magenta scallops, all done in lacquer with an enamel clearcoat.

Interior comfort is provided by a set of '82 Olds Cutlass reclining bucket seats, separated by a homemade console. The rear seat is a cut-down version of a rear bench out of the same Olds. Additional creature comforts include air conditioning, power windows, power brakes, power steering, cruise control, AM/FM stereo cassette, and a power trunk release. All the gauges are original, and they all work perfectly.

Mechanical stuff includes a 1973 Chevy 400 small block that has been treated to the addition of a Crane cam. A turbo 400 automatic transmission takes care of gearing. The rear end is out of a late-model Plymouth, and front disc brakes and spindles (which bolted right on) are from a '77 Dodge Monaco.

All the mechanical, body, paint and interior work was done over the course of two years by owner Kasternakis, who is obviously a very talented guy. Special thanks goes to George's dad, Mike for help and encouragement through this as well as a long list of previous projects.

The DeSoto never fails to draw a crowd and brings home a fair share of trophies. It also draws a lot of strange comments, like: "What is it?" and, "I think it's a Chevy with fins." According to George, most young people don't know what DeSoto is, never mind what it looks like now that he has had his way with it. And they'll probably never see another.

Vehicle: 1957 DeSoto FireFlite   Owner: George Kasternakis, Freehold, New Jersey

1958 CHRYSLER CUSTOM

by Dave Hill

To anyone who has been into the custom car hobby for more than a few years, Paul Glavaris' '58 Chrysler sled is nothing new. Built years ago by Hall of Fame member Gene Winfield, the car has been seen many times. The fact that it remains unchanged, in as-built condition, yet has never been in extended storage, is what is news. The car is a classic, pure and simple. It was styled right, painted right, and most important of all it was built right. It has stood the test of time.

Paul is a master stonemason from San Jose, California. His brickwork is designed to be ageless, and is built to last. When he and his wife Donna decided to join the custom movement a few years ago, they knew they needed a car that met the same standards. They succeeded. The Chrysler still turns heads everywhere it goes, and it takes its share of awards at the many runs they attend each year.

Take a long look at this car. Study its lines, details, paint color and style. The grille may be a bit garish for today's look, but that was very much the vogue in the '60s. The rest of the car is as pure, clean and simple as you can get. For a car as big and overdone as a late '50s Chrysler, that is one heck of an accomplishment.

This car was lowered by easing off the torsion bars up front and installing lowering blocks in the rear. Same-size tires and wheels were used both front and rear — True Spoke knock-off 15x7 wheels and Vogue 6.70x15 tires.

The top was chopped 3-1/2 inches and a '70 Dodge Challenger rear window installed. Up front, the hood was nosed, and headlights are from a '72 Oldsmobile Delta 88. Winfield handmade the grille using different size bullets, and the front fenders were extended. Rear treatment is a combination of '57 Chrysler with 2-inch extension and 2-inch french with back-up lights eliminated. The whole car was dechromed, and you'll notice that the door handles were removed. Gene painted the car in lacquer using white pearl, gold and tangerine pearl blend.

Interior work was done by Skip Dumont of Concord, California. The upholstery is white pearl Naugahyde, and carpet is '77 Cadillac Eldorado black. Seats are cut-down Capri, and the steering wheel is a LeCarra model. A Panasonic custom sound system provides the tunes.

Under the hood lives a 300-horsepower 392 hemi with 4-barrel induction. Chrome goodies dress up every conceivable thing in the engine compartment. A push-button Torqueflite takes care of gearing, and glass-pack mufflers take care of exhaust notes.

According to Paul, his future plans for the car are, "As long as the paint holds up, leave it alone." Way to go, Paul.

Vehicle: 1958 Chrysler New Yorker 2-door hardtop   Owner: Paul Glavaris, San Jose, California

1960 DODGE

by Buster Congdon

Whenever I build a car, I try to hit on a certain theme. In this case, I wanted people to see what this car would look like if it was customized in 1960. Another priority was to build it on a low budget. I didn't want to dump a lot of money into a car that might not be too desirable. With a lot of support from my wife, Shannon, I got started.

The whole car was stripped to the bare metal and all the rust holes were repaired. All body seams were filled, the moldings on the sides were removed and the holes welded. Door handles were taken off and the doors smoothed. Now, doors open with screw motors, with the switch hidden under the windshield on each side. I just wave a magnet past a certain point on the windshield and the door opens. This kit is sold by Ball's Hot Rod from Syracuse, New York, and works excellent.

Even though the roof was chopped 3-1/2 inches, the front and rear windows were not cut. The windshield is sunk 3-1/2 inches. I cut the cowl out and rebuilt it to fit the windshield at this point. This allowed me to mount the door opening switch in the sunk area of the windshield. The windshield automatically moved back and allowed me to drop the wiper motor and sink the wipers below the hood line. The cowl panel is molded to the fenders and the old wiper holes welded and smoothed.

The dash was removed and cut down to fit the windshield at the 3-1/2-inch point. Then it was taken apart, stripped to bare metal, and refinished, assembled and put back into position. Then all the garnish moldings were cut down and refitted. Quarter window garnish moldings were a problem, but I wanted them to look original. They couldn't be welded because they were white metal. After trying many different welding techniques, I made part of them out of fiberglass and that worked very well.

The hood was nosed and has polished aluminum inserts urethaned to the underside to serve as mirrors to reflect the image of the engine. Anything left on the car that was chrome was replated and installed last. The whole car was primed with a self-etching primer and then primed with Ditzler's K 200 and block sanded. Keeping in mind that this is a low-dollar car, I thought why not find a nice late model interior and fit it to the car? In my back yard was a 2-door 1984 Oldsmobile 88 that was wrecked. I had purchased the car for $150 to get the motor for another car. I took the complete interior out, one piece at a time as I needed it. I took the upholstery off the door panels and quarters in the Dodge and made new backup panels and cut them to fit the Dodge panels. I then made some inserts to cover the armrest holes. Visors from the Olds fit like they

Vehicle: 1960 Dodge Seneca Dart   Owner: Buster Congdon, Colchester, Connecticut

190

were made for the Dodge. Next, I stole the headliner from the Olds, and made side panels to fill openings on both sides. The rear seats fit almost perfectly, with only minor modifications needed. The floor was lowered in the front to fit the front seats. Carpet was bought for $69 and fit like a glove.

I wanted the dash to look stock, but I wanted a cassette radio, so it's in the glove box, which was modified to accommodate the radio.

The next step was the drivetrain. To me, a good parts car is like gold, if you have the correct one. Out back was a '77 Plymouth Fury with a good drivetrain, so I pulled the motor and transmission out, installed various new parts, painted it and put on an aluminum intake manifold with 600-cfm Holley. After this, I painted and detailed the engine compartment and bolted the motor in. The only problem was the right front motor mount, which was bolted with 2 bolts instead of 3, so I had to make a spacer and run a longer bolt through the block and the mount.

The transmission crossmember was fabricated with parts from both the Dart and Fury. The rear end is also from the Fury. I just cut off the spring pads from the Fury axle and welded the Dart units in the appropriate spots and bolted the axle up with 4-inch lowering blocks. The driveshaft came from a '71 Plymouth Satellite 4-door sedan, and fit perfectly.

The original transmission didn't have Park in it, which was another reason for the change in drivetrain, but I couldn't use the push-button shifter (this broke my heart), and I didn't want a shifter on the floor, so I mounted a ratchet cable shifter under the dash on the left side of the steering column. This works well and gets the job done.

Brakes consist of rear drums from the Fury, and front discs and spindles from a '76 Dodge Aspen. With the proportioning valve, they bolted right in. A '72 Duster power brake unit, donated by a friend, also bolted right in.

Finally, the paint job. Hues are Ditzler radiance colors — the main color being a bluish candy purple, and the scallops are pink blended into lavender. Then everything is clear-coated.

This car was fun to build because it was different, and everyone had strange opinions while it was being built. But you know, they were still interested in what was being done. And that's what it's all about.

1963 PLYMOUTH

Grandma never had it so good! And this particular Plymouth finally got the chance to live the life it was made for. With blacked-out grille and bumper, the Belvedere looks the part. And with the blown '76 Wedge 440, it can play the part as well.

1963 was a wonderful year for Chrysler Corporation cars. The MoPar name dominated the strip, and it also dominated the hearts of some who were standing on the sidelines nurturing dreams of someday owning one of those muscle machines.

Some of us do more than just dream. Tom Peterson is one who knows how to turn his dreams into reality. Earlier in this book, you've seen Tom's '29 Dodge resto-rod, so you have a clue as to the quality of work he does. Driven by his dream, Tom was suddenly confronted by the reality of a clean one-owner grandma-driven pink '63 Dodge Belvedere up for sale right in his hometown. He dove into this project with all the enthusiasm of a youth who has been forced to wait too long for his go-fast car.

But take a look at the lead photo. Does that look like a grandma-driven Plymouth to you? If it does, I want to meet your grandma! Actually, there is little resemblance between this blown pro-streeter and the $2500 plain Jane Belvedere that Tom originally bought. Four months of dedicated garage work and $9500 did a lot to change the personality of this car.

In fact, folks around the neighborhood can hardly believe this is the same car Tom started with. When he drives past, exhaust system rumbling, blower scoop shaking, people smile and wave and then they turn to each other and whisper. As for Tom, he doesn't care what people think; this is his dream come true.

Vehicle: 1963 Plymouth Belvedere   Owner: Tom Peterson, Brigham City, Utah

Well, grandma, look what's under the hood. Tom built this blueprinted engine to be very streetable, with 7.5:1 TRW pistons in .030" overbore cylinders, a Sig Erson cam and hydraulic lifters. Twin Holley 750 carbs rest atop the polished GMC blower, which packs the atmosphere down through a BDS intake manifold. Power is routed through a '76 Torqueflite that has been set up for full manual shifting. A B&M Super Hole Shot high-stall torque converter gets the engine up in the horsepower band for quick get-aways.

With enough torque to almost spin the motor beneath the hood when the throttle is mashed hard, Tom installed a limiting chain to keep the engine from tearing loose from the motor mounts.

Front disc brakes came out of a '73 Plymouth Satellite. The stock '63 spindle bolts were removed from the spindle upright, and the later model spindle bolts dropped in place. The disc brake installation was quick and easy. Start to finish, the entire car was built in only 4 months.

Inside is strictly business, with the diagonal leg of the roll cage splitting the difference between the Ford Fairmont front bucket seats. The dash-mounted Mallory tachometer informs Tom of upcoming shift points, and the B&M shifter is linked to a manual-only Torqueflite for precision shift control.

A peek underneath reveals the header-fed exhaust system, including a set of FloMaster Pro Street mufflers. These mufflers do a surprisingly good job of keeping the noise level down while providing excellent exhaust flow characteristics.

Left- Currie built the Ford 9-inch rear axle (narrower to accommodate the fat rear tires) and a 4.11:1 ratio gets the car off the line quickly. Spring perches had to be moved to align with the new location of the springs (shown here).

Fat tires need a place to live, so the fenderwells were widened substantially, as can be detected by glancing inside the trunk. Tom has also located his battery in the trunk, leaving more room under the hood for other goodies.

POTENT POLARA

by John Lee   photos by John and Damon Lee

When most of his friends are driving Camaros, Mustangs and late model four-bangers, why would 18 year old Jay Hull want to build an "old" '64 Dodge Polara 500?

'Cause his dad wouldn't let him drive <u>his</u> '64 Polara 500 Max-Wedge 426 four-speed!

The Max-Wedge was about the hottest thing on the drag strip and the street when it was new. A couple years later Chrysler Corporation bored the 426 out to 440 cubic inches, and except for the expensive and exotic 426 hemi, that became the basis for the company's high-performance and big car powerplants for more than a decade.

Jay and his dad, John, decided a moderately built 440 would be the way to go for what is primarily a street driven car.

A '72 Imperial block was chosen as the basis, as it came stock with a forged steel crank. Clover Auto Supply of Lincoln, Nebraska balanced the crank and bored the block .030-in. Then TRW forged aluminum pistons boasting 10.5:1 compression were installed with TRW rings. Stock rods were magnafluxed, shot peened and polished.

Charles Spanel of Capital City Auto Recyclers treated the stock valves to a three angle grind and installed them with bronze guides into heads milled .015-in. and polished. The MoPar Performance cam is described as "the hairiest hydraulic-lifter cam available." It offers .509-in. lift, 292 degrees duration and 76 degrees of overlap. Double Crane valve springs are used.

Induction is by way of a 750-cfm. Edelbrock four-barrel that's essentially a remake of the venerable Carter AFB. It's bolted to a Holley Street Dominator manifold. Spark is furnished by an electronic ignition conversion kit from MoPar Performance. Hedman headers funnel gases to a 2-1/2" dual exhaust system with turbo mufflers, custom built by Exhaust Pros of Lincoln.

Chrome valve covers and air cleaner dress up the engine's top side, while a torque strap helps stabilize it. The stock radiator provides cooling. MoPar expert Keith Brown of Lincoln is credited with "expert advice" on the mechanical build-up.

A Hurst Quarter-Stick directs gear changes in a 727 Torqueflite fitted with a B&M shift kit that includes a manual shift valve body. Final drive is through 8-3/4" Sure-Grip rear end from a '65 Coronet, containing

Vehicle: 1964 Dodge Polara   Owner: Jay Hull, Lincoln, Nebraska

4.10:1 gears. To provide clearance under the fenders for wide wheels, CT Engine & Chassis of Fremont, Nebraska used a MoPar Performance kit to move the leaf springs inboard three inches on each side. When none of the driveshafts they had around would stretch far enough, Jay and John had Lincoln Radiator custom build one with Spicer U-joints. Inline Suspension rebuilt the front end.

Weld Drag Lite wheels are 10x15 in the rear mounting Mickey Thompson S/S L60x15 rubber with 12" tread, and 5x15 in front with P215-70R15 BFG radials. Stock drum brakes are run at both ends, along with manual steering and air shocks in the rear.

Dodge built 18,400 Polara 500s for '64, mostly two-door hardtops with some convertibles. The sporty 500 line featured standard bucket seat and console interior and special swirl-pattern side trim inserts. Except for removing a couple of emblems and slightly enlarging the rear wheel openings for tire clearance, Jay left the rare body and trim intact.

Mike's Body Shop replaced rusted quarter panels with solid ones and straightened the body to perfection before coating it in Daytona Blue Dupont Centura enamel. An Auto Meter tach on the steering column, Stewart-Warner gauges in the dash and a fuel pressure gauge on the hood keep track of engine functions. Interior renovation is next on Jay's agenda.

Excellent rodding prospects, '60s Dodges and their stable mate Plymouths are still quite readily available. Jay's Polara, not too rough and with an original 318 in the engine bay, set him back only $100. And they're easy to modify, especially with factory-backed hop-up equipment from MoPar Performance.

SIX-PACK RUNNER
Plymouth's Factory Hot Rod

by John Lee

In 1968, Plymouth pulled a sneak attack on the competition with introduction of the Road Runner and, in the same stroke, established a new class of musclecar — the econo-supercar. For a total outlay of $2,913 you got a stylish intermediate coupe with a potent 335-horsepower 383 V8, four-on-the-floor transmission, 8-3/4 inch rear end, big brakes, heavy-duty suspension and wide-oval tires.

Over 44,000 people thought that was a neat deal in '68, and the car that was inspired by a Warner Brothers cartoon character was off and running.

In their test, Hot Rod Magazine coaxed 98 miles per hour in the quarter mile with an e.t. of 14.74 seconds out of one of the first production models. They predicted Road Runners would be turning 103 in the 14.30's before the year was out. That would be enough for most buyers, but those willing to shell out a little more long green could move up to a 375-horsepower 440 or even a mighty 425-horse 426 hemi.

First offered only as a pillared coupe with flip-out rear quarter windows, the original Road Runner was joined in the spring by a two-door hardtop model. As it returned for its second year in 1969, a convertible was also added, but by the end of the model run it had accounted for only 2,128 sales.

A new option for 1969, with which our feature car is equipped, was the 440 6-barrel, also known as the Super Commando. A trio of Holley 2-barrel carbs mounted on an Edelbrock manifold were good for another 15 horses, kicking the advertised output up to 390. While Road Runner markings had been fairly subtle in the beginning, the Super Commando was outfitted with a removable fiberglass hood with a huge air scoop, all finished in matte black that shouted "performance" in no uncertain terms.

A 4-speed was standard, and normal rear gears were 3.55:1 with lower ratios optional.

The yellow '69 Road Runner coupe Jim Kraus of Plattsmouth, Nebraska found parked in a driveway had been stored for 10 years and showed a total of only 27,000 miles. The body was in great shape, needing only a repaint, which Jim had done in 10 coats of

Vehicle: 1969 Plymouth Road Runner Coupe   *Owner: Jim Kraus, Plattsworth, Nebraska*

Plymouth Road Runner is a factory hot rod of the first order, and it displays only enough muscle outwardly to let everybody know that serious horsepower lives under the hood.

lacquer. The black vinyl top and interior are all original, and a Kenwood stereo has been installed.

During an overhaul to be certain everything was the best it could be, the 440 was given a clean-up bore job and the whole assembly was balanced and blueprinted. Holley aluminum valve covers were added for dress-up. A Hurst shifter replaced the rather anemic factory stick. Jim also upgraded the rolling stock with Cragar SS wheels and Goodyear Eagle ST radials.

While the coupe outsold the hardtop by 14,000 units in 1968, the reverse was true for 1969. A total of 33,743 coupes were sold, up 4,500 from the previous year. Hardtop sales jumped from 15,359 in its short first year of production to 48,549 for the second year.

The days of the $3,000 super car are long gone, but with one as near new as this, Jim Kraus doesn't have any trouble remembering them.

Left- A new option in '69 was the 440 six-pack, also known as the Super Commando. One way to recognize it is the flat-black hood with functional scoop, complete with 440 6-bbl decal on the side. It fairly shouts "performance".

Below- No-nonsense taillights were intended to be the only thing seen by the competition. Dual exhaust and the words Road Runner are performance tip-offs. Note the little road runner decal centered on the rear of the trunk lid.

One of the optional powerplants is the 375-horsepower 440 cubic inch V8. Equipped with a trio of 2-barrel carburetors, this became know as the 440 six-pack. Holley valve covers dress up this particular engine.

A set of Cragar SS wheels and Goodyear Eagle ST radials deliver traction to the ground with high-performance style befitting a factory hot rod.

Black vinyl interior is all stock, including the factory four-on-the-floor. Only a Kenwood stereo system has been installed to upgrade the tunes department.

1970 DODGE CORONET

Ray Brady is a MoPar man through and through. It was only during a teenage lapse in judgement that he strayed from the True Way and ended up with a '47 Chevy coupe as his first car. But, when a kid is 16 years old, he doesn't really care what his first car is. So, Ray, you are forgiven.

Since that time, Ray has had a '52 Plymouth, a '55 Plymouth, a '65 Dodge Coronet 500, '68 Dart GTS, '70 Dodge Coronet hardtop, and now a '70 Dodge Coronet coupe. In all these years, Ray has always personalized his vehicles so that they aren't just another red car. In this case, he went the custom low-rider route.

When Ray started on this project, he researched how many '70 Dodge Coronet coupes had been built. In 1970, the coupe was the lowest production model of the Coronet series, with a total production of only 2978 units. Ray's was number 907 off the line. Knowing that there weren't very many of this model to begin with, and having put his personal touch on this one, Ray is confident that he will never run into another coupe exactly like his.

The car has been lowered 4 inches by turning down the torsion bars in the front and installing lowering blocks in the rear. All body seams have been welded and filled. The front features a handmade bar grill, while the rear sports '59 Cadillac taillights mounted in handmade buckets.

On the hood are 192 louvers, and under the hood is a stock slant six with a pair of Holleys on an Offenhauser intake manifold. Exhaust is handled by a set of Clifford Research headers and 2-1/4" pipes.

Custom exterior accessories include dummy spots, peep mirrors, lakes pipes and Moon discs. Sikkens paint is white with blue scallops. On the inside, blue and white roll and pleat interior gives comfort to passengers. A custom dash includes a speedometer that reads S L O W   F A S T instead of using numbers to indicate speed.

This car was driven every day up until a short time ago, when Ray located a beater for daily use (a Dodge, of course). Now, Ray drives this car only when he wants to, instead of having to use it as his only source of transportation. Still, he believes that a rod or custom should be driven, instead of living under a cover in the garage and "driven" to a meet on a trailer. To Ray, driving is part of the fun of having a car that isn't just another car, but something special that you created. And Ray ought to know — he's a MoPar man.

Vehicle: 1970 Dodge Coronet Coupe   Owner: Ray Brady, Baltimore, Maryland

SOURCES

Quality Engineered Components
1150 Ryan Court
West Linn, Oregon 97068-4034
(503) 656-4545

Quality Engineered Components adapter mounted to engine. This shows the factory-style flex plate installed, which covers part of the adapter. These particular pieces are an earlier generation.

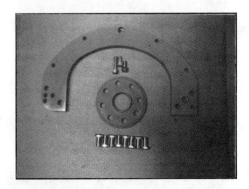

This is the Q.E.C. adapter package. The block plate is machined on all sides, although the inside and outside edges are for appearance only. Three special-sized fasteners are provided for the transmission mounting as well as the grade-eight bolts for the flex plate.

As the saying goes, hemi engines are "where ya find 'em". This industrial engine is still mounted in the air raid siren contraption where it was originally installed circa 1952. Inspection of the engine internals indicated very minimal usage. Products from Quality Engineered Components help make it possible to salvage such an engine as this and install it in a hot rod.

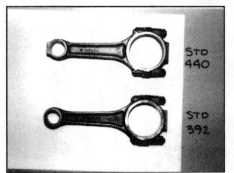

Comparison between the stock 392 connecting rod and a standard 440 connecting rod. The 440 rod is a bit huskier than the 392 and is preferred for most rebuild applications. Because the 440 rod is shorter than the 392 rod (6.75" vs 6.92") it can only be used with custom pistons. The thickness of the journal end is slightly thicker on the 440 rod, which makes sizing for oil flow clearance easy. The 440 rod should be reamed and bushed for the floating 392 pin, which is preferred over the pressed-in 440 pin.

This shows the Q.E.C. alternator mounting parts as assembled on the engine. The thermostat housing must be slightly modified to accept the brackets. This mount is for use with the '57-'58 water pump housing.

The Q.E.C. power steering pump mounting bracket as installed on the engine. This bracket is for use with the '57-'58 water pump housing and any B-RB pump with the factory-installed mount.

The Q.E.C. windage tray and mounting package. This package requires that four small holes be drilled into the block. The procedure is fully explained in the installation instructions.

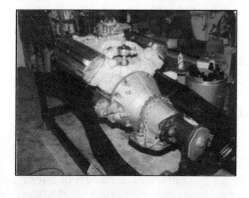

Side shot of 392 with transmission installed. The adapter is visible. This also shows the cast iron intake manifold with two Holley carburetors. Also shown is the late electronic distributor, the alternator mount, custom motor mount brackets (this is a W-150 frame), and the Q.E.C. fuel pump.

The stock manifold, after modifications to remove the generator bracket and enlargement of the throttle bores to match a Holley gasket (1-11/16" diameter bores). In order to use the Holley carburetor, a bolt pattern adjuster/spacer must be used.

This shows the dual Holley installation on a stock cast iron manifold. The aftermarket aluminum manifolds have closer center spacing and the Holley carburetors will not fit. The spacers used have four throttle bores the same size as the modified manifold bores.

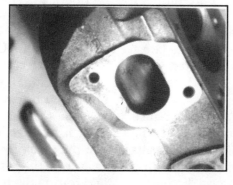

Minor porting work was done in the exhaust system. Note the difference between the bowl areas and see how the exhaust port is smoothed out. The intake is not modified except for minor cleaning in the bowl.

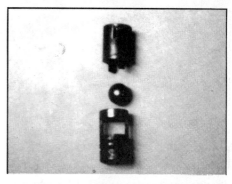

Shown is the oil filter by-pass and anti-drain-back valve. The valve arrangement can be used as is. The by-pass valve will provide for adequate filtration and also ensure oil supply to the lifter galley upon initial starting each day. Additionally, if the engine is not started for extended periods, the air trapped in the drained system may remain for up to twenty minutes of running time.

The 1954 331 cu.in. Chrysler was easily installed in this 1973 Dodge half-ton pickup. Changes include: transmission adapter, power steering mount, alternator mount, and remote oil filter.

The 331 intake manifold has been modified to accept the 1973 carburetor by simply re-drilling for the smaller bolt pattern and plugging the original holes. Throttle linkage from a 440 engine was attached to the manifold.

201

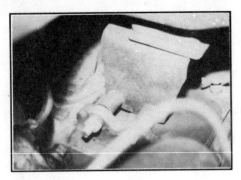

The driver-side motor mount bracket is from a 1966 Dodge pickup truck and required only minimal adjustment.

The passenger-side motor mount is also from a 1966 Dodge pickup truck and is used as is.

MOPAR ENGINE MANUAL

by John Lee

Owners wanting to make their Chrysler Products run faster, have always had lots of support from the factory.

Remember the Ramchargers back in the '60s? That club, made up of Chrysler engineers, could be found at the weekend drags testing new innovations that would eventually show up on the company's stock products, or be offered over the parts counter. Often, items developed by aftermarket companies to improve Plymouth, Dodge and Chrysler performance show up in the factory parts catalog.

Chrysler even tells you how to put all this hardware and knowledge together, in the book MOPAR ENGINES, which costs $20 and is available over the MoPar Performance parts counter as part number P4452790.

The subtitle is "Speed Secrets & Racing Modifications for Chrysler V8 & 6-Cylinder Engines," but the latest revision also covers the later 2.2-liter, 2.6-liter, Colt-Arrow and Omni-Horizon four-bangers and the new 3.6-liter V6.

Compiled by Larry Shepard, MoPar Performance staff engineer whose involvement goes back to the glory days of the 426 hemi, MOPAR ENGINES details each family of engines with specifications for rebuilding and hop-up recommendations. Though most discussion is devoted to the more popular small-block and B-RB big-block V8s, there is also coverage of the early hemis, old-style 277/301/318 V8s from the '50s and early '60s and the venerable slant six.

MoPar Performance standard and extra-duty part numbers are provided, along with instruction on how to use or modify them.

Separate chapters are devoted to such topics as blueprinting, supercharging, six-pack carburetor adjustment, ignition systems and nitrous oxide application. A section of the book tells you exactly what combination of parts you need to assemble an engine that will put you into your chosen drag racing bracket.

MOPAR ENGINES is a must for anyone planning any serious Chrysler engine building.

DISC BRAKE CONVERSION KIT

California Suspensions, along with JFZ, has developed a disc brake conversion that is a bolt-on for '67 to '72 B and '70 to '74 E body drum brake spindles. The kit consists of 12-inch vented rotors that fit the stock hubs, 4-piston calipers, caliper brackets that bolt to the drum brake spindles, and necessary hardware. If you're in search of the ultimate in braking ability, a rear disc conversion is under development and will be available soon.

In addition to brake kits, California Suspensions offers front and rear suspension parts, urethane bushings, sway bars, steering components, and custom torsion bars.

California Suspensions is located at 936 Detroit Ave., Suite C, Concord, California 95418. They can be reached by phone at (415) 685-7487.

REPLACEMENT HEAD GASKETS

Tom Hannaford at Antique Auto Parts Cellar, P.O. Box 3, South Weymouth, MA 02190, (617) 335-1579, has an asbestos substitute developed by Armstrong for high heat/high flange pressure applications. That's just the ticket for head gaskets. Put a bunch of mold-release on the gasket (copper coat or Teflon works, too) and torque the head down. Let it sit overnight and re-torque it the next day. Fire up the motor and re-torque it again. The stuff is great, but if you don't put plenty of mold-release on first, you'll never get the head back off afterwards. Tom can duplicate any head gasket, new or used, that you send him. If there is a sufficient demand, he will have a die made and stock these gaskets. He currently stocks the overbore gaskets for '51 to '54 Chryslers.